Staging Musical Theatre

ELAINE A. NOVAK & DEBORAH NOVAK

BETTERWAY BOOKS
CINCINNATI, OHIO

D1401146

Staging Musical Theatre. Copyright © 1996 by Elaine Adams Novak and Deborah Novak. Printed and bound in the United States of America. All rights reserved. No part of this book may be reproduced in any form or by any electronic or mechanical means including information storage and retrieval systems without permission in writing from the publisher, except by a reviewer, who may quote brief passages in a review. Published by Betterway Books, an imprint of F&W Publications, Inc., 1507 Dana Avenue, Cincinnati, Ohio 45207. (800) 289-0963. First edition.

Other fine Betterway Books, are available from your local bookstore or direct from the publisher.

00 99 98 97 96   5 4 3 2 1

Library of Congress Cataloging-in-Publication Data

Novak, Elaine Adams.
  Staging musical theatre: a complete guide for directors,
  choreographers, and producers / Elaine Adams Novak,
  Deborah Novak.
      p.   cm.
  Includes bibliographical references and index.
  ISBN 1-55870-407-8 (alk. paper)
  1. Musical theater—Production and direction
  I. Novak, Deborah. II. Title.
MT955.N75 1996
792.6'4—dc20   96-18158
                                                CIP
                                                MN

Edited by Argie Manolis
Designed by Angela Lennert Wilcox
Cover photography by Sandy Underwood

On the cover: Dorothy Stanley and Brian Sutherland in the Cincinnati Playhouse in the Park production of *She Loves Me*.

Betterway Books are available for sales promotions, premiums and fund-raising use. Special editions or book excerpts can also be created to specification. For details, contact the Special Sales Manager, F&W Publications, 1507 Dana Avenue, Cincinnati, Ohio 45207.

We wish to acknowledge the support and assistance given by our family, Edwin Novak and John Witek; by our friends at Marshall University and elsewhere, Eugene Anthony, Kevin Bannon, Milton Brooks, Deborah Carder, David Castleberry, Susan Dolen, John Dolin, Shirley Dyer, N.B. East, Linda Eikum-Dobbs, William G. Kearns, Mary Marshall, Janis Martin, John Mead, Maureen Milicia, James Morris-Smith, Mike Murphy, Gregory Rinaldi, Larry Stickler, Kay Wildman, Donald Williams and Sara Wilson; and by our editors at Betterway Books, Michelle Knippenberg, Argie J. Manolis and David Tompkins.

Preface

Perhaps—

> you are a choral, band, speech or gym teacher at a high school or college who has been given the task of putting on the annual musical;
>
> you are a singer, dancer or actor who has been asked to direct or choreograph the community theatre musical or church pageant;
>
> you are a piano, dance or acting teacher who has been chosen to direct a civic organization's or club's musical presentation—

if so, how do you approach the job of staging a musical?

This is a practical how-to handbook for those who would like to learn to produce or direct musical theatre. It takes the reader step-by-step through the process of putting on musicals and provides additional material on revues and operas. It is appropriate for those studying alone or in musical theatre classes or workshops.

It is not easy to do this work well, but if you are asked to be a stage director, musical director, conductor, choreographer, producer or stage manager of a musical production, you can find helpful information in this book to get you through the planning, casting, rehearsing and performing. It is hard work,

but it can also be exhilarating, rewarding and fun.

The introductory chapter describes the principal forms of musical theatre (the musical, opera and revue). Chapter two is concerned with acquiring a team of key personnel for the production, selecting a musical and preproduction planning. The third chapter deals with how to research and analyze a musical, while the fourth is about how to interpret one. Chapter five takes up the planning needed for the technical elements, and chapter six is on completing the production team by organizing the managers. Holding auditions and casting are the subjects of chapter seven. Rehearsing and performing are discussed in the next five chapters: beginning rehearsals (chapter eight), the musical director/conductor's rehearsals (chapter nine), the choreographer's rehearsals (chapter ten), the stage director's blocking rehearsals (chapter eleven), and developing, polishing, final rehearsals and performances (chapter twelve). Chapter thirteen concerns staging revues, and chapter fourteen, staging operas. Chapter fifteen offers two scenes with music that aspiring stage and musical directors, choreographers and performers can use for practice. An appendix, which gives information on notable musicals, revues, operas, comic operas and operettas, a bibliography and a glossary of theatrical terms complete the book.

Table of Contents

CHAPTER ONE

Introduction

Staging musical theatre requires the collaboration of a great number of talented people. First, we have the writers—the *bookwriter, composer* and *lyricist*—who create the book, music and lyrics, which they sell to a *producer*. The latter, who is the top business-person in a professional organization formed to produce the musical, raises the money for the presentation and hires everyone needed. Among those to be engaged for a professional production are:

- *Stage director*, who controls the artistic elements of the presentation
- *Musical director*, who is in charge of all musical matters
- *Choreographer*, who creates and directs the dancing
- *Stage manager*
- *Actors, singers* and *dancers*
- *Designers* of scenery, lighting, sound, costumes, makeup and hairstyles
- *Conductor, orchestrator, arrangers, rehearsal pianists* and *orchestra*
- *General manager, company manager, press agent* and others who aid the producer
- Various *assistants* to those listed above

For an amateur production, the producer obtains the right to present a work from the *licensor* and establishes an organization that may be different from the professional one above. These processes are described in chapter two.

In any school/community musical production, the producer, stage director, musical director/conductor, choreographer, designers and technical director lead the other workers.

What does it take to be a good leader? Like the coach of an athletic team, the leaders must be organizers, teachers, cheerleaders and disciplinarians. And they need intelligence, creativity and sensitivity. But it would not be desirable for all of these leaders to have different interpretations of the show. For this reason, the stage director is given the responsibility for controlling the overall artistic impression of the production. The stage director must envision the work onstage and have the patience, the stamina and the communicative skills to get everyone working on the musical to bring it to life.

Staging a musical is different from directing a stage play. Representational plays can be realistic, even naturalistic, in presenting an imitation of life to the audience; but musical theatre is not realistic. Consider how in a musical two lovers talk, then suddenly break into song accompanied by a full orchestra and chorus! Musical theatre uses a presentational style as the actors present a performance involving song, speech and dance. This combination of music, words and movements in a presentational style provides an extra dimension that enlarges the effect on the spectators. Undoubtedly, this has helped to make the musical one of America's top forms of entertainment. It also gives the leaders additional problems in analyzing, interpreting and staging the work—matters that will be addressed later.

FORMS OF MUSICAL THEATRE

Musical theatre is a comprehensive term that embraces three main divisions: the *musical*, *opera* and *revue*; but at times it is difficult to classify a particular show. Because both the musical and opera tell a story using music, singing, acting, dancing and spectacle, the dividing line between them may be difficult to determine. Usually, though, in an opera the music and singing are the most important elements, while in a musical the book, the acting, dancing and production may receive as much or more attention than the singing and music. Also, in grand opera, all or most of the lines are sung, but in a musical there are usually spoken passages. The revue is different from the other two because it does not have a plot or story line to tie the entire show together, although there may be a theme to provide some unity.

Musical

The old label for a musical was musical comedy but because some shows since the 1920s have had serious themes, the usual name now is just *musical* or *Broadway musical* or *American musical*. The last two are tributes to the fact that the U.S. led the way in the development of this form of entertainment.

The term *musical* now encompasses the following types of theatrical productions:

• **Musical comedy**—An entertaining show that makes an audience laugh, musical comedy may be based on exaggerations, surprises, incongruities, or deviations from normality and always has a happy ending. It may have some serious scenes—just as a serious drama may have comic moments—but the protagonist (the leading character) is happy at the end. An example is *Annie Get Your Gun*.

• **Musical farce**—When there is an emphasis on highly improbable comic actions in the plot, the show may be labeled a musical farce. Characteristics are funny chases, misunderstandings, mistaken identities and a happy ending, such as *A Funny Thing Happened on the Way to the Forum* provides.

• **Musical satire**—A comedy that makes fun of the customs, beliefs or institutions of a particular time period or place may be called a musical satire. An example is *Of Thee I Sing*, which satirizes American politics.

• **Musical fantasy**—When an imaginative musical takes us away from reality to an unrealistic environment with strange settings and unusual characters, it may be named a musical fantasy. For example, in *Brigadoon* two Americans wander into a two-hundred-year-old Scottish village that exists for only one day every hundred years.

• **Musical tragedy**—Tragedies are noted for their excellent characterizations and an unhappy ending as the protagonist falls to defeat. There are few musical tragedies, but *West Side Story*, which is loosely based on Shakespeare's *Romeo and Juliet*, is an example.

• **Musical melodrama**—Here the characters are likely to be archetypical representations because a complicated plot with contrived activity is more important to this genre than in-depth characterizations. The show often includes a hero, a heroine and a villain, and at the end, good overcomes evil as the villain is defeated. An example is *Sweeney Todd*.

• **Musical drama**—When a serious musical does not fall into the traditional forms of tragedy or melodrama, it may be called a musical drama. Look at *Carousel*.

• **Rock musical**—This is a show that features rock music, such as The Who's *Tommy*.

• **Concept musical**—This kind does not have a typical plot structure but examines a theme with episodes serving to illustrate the main idea or concept. For example, in *Company*, Robert, the leading character, a New York bachelor, is concerned about marrying. There are scenes with his girlfriends and married and divorced chums in which he investigates the subject of marriage.

• **Operatic musical, popular opera or theatre opera**—This is a production, such as *Evita* or *Les Misérables*, that has few or no spoken lines and can, therefore, be called a musical or an opera.

Opera

The principal types of operas are *grand operas*, which are large spectacular productions like *Aïda*, in which the entire text is set to music; *operettas*, which may have spoken dialogue and present an adventurous, romantic plot, humor and melodic music, as in *The Student Prince*; and *light* or *comic operas*, which also have spoken passages and emphasize wit and comedy, such as *The Mikado*.

Revue

A *revue* may have songs, dances, music, comedy acts, blackout sketches and specialty numbers, all carefully routined for maximum effect. It may have a theme, but it does not have a plot. In past years, minstrel shows, burlesque, vaudeville, variety shows and spectacular productions like the *Ziegfeld Follies* were popular revues. Today, revues can be found in nightclubs, cabarets, off Broadway and sometimes on Broadway with shows such as *Ain't Misbehavin'* and *Jerome Robbins' Broadway.*

Whatever type of production you choose, this book will guide you from the planning stage to opening night.

CHAPTER TWO

Planning to Stage Musicals

To present a successful musical, the producer and other leaders must start early to plan (see Figure 2-1, Producer's Duties Before Auditions). One of the first chores is to obtain money for the production. If your organization wishes to apply for a national, state or local grant to help finance the show, you may find that some applications have to be submitted six months or more prior to the production.

Another early job is to reserve theatres and rooms that will be needed for auditions, rehearsals, the building and assembling of technical elements and performances.

Starting about three months before auditions, you should begin to acquire key personnel, select a musical and make arrangements for mounting the show. These are the concerns of this chapter.

ACQUIRING KEY PERSONNEL

Figure 2-2 shows a typical organizational chart for an amateur musical production. Keep in mind that some school/community organizations may not have enough qualified people for all of the positions listed and that one person may have to hold two, three or four jobs. It is not unusual for one person to be the producer, stage director and choreographer—or the designer of scenery, props, lighting and sound—or the musical director, conductor, and publicity manager—but all of the jobs will be described individually.

Producer

The primary duty of the producer is to organize the financial elements of the enterprise. As the person who controls the money, the producer may have great influence on the entire production. The work involves the following:

- Raising money for the musical's presentation
- Obtaining rooms or theatres for auditions, rehearsals, building and assembling technical elements and performances
- Obtaining all personnel by recruitment, auditions or employment with the advice of other leaders
- Selecting a musical with advice from others
- Deciding on the prices of tickets, which may include special rates for children, senior citizens and large groups
- Preparing a budget
- Signing contracts for the right to present the musical, for hiring employees, for the purchase of supplies and equipment, and for the rental of various items that may include a theatre, scenery, props, costumes, and lighting and sound equipment
- Establishing procedures for handling income and paying all expenses
- Directing publicity and promotion
- Supervising the managers of business, tickets, refreshments/souvenirs, programs and house
- Overseeing all work on the production to be

FIGURE 2-1 **PRODUCER'S DUTIES BEFORE AUDITIONS**

9 to 3 months to auditions	3 months to auditions	2 months to auditions	1 month to auditions
Apply for possible grants. Raise money for production. Reserve theatre and rooms for auditions, rehearsals, performances, construction. Read and evaluate possible musicals to present.	Acquire key personnel: stage director, musical director, choreographer, designers, technical director. Select musical and order material. Decide on prices of tickets. Prepare tentative budget. Make arrangements for touring the production to other theatres.	Inquire about renting, borrowing or buying scenery, props, costumes, lighting and sound equipment.	Complete the production team by acquiring managers of publicity, business, stage, tickets, programs, refreshments and house. Finalize budget. Establish procedures for handling money. Start publicity. Announce auditions. Order supplies: lumber, canvas, paint and other materials for building scenery, props, costumes. Order or make tickets, posters, flyers, postcards. Start selling ads for programs.

To find out if your organization may be eligible for a grant, contact your state arts agency. The exact name will vary from state to state—it may be an arts council, commission, board, foundation or division—but an inquiry to your state capital should put you in touch with the correct agency. Ask the agency to send you guidelines for any grants for which your group may apply.

sure that everyone is staying within the budget, that contract obligations are met, and that laws and regulations are obeyed
- Booking the production into other theatres for additional performances
- Closing the show, which includes seeing that all rented and borrowed materials are returned and that those bought or built are properly disposed of, stored or sold

While the producer is the business head of the venture, this person may or may not get involved with the artistic aspects, depending on his or her preference. Cameron Mackintosh, an English producer who has mounted many productions including *Cats*, *Les Misérables*, *The Phantom of the Opera* and *Miss Saigon*, has described the job of producer as the wooden spoon in the middle of the ingredients that keeps everything stirred up.

The producer may need assistants, such as managers of publicity, business, tickets, refreshments/souvenirs, program and house. (For more information about the work of the producer, see chapters six, seven, twelve, thirteen and fourteen.)

Stage Director

The stage director supervises the artistic aspects of the musical, which include these:
- Advising on the selection of a musical and the acquisition of personnel
- Researching and analyzing the musical
- Deciding on the musical's interpretation and communicating the concept to everyone in-

volved with creating the production
- Holding auditions and casting the show with the advice of the musical director and the choreographer
- Coordinating the work of the musical director/conductor, choreographer, designers and performers
- Planning a rehearsal schedule with the help of the stage manager
- Seeing that an accurate prop list is compiled
- Approving plans for the scenery, props, lighting, costumes, sound, makeup and hairstyles
- Rehearsing the performers, which entails staging everything except the dances
- Supervising and criticizing all artistic work with the goal of obtaining unity

The stage director's principal assistant is the stage manager, but the stage director may also want an assistant director and, perhaps, a secretary to take notes during rehearsals of things to correct and accomplish. (See chapters three, four, five, seven, eight, eleven, twelve, thirteen, fourteen and fifteen for more information about the work of the stage director.)

Musical Director/Conductor

The musical director is responsible for every note of music in the production:
- Recommending to the stage director the number and vocal ranges of singers needed
- Holding singing auditions
- Advising the stage director on the casting of singers
- Deciding on the instrumental configuration of the orchestra
- Assembling an orchestra
- Supervising all singing and all orchestral rehearsals

The musical director may also be the conductor of the orchestra at all orchestral rehearsals and performances. The conductor is charged with these tasks:
- Devising the orchestra's rehearsal schedule and informing the musicians of it
- Cueing musicians and performers
- Controlling tempos, rhythm, and the loudness and softness of the music according to interpretations established in rehearsals
- Setting standards for orchestra members re-

FIGURE 2-2 **ORGANIZATION FOR AN AMATEUR MUSICAL**

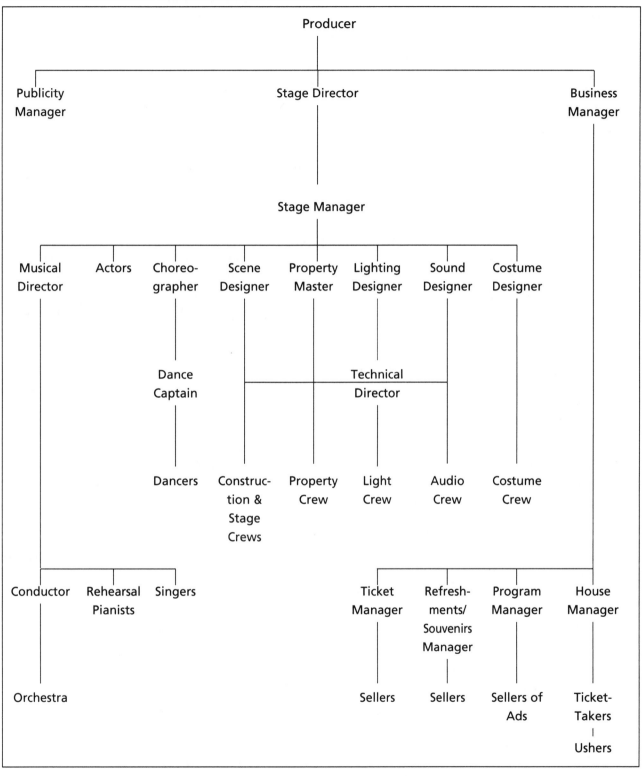

garding clothes, punctuality, warming up, and behavior while in the pit

Aides to the musical director/conductor may include choral and vocal directors, an orchestra manager, rehearsal pianists and other assistants. (See chapters three, four, seven, eight, nine, twelve, thirteen, fourteen and fifteen for more information about the work of the musical director/conductor.)

Choreographer

The choreographer is in charge of the following:

- Recommending to the stage director the number and types of dancers needed
- Conducting dance auditions
- Advising the stage director on the casting of dancers
- Creating and teaching the dance routines
- Rehearsing everyone who dances
- Assisting with the blocking of singing numbers, if the stage director asks for help

The choreographer may have an assistant choreographer, a dance director and a dance captain, who is a performer selected by the choreographer to keep the dances as they were when they were choreographed. (For more information about the work of the choreographer, see chapters three, four, seven, eight, ten, twelve, thirteen, fourteen and fifteen.)

Designers

The designers of a musical devise the scenery, properties, lighting, sound, costumes, makeup and the hairstyles.

Scenery

The scene designer prepares an appropriate environment for each scene:

- Supplying specifications for the construction and painting of the scenery
- Selecting or designing the set properties
- Supervising all special effects (including projections)
- Overseeing the placement and shifting of sets and props

The scene designer is assisted by the technical director, master carpenter, construction crew, property master and crew, and the stage crew, which consists of stagehands (or grips) and riggers.

Properties

The property master and crew care for two types of properties:

- Set (or trim) props, which are attached to the scenery (like draperies and wall decorations) or an integral part of the scene design (such as furniture and lamps). These are selected by the scene designer or constructed to this designer's specifications.
- Hand properties, which are handled by the performers (such as a book, newspaper or food). These are acquired or made by the property crew to the stage director's specifications; however, if the prop is considered to be part of a costume (like a cane or fan), the costume designer may select it.

The property crew is also responsible for mechanically produced stage and sound effects (for example, gunshots, fog, smoke, and the rings of telephones and doorbells).

Lighting

This designer plans the stage lighting, which involves the following:

- Acquiring needed lighting equipment
- Making light plots and instrument schedule
- Supervising the placement and focusing of the lighting instruments
- Overseeing the operation of the control board

The lighting designer is assisted by a master electrician and lighting technicians.

Sound

The sound designer is responsible for these tasks:

- Amplifying performers' voices and musical instruments
- Mixing sounds
- Creating or obtaining recorded music and sound effects (such as distant church bells or an airplane flying overhead)
- Supervising the operation of the control console, which is often placed in the house so that the operator can ascertain easily how the spectators are perceiving the sound

The sound designer's assistants are called audio technicians.

Costumes

The costume designer acquires all costumes and accessories (such as gloves, shoes, hats and jewelry) worn in the musical. He or she may design costumes to be made by seamstresses and tailors, purchase ready-made items, rent them from costume houses or other producing companies, or borrow them. This designer supervises:

The work of other important members of the production team is described in chapter six, "Organizing the Managers."

- Fittings of costumes
- The dress parade at which performers wear their costumes for the stage director and others to approve
- Performers' hairstyles, mustaches and beards

The costume designer is assisted by a wardrobe supervisor and costume crew.

Makeup and Hairstyles

Normally, performers are responsible for their own makeup and hairstyles; however, if the styles are unusual, professional makeup artists and hair and wig stylists may be brought in to design and do them. (For more information about the work of designers, see chapters three, four, five, nine, twelve, thirteen and fourteen.)

Technical Director

The technical director is in charge of coordinating all technical elements. This person supervises these activities:

- Purchasing supplies and equipment (within the guidelines of the budget)
- Constructing and painting sets (as designed by the scene designer)
- Building, borrowing, buying or renting properties
- Shifting, repairing and striking scenery and props
- Work of all technical crews, assisting where needed

(For more information on the technical director, see chapters four, five and twelve.)

SELECTING THE MUSICAL

In a professional production, the producer has the most to say about the selection of the musical. In school/community theatre, however, the stage director usually makes the selection with the advice of others: the producer, board of directors, musical director/conductor, choreographer, designers, technical director, or even the entire membership of an organization. In school situations, the chairpersons of theatre, music and dance departments, the dean and, perhaps, higher-ups may have to approve the choice.

Before presenting the musical for this approval, the stage director or producer should survey available musicals and select several for perusal. To do this, keep a list of possible shows, adding to it whenever you see a musical, hear a recording, or read a script or critical reviews of a show that interests you. Also, ask the musical director/conductor, choreographer, designers, and other knowledgeable theatre people for their recommendations. Look at the descriptions of notable shows in the appendix of this book and consult catalogs from the following companies, which handle the amateur rights for most musicals and revues:

Music Theatre International
545 Eighth Ave.
New York, NY 10018-4307
(212) 868-6668
Fax (212) 643-8465

Rodgers and Hammerstein Theatre Library
For *amateur* performance rights:
229 W. Twenty-eighth St.
New York, NY 10001
(212) 564-4000
Fax (212) 268-1245
For *professional* performance rights:
1633 Broadway, Suite 3801
New York, NY 10019-6746
(212) 541-6600
Fax (212) 586-6155

Samuel French, Inc.
45 W. Twenty-fifth St.
New York, NY 10010
Musical Department: (212) 206-8125
Fax (212) 206-1429

Tams-Witmark Music Library, Inc.
560 Lexington Ave.
New York, NY 10126-0394
(800) 221-7196 or (212) 688-2525
Fax (212) 688-3232

By reading brief descriptions of shows, you can tell something about the plot, characters, musical numbers and instrumentation. But no matter how great the work seems to be in the description or how favorably you remember a production of it, you should always study the script and music before making a decision.

To get perusal material (for which there is a mailing and handling charge), write or call the company that can provide a license agreement for that musical. At the same time you can inform them of the following:

- Name, address, telephone and fax number of the producing organization
- Your name, address and telephone number
- Your admission prices
- The name and seating capacity of the theatre in which your show will be presented
- The dates and number of performances
- The expected attendance at each performance
- Whether you will require an orchestration

The licensor will then tell you the amount of royalties and rental fees or purchase prices of the scripts, dialogue and vocal parts, scores and orchestrations. For some musicals it is possible to obtain a rehearsal tape of the music. If you are interested in this service, ask the licensor if it is available.

To select a show, think about the following.

Does the Musical Excite You?

You must like the work or you are never going to be able to persuade a musical director, choreographer, designers, cast and crews that this is a stimulating project. Is the musical of sufficient quality to interest a large number of people for weeks or months? Will their experiences during this production be worth their while?

Can You Cast It?

No matter how much a show thrills you, you must be practical enough to consider whether you have the people who can portray these characters and do the required singing and dancing. For example, if you do not have a good choreographer and about twenty male dancers, you should not attempt *West Side Story*.

You must also consider the accompaniment. Do you have the musicians to play the instruments re-

quired by the orchestration? Discuss this with the musical director/conductor. You may want to consult the licensor to see if a simpler orchestration is available. It may be possible to accompany the show with one or two pianos or keyboards and, perhaps, a rhythmic ensemble.

Can You Stage It?

Here are the questions to answer:

- Do you have an adequate place in which to present this musical?
- Is the acting area large enough?
- Is there an orchestra pit or a place somewhere for the accompanying musicians?
- Is there enough room backstage to accommodate the scenery, props, lighting and sound equipment, costumes, performers and crews?
- Do you have designers, crews and enough space to build the technical elements?

Again, consider *West Side Story*. This musical needs eleven different sets for fifteen scenes. Another example is *Little Shop of Horrors*, which uses puppets of different sizes from small to enormous. Some musicals, such as *The Music Man*, require a large number of period costumes. If you do not have designers, construction crews and facilities to handle these requirements, you should select another show. Take note, though, that you may be able to rent costumes and some difficult necessities, such as puppets, scenic drops, or lighting or sound equipment from theatrical supply houses or other producing companies.

Do You Have Sufficient Preparation Time?

It is difficult to prescribe the amount of time that will be needed to prepare any musical because there are various factors that affect this:

- The difficulty of the show in the singing, dancing, acting and orchestral requirements
- The difficulty of the musical in the technical requirements: sets, props, lighting, sound, costumes and makeup
- The number of people needed for the cast, orchestra, production staff and crews (In general, more people make it more difficult.)
- The experience, competency and efficiency of the personnel

Generally, most school/community organizations that rehearse about fifteen hours per week will probably need six to eight weeks for a large musical.

Before making your selection, you should calculate how much preparation time your group will need for a particular show and compare this with the amount of time available to you.

Will It Be Popular With Your Audiences?

This is an important question if you are dependent on ticket sales to pay your bills and stay in business. No one knows for sure what audiences for school/community shows want to see, but usually they will buy tickets to well-known favorites and newer shows that have won awards and been reviewed favorably in magazines and newspapers. They are often less inclined to spend money to see a musical that they know nothing about, unless you can interest them through publicity about the outstanding attributes of your production.

Will It Fit In With a Season of Shows?

If you have to plan a season of musicals and plays, you will probably want to get variety in the offerings. Some groups do present all comedies or all serious plays, but most school/community organizations try to get a mixture of comedy, farce, romantic comedy, satire, drama, melodrama, tragedy and fantasy. The planners may also want to select shows in various styles or from different time periods or countries. For some seasons they may want a theme (for example, an all-American season of plays and musicals), and that will affect the choices.

To put together an enticing season, all of the directors of the individual shows may have to meet to present their selections with their reasons for choosing them. The directors may be asked to arrive at a conference with several titles in hopes that one may be compatible with what other directors want to do.

Do You Have the Money to Produce It?

Some musicals are very expensive to produce and others are not. To decide if your selection is feasible, prepare a tentative budget for the production. First, estimate your probable income. Next, figure the probable cost of the items that apply to your situation. (See Figure 2-3.)

Now compare your estimated income and expenditures, and if the result is favorable, you may have found your show.

MAKING ARRANGEMENTS FOR THE PRODUCTION

After the musical has been selected, the producer is responsible for making arrangements with the writers or with a licensing company. If you are presenting a new, original musical that has never been produced before, the producer will sign contracts with the bookwriter, composer and lyricist for the production, obtain an orchestrator and arrangers to prepare the music, and have scripts and music duplicated. It is more likely, however, that the producer will sign a contract with a licensing company to present a well-known musical, such as the ones listed in the appendix.

Contract With Licensor

The licensor's contract will specify the amounts of royalty, rental or purchase prices of materials, refundable deposits and extra materials, plus stipulations like program credit for the authors, licensor and others. It will also state when these amounts of money must be paid. The stage director and musical director/conductor should be certain that enough scripts, vocal books, scores and orchestral parts are ordered. If more than the standard set of materials is needed, there will be an extra charge to rent or buy additional copies. For some shows, you can rent from the licensor the choreography used in a Broadway production. Some choreographers like to have this help, but others may prefer to work with their own ideas.

The producer, stage director, musical director and choreographer should read the license agreement carefully. Note that in most contracts the licensee agrees to perform the musical in accordance with the material furnished by the licensor and, to

FIGURE 2-3 **INCOME AND EXPENDITURES**

INCOME

Sale of tickets	$ _____
Sale of advertising in programs	_____
Sale of refreshments and souvenirs	_____
Grants from local, state or national foundations	_____
Gifts from patrons and sponsors	_____
Other income	_____
Total	$ _____

EXPENDITURES

Royalty	$ _____
Rental fees/ purchase prices of scripts, music	_____
Scenery	_____
Properties	_____
Lighting	_____
Sound	_____
Costumes, wigs, shoes, accessories	_____
Makeup	_____
Orchestra's music stands, chairs and lights	_____
Rental of audition and rehearsal rooms, building spaces and theatres	_____
Transportation charges of scenery, props, costumes, supplies and equipment	_____
Promotion and publicity: flyers, postcards, newspaper ads, radio and TV commercials, posters, signs, billboards, photographs and personal appearances	_____
Postage	_____
Telephone	_____
Office expenses	_____
Tickets	_____
Programs	_____
Refreshments and souvenirs to be sold	_____
Salaries of employees	_____
Janitorial services	_____
Touring production: transportation, meals, lodging	_____
Insurance	_____
Taxes	_____
Other expenses	_____
Total	$ _____

Names, addresses and phone numbers of costume houses and theatrical supply houses may be obtained from the yellow pages of your phone book. If you cannot find any listings, call your nearest college theatre department or producing company for their recommendations. Also, your library may have the following publications, which have this information:

The New York Theatrical Sourcebook
Broadway Press
350 W. Eighty-fifth St.
New York, NY 10024-3832

TCI Buyers Guide
P.O. Box 470
Mount Morris, IL 61054-0470

Regional Theatre Directory
P.O. Box 519
Dorset, VT 05251

quote the Tams-Witmark Library, Inc., license agreement, "agrees to make no additions, transpositions, or interpolations of any kind in, and no substantial deletions from, the music score or book."

Touring
If the production should tour to other theatres, these arrangements should be finalized early.

Renting, Borrowing, Buying Items
About two months before auditions, inquiries should be made about renting, borrowing or buying needed items. If costumes and wigs are to be rented, the producer or costume designer should write or call various costume houses requesting a costume plot and rental fees. To rent or purchase lighting or sound equipment, scenery, props or special effects, the producer, designers or technical director should contact theatrical supply houses for prices. Be sure to give them your dates and your number of performances.

One Month to Auditions
About one month before auditions, the producer should make certain that
- The production and office staffs are filled (see chapter six, "Organizing the Managers").
- The budget is finalized
- Supplies such as lumber, canvas and paint have been ordered for the technical elements
- Tickets, flyers, postcards and posters are being made or have been ordered
- Ads are being sold for the program
- Publicity about the musical and auditions has been started

CHAPTER THREE

Analyzing Musicals

Before interpreting the musical, the stage director must research and analyze the book, lyrics and score. After that, he or she should be ready to decide on the style and concept for the production, which are discussed in the next chapter. In addition, the musical director/conductor, choreographer and designers need to research and analyze the subjects that affect their work.

RESEARCHING THE MUSICAL

The stage director should begin by researching the authors, past productions of the work, the source, and the place and time period in which the musical is set. First, find out about the *bookwriter* (also called *librettist*) who wrote the *book* (or *libretto*) that contains the plot, characters, thoughts, dialogue and stage directions; the *lyricist* who devised the lyrics for the songs; and the *composer* who created the musical score. Look for answers to the following:

• Who are the authors? Have they written other shows? It will help you understand the musical if you will get acquainted with the writers through reading about their lives and other productions.

• What was the authors' intention or purpose in creating this piece? While you may not have the same purpose in presenting the show, you should be aware of the writers' reason.

• When was this musical written and where was it first produced professionally? Where else has it been presented?

• Who produced, directed and choreographed

Your library may have *Theatre World*, which is published annually and offers photographs and information about productions of Broadway, off-Broadway, touring and resident companies. Also, pictures of shows may be found in published editions of the musical script or score and in theatrical and news magazines.

the first professional production? Who starred in the show? How many men, women and children were in the cast? Who were the designers?

• What did the original production look like? What about touring companies and revivals?

• What were the critics' comments about the original production? About revivals?

• Was a cast recording made of the original production or a revival? A videotape? A film? Watch and listen to those that are available. Is there a professional or amateur production that you can see? You may get some ideas that you can use in your production.

• What is the source for this musical? Is it a play (for example: *My Fair Lady* is derived from the play *Pygmalion*), a novel (*Les Misérables*), stories (*Fiddler on the Roof*), the Bible (*Jesus Christ Superstar*), poems

If these were New York City productions, look in your library for *New York Theatre Critics' Reviews*. The reviews should be under the date of the opening performance in New York.

(*Cats*), a film (*A Little Night Music* from *Smiles of a Summer Night*), a television show (*Ballroom* from *The Queen of the Stardust Ballroom*), history (*1776*), the life of a person (*Fiorello!*), a comic strip (*Annie*), the work of an artist (*Sunday in the Park With George*), or is it an original concept (*A Chorus Line*)? If possible, examine the source.

• What was life like in the place and time period depicted in the musical? What were the customs and manners of the day? What kind of clothes, shoes, hairstyles and makeup did people wear? What dialects or accents should actors use to portray these characters? For answers, consult historical accounts, other works set in the time period or country, and reference books.

ANALYZING THE BOOK, LYRICS AND SCORE

After research, the stage director should be ready to analyze the work. As you read the script and score, prepare a *rundown* or *outline* that provides the place, time, orchestra numbers, songs, dances and characters in each scene. (For an example, see Figure 3-1 which is a rundown for the first three scenes of *Brigadoon*.) This outline quickly gives the stage director an idea of:

• The places and times of the scenes
• The placement and types of musical numbers
• The number and kinds of sets needed
• The characters in each scene, song and dance
• The flow of the musical from one scene to another

It helps the stage director to visualize the production. It also provides information needed to get ready for casting and for conferences with the designers, choreographer and musical director.

Next, the stage director should study the script and score again and answer the following questions. These responses will determine your overall approach to directing the production.

• Does the title give a clue to the theme, major characters, location or time period? (Consider *Les Misérables*, *Hello, Dolly!*, *Oklahoma!* and *1776*.)

• Is the genre a comedy, farce, satire, fantasy, tragedy, melodrama, drama or something else? (See chapter one for definitions.)

• What is the plot? Can you tell the story of what happens in the musical from the beginning to the end? Are there subplots?

• Who is the protagonist (the central character), and what does he or she want? Is there more than one protagonist? Is there an antagonist (someone who is opposed to the protagonist)? Again, there may be more than one antagonist, and sometimes the protagonist and antagonist are the same person, if he or she has an internal conflict. Is there conflict between the protagonist(s) and antagonist(s)? Why?

• What has happened immediately before each scene of the musical? These occurrences will affect what each character is thinking and feeling as he or she begins the scene.

• What is the writers' objective for each scene? Some possible objectives include these:

To establish mood and style

To give exposition

To advance the plot

To reveal characters and relationships

To express a theme or major idea

To focus attention on a musical number

To provide spectacle

To add comedy, pathos, foreshadowing, excitement, conflict, obstacles, complications, suspense or surprises

To build to minor climaxes and eventually a major one.

• Do you understand the subtext (the underlying meaning) of scenes?

• Who are the characters and how are they related? What is each character's superobjective (major goal) for the entire show, objectives, motivations, and actions for each scene in which the character appears, and attitudes toward others?

• Do you understand words and references in

FIGURE 3-1 **STAGE DIRECTOR'S RUNDOWN FOR ACT I, SCENES 1-3, OF *BRIGADOON***

ACT I

Overture by orchestra (Music #1)

PROLOGUE (Music #2) "Once in the Highlands"—Singing Chorus (offstage)

SCENE 1—A forest in the Scottish Highlands. 5 A.M. in May.

Characters: Tommy, Jeff

(Music #3) "Brigadoon"—Singing Chorus (offstage)

INTERLUDE—A road in the town of Brigadoon. A few minutes later.

(Music #4) "Vendors' Calls"—Singing Chorus (Maggie and two youths cross stage)

SCENE 2—The square of Brigadoon—MacConnachy Square. Later that morning.

(Music #5) "Down on MacConnachy Square"—Sandy, Meg, Singing Chorus

(Music #6) "Waitin' for My Dearie"—Fiona and Female Singing Chorus

(Music #7) "I'll Go Home With Bonnie Jean"—Charlie, Singing Chorus

(Music #7A) Dance—Maggie, Harry, Dancers

(Music #8) "The Heather on the Hill"—Tommy, Fiona

(Music #8A) Reprise: "Down on MacConnachy Square"—Singing Chorus

Characters in addition to those named above: Jeff, Angus, Archie, Stuart, MacGregor, Andrew, Jean, Fishmonger

(Music #8B) Change of scene

SCENE 3—The Brockie open shed. Just past noon.

Characters: Jeff, Meg

(Music #9) "The Love of My Life"—Meg

(Music #9A) Change of scene

---

the dialogue and lyrics? If not, consult a dictionary, encyclopedia, atlas or other reference books.

• What does the work mean to you? What theme and major ideas do you want to communicate to an audience?

• What are the technical (scenery, props, lighting, sound, costumes, makeup and special effects) requirements?

• Examine the placement of musical numbers. What did the bookwriter, lyricist and composer hope to accomplish by placing a song, dance or music in these locations?

Analyzing the Plot

The plot is the plan or outline of what happens in a work. In writing a plot, the bookwriter devises a sequence of events to tell the story, depict the characters, express the thoughts and focus attention on the musical numbers.

Plots vary in structure, but many bookwriters use a cause-to-effect arrangement that has a short beginning, a lengthy middle that builds to the major climax, and a brief ending.

At the beginning of most musical plots, the author may try to establish the style and mood, introduce major characters and give exposition (the place, time period and other information that the audience needs to know to understand the work). A problem may be presented to the protagonist that introduces the theme or major dramatic question. There may also be an inciting incident that gets the main action started.

In the long middle section, there is usually conflict between protagonist and antagonist and the building of suspense with complications and obstacles that keep the protagonist from achieving his or her goal. There may also be surprises and reversals as the action builds to minor climaxes and eventually to the major climax, which is the point of the greatest emotional involvement on the part of the audience.

The ending, which may be termed the resolution or denouement, relieves the tension and often satisfies the spectators' expectations by answering questions that were raised during the play.

For an illustration of this common plot structure, look at *1776* by Peter Stone and Sherman Edwards. This is a seven-scene plot that may be done without an intermission or with an intermission after the fifth scene.

The first scene gives exposition through song and dialogue about the place (Philadelphia), the time period (May, 1776), the climate (hot) and the mood (argumentative), introduces the protagonist (John Adams) and reveals his relationship with the rest of the Continental Congress. It also introduces his loving wife, Abigail, who is home in Massachusetts but talks to him throughout the play in his imagination. John's goal is to get Congress to vote for independence from Great Britain. His problem is that most members of Congress oppose this action. The major dramatic question is this: Will John succeed in his campaign for independence?

Scene 2 introduces Benjamin Franklin, who is one of three representatives from Pennsylvania. Ben, who supports Adams in the fight for independence, has the idea of asking Richard Henry Lee to travel to his home state of Virginia to persuade the House of Burgesses to pass a resolution proposing independence. This is the inciting incident that sets the main action in motion.

In the middle section of the plot, Lee returns from Virginia and presents the resolution. Immediately, another representative from Pennsylvania, John Dickinson, and the Conservatives oppose the resolution and ask that it be postponed indefinitely. This is just one of the obstacles that Adams faces in the conflict between those in favor of independence and those who are against it. To stop a vote that would mean defeat of the resolution, Adams asks for a postponement to write a declaration of independence. This is approved and a Declaration Committee decides that Thomas Jefferson should write the declaration.

More obstacles and complications occur and the

suspense builds as numerous people object to various parts of this document. Eventually all states approve it except Pennsylvania: Franklin is for independence, Dickinson is against it, and the third representative, James Wilson, has the deciding vote. After more suspense, Wilson casts his vote in favor of independence, and the resolution is passed. With Adams achieving his goal, the major climax of the musical is reached.

In the ending, Dickinson leaves the chamber because he cannot sign the document, and Congress then proceeds to the dramatic signing of the Declaration of Independence.

In addition to the main action of the plot, there are three small actions that contribute greatly to the musical. Two concern the relationships of Adams and Jefferson with their wives, and the third involves the Courier who brings messages from George Washington. The Courier has one of the best moments in the musical when he talks about the death of his two best friends and sings the moving "Momma, Look Sharp."

While this linear pattern for a plot with subactions or subplots fits many musicals, it does not describe all of them. Some, such as *Baby* or *Follies*, are episodic in that a series of episodes illustrates the theme or concept for the musical. Another unusual plot structure was used for *Merrily We Roll Along*, in which the story progresses backwards from 1980 to 1955.

Analyzing the Characters

Through the actions of the plot, dialogue and their songs and dances, the major characters reveal the complexities of their natures. The smaller parts tend to be simpler characters because they are not onstage long enough to show us well-rounded persons; chorus members in some musicals may not be individualized at all.

The stage director should prepare a list of characters and note in which scenes each one appears. Also for later convenience in calling actors to rehearsals, you may indicate on this chart whether the character speaks, sings or dances with a group, or sings or dances solo (see Figure 3-2).

To analyze each character, the stage director needs to read the script carefully for ideas. Look

FIGURE 3-2 **STAGE DIRECTOR'S CAST CHART FOR *1776***
CHART SHOWING WHO IS IN EACH SCENE AND WHAT THEY DO

Character	Actor's Name	1	2	3	4	5	6	7
John Adams								
John Hancock								
Charles Thomson								
Dr. Josiah Bartlett								
Stephen Hopkins								
Roger Sherman								
Lewis Morris								
Robert Livingston								
John Dickinson								
James Wilson								
Caesar Rodney								
Col. Thomas McKean								
George Read								
Samuel Chase								
Richard Henry Lee								
Thomas Jefferson								
Joseph Hewes								
Edward Rutledge								
Andrew McNair								
A Leather Apron								
Abigail Adams								
Benjamin Franklin								
A Painter								
Dr. Lyman Hall								
Courier								
Rev. John Witherspoon								
Martha Jefferson								

√ = Speaks   E = Extra (does not speak, sing or dance)   S = Sings with group   SS = Sings solo   D = Dances with group   DS = Dances solo

especially at the following:

- How the writers describe the role; descriptions may appear at the first entrance of the character and in other stage directions
- What the character says about himself or herself
- What other characters say about her or him (provided they are speaking the truth)
- What the character has done in the past and does during the musical
- How the character changes during the musical

The stage director should write a description of each character, deciding on the following:

- His or her function in the play: Is this character the protagonist; antagonist; friend, relative or enemy of one of the principals; confidant(e); comedian; servant; member of the singing or dancing chorus; extra; or something else?
- Physical appearance: age, height, weight, color of hair, hairstyle, clothing, shoes, posture, movements, stage business, rhythm of movement and speech
- Personal habits: smoking, scratching, gesturing with a cane or fan and the like
- Vocal characteristics: dialect, accent, quality, pitch, loudness, rate
- Nationality, ethnic origins, family relations
- Intellectual characteristics, education
- Emotional characteristics
- Personality
- Social and economic status, occupation, hobbies
- Religion
- Politics
- The character's major goal for the entire play
- The character's objective(s), motivation(s) and action(s) for each scene that the character is in
- The obstacles encountered by the character in trying to reach the objectives
- The character's attitude toward every other character in the musical with whom he or she is involved
- The changes that the character experiences from the beginning to the end of the show
- Singing range of character
- Types of dancing character must do

A complete description of each character can help the stage director immensely in casting the musical because it tells one what to look for. A description can also help in rehearsals as the stage director talks with each actor about the role. The following is an example of a description that a stage director might write about the leading character of the musical *1776*, John Adams:

John Adams Protagonist. Age 40; 5'8" tall; tends to be slightly overweight; wears a dark brown wig, tied in back, and practical clothes of the day: suit coat, breeches, vest, shirt with lace fall at neck and lace cuffs, shoes with buckles; carries a walking stick. His posture is erect; his movements are quick; he often uses his cane to make a point; his rhythm of movement and speech is fast and dynamic. Adams is a representative to Congress from Massachusetts, so his speech may reflect a slight northeastern dialect. When excited, he often uses a loud, piercing, rather high-pitched tone. As for personality, his colleagues find him impatient, blunt, obnoxious and vain, but his wife and family know him to be affectionate and kind.

Born Braintree, Massachusetts, on October 30, 1735

Father A farmer and militia officer

Mother From a prominent Massachusetts family of merchants and physicians

Education Graduated from Harvard College in 1755

Occupation Attorney in Boston

Wife Abigail Smith Adams, to whom he is devoted

Children Four

Major goal for the play To get the Continental Congress to declare its independence from Great Britain

Scene 1 Adams's objective is the same as his major goal. He is motivated by his deep commitment to independence. His action is to complain about the Continental Congress, which has been in session for one year and has done nothing. Obstacles are some representatives in Congress, headed by John Dickinson, the chief antagonist, who believe that the country should remain a part of Great Britain.

Scene 2 Adams's objective and motivation are the same; his action is to go along reluctantly with Franklin's idea to get Lee to go to Virginia and persuade the Virginia House of Burgesses to pass a resolution proposing independence.

Scene 3 His objective and motivation are the same, but his action is to hold his tongue in Congress until Lee returns with the proposal. After Lee presents the resolution, Adams's action is to defend it when Dickinson speaks against it. When it appears that the resolution will be defeated, Adams's action is to devise a way to get a postponement. He and Franklin then come up with the idea that a declaration of independence should be written. Adams's next action is to persuade Jefferson to write the declaration.

Scene 4 This action continues in Scene 4. Jefferson, who misses his wife, is in no mood to write a declaration, and this is another obstacle that Adams overcomes by sending for Martha Jefferson.

Scene 5 Adams's action is to convince the members of Congress who do not believe in separation from Britain that they should be voting for the resolution.

Scene 6 While the Declaration of Independence is read to Congress, Adams's action is to gloat over how well things are going.

Scene 7 In the last scene, his action is to get Congress to approve the Declaration of Independence. Finally, Congress votes its approval, and Adams achieves his goal. In the denouement, Adams proudly signs the document along with the other members.

Attitudes He is friendly toward everyone who is in favor of declaring independence. His attitude toward others is that they must be persuaded, by one way or another, to vote for independence.

Changes The biggest chance that Adams experiences from the beginning to the end of the show is the shift from working constantly and diligently to get Congress to declare its independence to a feeling of relief and satisfaction after the resolution on independence is approved.

Singing Adams is a tenor with nine solos.

Dancing During "He Plays the Violin," he waltzes expertly with Martha Jefferson.

The above description is longer than usual because Adams is a prominent historical figure about whom much has been written. When writing a description

of a nonhistorical character like the Courier or Leather Apron, the stage director will need more imagination in order to decide on such items as ethnic origin, education and personality, and the overall length of the description will undoubtedly be much shorter.

Analyzing the Thoughts

The thoughts of a musical may include the theme or main underlying idea, messages to the audience and other points. You must read the book and lyrics carefully to discover them in the dialogue, songs, dances, or movements of the performers. Consider *Fiddler on the Roof*. The theme may be that traditions are crumbling, as described in the opening number "Tradition," but another major idea is that, despite injustices perpetrated by the rulers against a weak minority, the latter will survive. At the end of the musical, Jerome Robbins, the director-choreographer of the first Broadway production, visually showed the breaking up of the Jewish community as they leave to start new lives in other places.

The term *concept*, as in *concept musical*, is more than a theme—it's how the theme is implemented. *A Chorus Line*, which was conceived by Michael Bennett as a salute to Broadway chorus dancers, shows the world their hopes, their aspirations and their difficult lives. While this may be the theme, the concept is to use a Broadway dance audition as the place to expose their struggles for survival.

To decide how to interpret a musical production, the stage director should think about the theme and other ideas to be communicated to the audience. In researching how other directors have interpreted the work, you may find that opinions vary. For example, you may read that *Evita* is about the fluctuations and manipulations of power, as reflected in the life of Eva Perón of Argentina. Others have written that it is about a local girl who makes good and then dies. The bookwriter, Tim Rice, has said that the only message in the show is that extremists are dangerous, especially attractive ones.

It is up to the stage director to arrive at the theme and other points to be made in the production and to make sure that everyone who works on the musical understands these views.

Analyzing the Words of the Dialogue

Through their words, characters reveal the plot, their thoughts and information about themselves and others. The stage director should examine every sentence to determine: What do these words mean? Is there an underlying meaning (often called the *subtext*)? In other words, is a character saying one thing while actually thinking differently? In rehearsals, performers are going to ask the stage director about meanings and pronunciations, so be prepared.

Jokes and *figures of speech*, such as *similes*, *metaphors*, and *allusions*, need study. *Sensory images* (words that stimulate the senses of sight, hearing, taste, touch or smell) may present problems. The writers' words should arouse images and feelings in the performer's mind and body, just as the words when spoken by the performer should create images and feelings in the spectators. Look at the sensory images in the following speech, which is delivered by a "fleshy poet," Reginald Bunthorne, in *Patience* by Gilbert and Sullivan:

> Do you know what it is to be heart-hungry? Do you know what it is to yearn for the Indefinable, and yet to be brought face to face, daily, with the Multiplication Table? Do you know what it is to seek oceans and to find puddles?—to long for whirlwinds and yet to have to do the best you can with the bellows? That's my case.

It is the stage director's job to see that the actor understands the desired interpretation of the words so that this will be communicated to the audience.

Analyzing the Music, Songs and Dances

The stage and musical directors and choreographer should analyze the composer's score. Look at the music to be played by the orchestra. Is there music for the following purposes?

- An *overture* to begin Act I
- *Entr'acte* music to begin Act II
- Music to *underscore* dialogue or movements
- *Songs* and *dances*
- *Bridges* or *crossovers* to cover set or costume changes

> Older shows often include music for *bridges* to hold the audience's attention while stagehands change the scenery or occasionally while performers put on different costumes. Sometimes actors cross the stage during these numbers (called *crossovers*) singing, dancing or speaking. Today's modern theatres, however, may have devices to speed up scene changes so you can often shorten or eliminate this music.

- *Curtain calls* and the *audience's exit* from the theatre

The stage and musical directors and choreographer should also confer about the following for each song and dance number:

- Who sings, who dances, who speaks, who else in onstage, and what are they doing? Do singers have to dance or just move rhythmically? Do dancers have to sing well?
- What happens in the plot before and after the number?
- What is the mood of the scene?
- What impact should this number have on an audience?
- Does it provide a climax to a scene?
- Does it give exposition, such as to the time and place?
- Does it advance the plot?
- Does it reveal characters and relationships?
- Does it state the theme or main idea?
- Does it tell a story?
- Does it add humor or comedy?
- Does it add variety and spectacle?
- Is this number in the musical solely to show off the talents of the performers?
- What is the overall musical style of the score?

The three leaders should also discuss the types of songs in the score:

- Is there a smooth-flowing love song, called a *ballad*?
- A fast-moving *up-tempo* song?
- A *narrative* song that tells a story?
- A *comedy* song that is meant to get laughs?
- A *dramatic* song that will arouse the sympathetic emotions of the audience?

Musical style refers to the music's distinctive manner of expression. As you analyze the score, ask yourself:

- Does it adhere to an established musical genre, such as jazz, pop, country or rock and roll?
- Does it exhibit a recognizable set of musical conventions, such as the blaring trumpets of the burlesque house in *Gypsy*?
- Does it pertain to a particular geographical region (*Li'l Abner*), a country (*Finian's Rainbow*), or a time period (*The Boy Friend*)?

- A *rhythm* song or *jump* tune that is fast with a strong beat?
- An *establishing* number to provide essential exposition to the audience about the locale, time period, plot, characters or theme?
- A *patter* song that requires singing many words quickly?
- A *musical soliloquy* to give information to the audience about what the singer is thinking and feeling?
- A large *production* number with lots of singers and dancers, spectacular scenery, beautiful costumes and effective lighting?
- A *reprise*, which is a repetition of an earlier song in the show? (The second—or third—time the song is repeated it may have new lyrics with a different meaning and/or it may be sung by another person.)
- An *eleven o'clock* number that provides a big finish shortly before the musical ends?

Look at the structure of each song. Is there a beginning that gets the listeners interested? A middle that develops the subject? An ending that provides a satisfactory conclusion?

Pay particular attention to the words of the lyr-

The name *eleven o'clock number* came into use when Broadway musicals started at 8:30 or 8:40 P.M. and ended about 11:05 to 11:15. Today, with a starting time of 8 P.M., most musicals are finished before 11 P.M., but the name eleven o'clock number persists.

ics. What are the singers' objectives, motivations, actions, thoughts and emotions during each song? Be sure you understand the sensory images, such as those in a solo by Mabel in *The Pirates of Penzance* by Gilbert and Sullivan:

MABEL Dear father, why leave your bed
　　　At this untimely hour,
　　　When happy daylight is dead,
　　　And darksome dangers lower?
　　　See heaven has lit her lamp,
　　　The midnight hour is past,
　　　The chilly night air is damp,
　　　And the dews are falling fast!
　　　Dear father, why leave your bed
　　　When happy daylight is dead?

The musical director should determine:

- The singing ranges (soprano, mezzo-soprano, alto, tenor, baritone, bass) of the soloists
- The total in each vocal range that should be cast in the singing chorus
- The types of voices needed: legitimate singers? belters? rock? popular? jazz?

The stage director and choreographer should decide who is going to block the movement in singing numbers. Dancing is handled by the choreographer, but other movement is normally done by the stage director. If he or she does not feel qualified to handle this, however, the stage director may assign this work to the choreographer.

Another subject for discussion by the stage and musical directors and choreographer is the types of dances in the musical. Look for the following:

- An *opening number* that establishes the mood, style, time and place and other exposition
- A *solo* dance that reveals the inner thoughts or aspirations of a single character
- *Duet* and *small group* dances that establish relationships
- *Production* numbers that have many dancers to provide spectacle and entertainment

Other questions to be answered for each dance are:

- Is there a beginning, middle, and end to the dance?
- How many solo and chorus dancers will be needed and what types of dancing must they

The choreographer may want to research previous productions. Look at still photographs of dancers from New York productions. The New York Public Library's Theatre on Film and Tape Archive has a video collection of dances from Broadway and off-Broadway shows. To use the collection, however, you must make an appointment and state your reasons for viewing. They are located at 40 Lincoln Center Plaza, New York, NY 10023-7498.

do? (Some common ones are: jazz, tap, ballet, pointe, acrobatic, soft shoe, ballroom and a mixture that is often called *stage dance* or *show dance*.)

- What are the dancer's objectives, motivations, thoughts and emotions during each dance?
- Where will each dance take place? Will this dance have exceptional technical needs (a large amount of space, stairs, ramps and platforms or unusual props, costumes, makeup, lighting or special effects)?

After studying the script and designs, the choreographer should study the score and learn the music precisely. You may ask the musical director and rehearsal pianist to make a tape of the dance music so you will have it for study and later rehearsals. To get a feeling for the orchestration, you may ask the musical director/conductor to go through the score, pointing out where various instruments will be playing and the dynamics of the music.

Analyzing the Spectacle and Sound

The stage director should analyze the *spectacle*, which includes all of the visual elements of the production (the performers' movements and dances as well as the scenery, properties, lighting, costumes, makeup and special effects), and the *sound*, which refers to the aural aspects of the production (performers' voices, music and sound effects).

For each scene, the stage director must decide how the production should look and sound. As preparation for talking with the designers, the stage director should prepare a *production analysis* that details the requirements of the scenery, props, lighting, sound, and special effects and their cues (see Figure 3-3). The stage director does not have to be an expert in technical theatre to do this, although some knowledge is helpful. For example, you ought to know the names of common types of sets, such as:

- A *wing-drop-border* set has wings (these are flats or drapes at the sides of a proscenium stage to mask the offstage areas), backdrop(s) and borders hanging overhead.
- A *box set* has three walls and a ceiling and is used for interior rooms on a proscenium stage. The audience views the action through the missing fourth wall of the room.
- An *architectural set* is a permanent structure that can be altered to suggest different locations by adding scenic pieces, draperies and properties.
- Another neutral type of set is a *unit set*, which may have flats, screens, curtains, platforms and stairs that can be rearranged to change locales.
- A *simultaneous set* displays to the audience two or more different places at the same time.
- A *space stage* is an open stage that features lighting and, perhaps, *projected scenery* (film, slide or television pictures that are projected from the rear or the front onto a surface that is part of the set).
- *Revolving stage sets* feature a revolve, which is a circular platform that can be turned to show different scenes.
- *Wagon sets* use rolling platforms and *elevator sets* use elevators to get scenery, properties and performers on and off stage.
- *Partial sets* have simple set pieces, fragmentary sets, screens or skeletal scaffolding in front of curtains, draperies, or the back wall of the stage.
- A *scrim* is a net or gauze curtain, drop or set that appears opaque when lighted from the front but becomes transparent when lighted from behind.
- A *cyclorama* is a curved curtain, drop or wall

FIGURE 3-3 **STAGE DIRECTOR'S PRODUCTION ANALYSIS FOR SCENE I OF *1776***

Scenes & Music	Scenery	Props	Lighting & Sound
#1 Overture	Front curtain is down.		Fade houselights out slowly. At end of over-ture, spot Adams.
Scene 1	At end of Adams's first speech, curtain flies out revealing Chamber.		
Chamber of Continental Congress. Time: May 8. #2 "Sit Down, John" by Adams and Congress.		May 8 on wall calendar; talley board, barometer; Hancock's large desk has inkwell, quill, sand shaker, books, flyswatter, gavel, matches, papers, 2 pipes, 2 mugs, hand bell, can tobacco; Thomson's small desk has letter opener, inkwell, quill, hand bell, sand shaker, book, papers; Bartlett's small desk has inkwell, quill, pipe, fan, book, papers, matches; McKean's table has fan, inkwell, quill, sand shaker; Dickinson's table has books, sand shaker, inkwell, 2 quills, playing cards; Hopkins's bench has fan; Rodney's bench; Hewes's chair has news-paper; 14 chairs; 5 stools; wastebasket; coat rack with few canes, hats, coats; Adams has cane; all men have handkerchiefs.	Indoor day lighting. At end of song, fade out lights on Congress and spot Adams.
#3 "Piddle, Twiddle" by Adams.			When Hancock speaks, spot Hancock and then Wilson. After Wilson's speech, spot Adams.
#4 "Till Then" by Adams and Abigail.			Spot Adams and Abigail. At end of song, spot Adams.

FIGURE 3-4 **STAGE DIRECTOR'S LIST OF COSTUMES AND WIGS FOR *1776***
(BASED ON COSTUME PLOT OF KRAUSE COSTUME CO., CLEVELAND, OH)

JOHN ADAMS (age 40): 1. Dark suit coat and breeches, vest, shirt with lace at neck and wrists, hose, shoes with buckles, hat, walking stick, and dark-colored wig.

2. Another suit coat in a medium-dark color and vest.

JOHN HANCOCK (40): 1. Dark, elegant suit coat, vest, breeches, shirt with lace at neck and wrists, hose, shoes with buckles, and dark-colored wig.

CHARLES THOMSON (47): 1. Conservative, dark suit coat, vest, breeches, shirt, hose, shoes with buckles, and dark-colored wig.

DR. JOSIAH BARTLETT (48): 1. Dark, simple suit coat, vest, breeches, shirt with lace at neck and wrists, hose, shoes with buckles, and dark-colored wig.

STEPHEN HOPKINS (70): 1. Simple suit coat, vest, breeches, shirt, hose, shoes with buckles, cane, black Quaker hat, and shoulder-length grey wig.

ROGER SHERMAN (55): 1. Tweedy, homespun suit coat, vest, breeches, shirt, hose, shoes with buckles, and dark-colored wig.

LEWIS MORRIS (50): 1. Elegant satin suit coat, vest, breeches, shirt with lace at neck and wrists, hose, shoes with buckles, and white wig.

ROBERT LIVINGSTON (30): 1. Dark suit coat, vest, breeches, shirt, hose, shoes with buckles, and natural-colored wig.

JOHN DICKINSON (44): 1. Elegant suit coat, vest, breeches, shirt with lace at neck and wrists, hose, shoes with buckles, cane, and natural-colored wig.

2. Another elegant suit coat.

JAMES WILSON (33): 1. Conservative suit coat, vest, breeches, shirt, hose, shoes with buckles, cane, and natural-colored wig.

CAESAR RODNEY (48): 1. Dark suit coat, vest breeches, shirt, hose, shoes with buckles, cane, long, green scarf, and white wig.

2. Cloak and riding boots.

COL. THOMAS McKEAN (42): 1. Bright suit coat, vest, breeches, shirt, hose, shoes with buckles, rough-hewn cane, and natural-colored wig.

GEORGE READ (43): 1. Light-colored suit coat, vest, breeches, shirt, hose, shoes with buckles, and white wig.

FIGURE 3-4 CONTINUED

SAMUEL CHASE (35): 1. Light-colored suit coat, vest, breeches, shirt, hose, shoes with buckles, and white wig.

RICHARD HENRY LEE (45): 1. Elegant suit coat, vest, breeches, shirt with lace at neck and wrists, hose, boots, tri-cornered hat, and natural-colored wig (brown with a little silver).

THOMAS JEFFERSON (33): 1. Light-colored suit coat, vest, breeches, shirt with lace at neck and wrists, hose, shoes with buckles, and copper-colored wig.

JOSEPH HEWES (46): 1. Light-colored suit coat, vest, breeches, shirt with lace at neck and wrists, hose, shoes with buckles, cane and white wig.

EDWARD RUTLEDGE (26): 1. Dandified, light-colored suit coat, vest, breeches, shirt with lace at neck and wrists, hose, shoes with buckles, and natural-colored wig.

ANDREW McNAIR (60): 1. Open vest, patched breeches, shirt, dark hose, shoes with buckles, and simple, natural-colored wig.

A LEATHER APRON (17): 1. Shirt, vest, breeches, hose, shoes with buckles, leather apron, and simple, natural-colored wig.

ABIGAIL ADAMS (32): 1. Pretty dress of the period, panniers, cap, petticoat, and natural-colored shoulder-length wig.

2. Another pretty dress in different color with shawl.

BENJAMIN FRANKLIN (70): 1. Elegant suit coat, vest, breeches, shirt with lace at neck and wrists, hose, shoes with buckles, hat, cane, eyeglasses, and balding, shoulder-length white wig.

2. Knitted booty.

3. Another elegant suit coat and vest.

A PAINTER (30): 1. Painter's smock and beret, breeches, hose, shoes with buckles, and simple, natural-colored wig.

DR. LYMAN HALL (55): 1. Dark, conservative suit coat, vest, breeches, shirt with lace at neck and wrists, hose, tri-cornered hat, shoes with buckles, and natural-colored wig.

COURIER (20): 1. Torn, tattered blue and buff military uniform coat, vest, breeches, shirt, leggings, spurs, and simple, natural-colored wig.

REV. JOHN WITHERSPOON (54): 1. Plain, dark suit coat, vest, breeches, shirt, hose, tri-cornered hat, shoes with buckles, and natural-colored wig.

MARTHA JEFFERSON (27): 1. Attractive light-colored dress of the period, panniers, cap, petticoat, cape, and natural-colored shoulder-length wig.

that surrounds the playing area on three sides and is often painted to look like sky.

As for the colors to be used in the scenery, if you have ideas be sure to mention them.

In lighting, there are some terms that a stage director may use in preparing a production analysis:

- *Blackout* means a fast darkening of the stage.
- *Fade out* or *dim out* is a slower blackening.
- *Fade up* or *fade in* means that the stage lights come up gradually.
- *Bump up* is used when you want the stage lights to come up quickly.
- In a *cross-fade* the lights go down in one area of the stage while they come up in another area.
- *Spotlighting* involves focusing a strong light on one individual or a group. This is often used for solos or duets in order to attract the audience's attention to the most important people onstage.
- A *follow spotlight* may be operated by a technician to keep these actors in a strong light as they move around the stage.

For the production analysis, the stage director should visualize the general lighting for each scene (for example, "day interior," "sunny summer day exterior," "cold evening exterior," and so forth) and how the lighting changes. If spotlighting is to be used, decide when and on whom the spots should be focused. If color is important, name the color of the lighting to be used (blue, amber, red, green, etc.). There are many colors available so be as specific as you like as to the exact color you want.

Any recorded sound effects (like an offstage car starting up and driving away) and special effects (such as flying Peter Pan) should also be noted in the analysis.

In addition, the stage director and the costume designer, with advice from the choreographer, should prepare preliminary descriptions of the costumes and wigs to be acquired (see Figure 3-4). If any unusual makeups are needed, these too should be noted.

For most school/community productions, performers may be requested to furnish their own shoes, stockings, socks, underwear, and (if the musical is set in contemporary or recent time periods) some of their own clothes. For sanitary reasons, they may also be asked to provide and apply their own makeup; however, if the makeup is unusual, both the makeup and instruction in how to apply it should be given to the actors.

CHAPTER FOUR

Interpreting Musicals

After researching and analyzing the musical, the stage director should now have a concept of how this show should look and sound in performance. This vision will dictate the style and interpretation given to the production. The musical director/conductor, choreographer, designers and all other workers should be made aware of this concept and should make their plans accordingly.

DETERMINING STYLE AND INTERPRETATION

Style is the quality that results from a distinctive manner of expression used by artists to present their ideas and emotions. For plays in the theatre, there are two major categories of styles: representational and presentational.

Representational stage plays, such as Anton Chekhov's *Three Sisters*, purport to show life as it is. Actors appear to be living their parts, and they ignore the spectators who are allowed to watch the events through the "fourth wall" of the room depicted onstage. The dialogue, actions and costumes are true to life, and the scenery appears to be the actual place. These plays, which are highly illusory, encourage the audience to empathize with the performers to the extent that the spectators may forget that they are in a theatre. This type of play may be labeled *realistic,* and if the designers are trying to be extremely realistic—attempting to put a "slice of life" onstage—it can be called *naturalistic.* An example of the latter is Maxim Gorki's *The Lower Depths.*

On the other hand, *presentational plays* are pre-sented to the spectators. Actors work directly to the audience much of the time, scenery may merely suggest a locale and there is little attempt at illusion.

Musical productions, which are highly presentational, may not have much illusion onstage, but illusion can be achieved in the minds of the spectators if they can watch a production with what Samuel Taylor Coleridge called a "willing suspension of disbelief." So long as the listeners accept the stage conventions used (such as singers and dancers suddenly appearing onstage with no motivation), it is possible for them to empathize with a musical as much as a representational play.

The *production style* should be selected by the stage director to complement the style of the writing; for example, an epic theatre musical, such as Bertolt Brecht and Kurt Weill's *The Threepenny Opera*, is usually given an epic theatre production. Alan Jay Lerner and Frederick Loewe's *My Fair Lady*, which is based on George Bernard Shaw's realistic play *Pygmalion*, will probably be given a selective realistic production.

The following are some names, descriptions and examples of production styles that are currently used for musicals.

Selective Realism

In this type, just the minimum number of essential elements of a locale is used. While the details may be faithful to the period in costuming, properties and decor, there is a greater emphasis on theatricality. *Les Misérables* by Alain Boublil and Claude-Michel Schönberg (with Herbert Kretzmer) employs this style.

Theatricalism

No attempt is made at illusion in this style. The audience knows that it is in a theatre watching a musical as lights may be visible, stagehands may change the scenery in front of the audience, some properties may be imagined and so forth. An example is *Stop the World—I Want to Get Off* by Anthony Newley and Leslie Bricusse.

Formalism

The designer may use steps, ramps, different levels, columns, drapes and screens to form a neutral type of stage that does not suggest any one place until it is established by the dialogue or lyrics or by the addition of a set piece or properties. Unit sets and permanent architectural settings are included in this category. A musical that may use this type is *Chicago* by John Kander, Fred Ebb and Bob Fosse.

Symbolism

In this style symbols are used onstage to suggest meanings to the spectators; for example, in *Starlight Express* by Richard Stilgoe and Andrew Lloyd Webber, the costumes connote trains or parts of trains to the audience.

Expressionism

This is a theatrical style that represents a place as seen through the eyes of the leading character. Typically, as the protagonist becomes disturbed or upset, the scenery, properties, lighting, costumes, makeup and sound become distorted to suggest how he or she views the environment. *Lady in the Dark* by Kurt Weill, Ira Gershwin and Moss Hart may use this style.

Impressionism

In an impressionistic design, the designer is trying to heighten the mood in a nonrealistic but atmospheric way. Like expressionism, spectators may see the environment as a major character does. An example is *The Phantom of the Opera* by Andrew Lloyd Webber, Richard Stilgoe and Charles Hart.

Constructivism

This style uses steps, ramps, ladders, platforms and beams to suggest skeletal structures. Only the scenic elements actually needed for the action may be onstage. Note the designs used for the Broadway production of *Company* by Stephen Sondheim and George Furth.

Epic Theatre

This is another theatrical style that uses slide, movie or TV projections, signs, turntables, treadmills, escalators, elevators and other technical devices. This style was developed for the epic plays and musicals of Bertolt Brecht and others who write about subjects of social significance. *Evita* by Andrew Lloyd Webber and Tim Rice uses this style.

Multimedia

Stereophonic sound, unusual lighting, special effects and slide, film or television projections on multiple screens may combine with live performers and music for another theatrical style. *Grease* by Jim Jacobs and Warren Casey is an example of this type of staging.

NEW INTERPRETATIONS OF TRADITIONAL WORKS

Because the musical was originally presented in a certain style does not mean that you have to produce it the same way. As noted in chapter one, some modern directors (especially of operas and comic operas), like to give new interpretations to old favorites and if the work is in the public domain, this is legally possible. For example, Peter Brook, a famous English director, changed the opera *Carmen* considerably when he offered *La Tragédie de Carmen* with a cast of only seven (four singing roles and three speaking parts).

Why do directors want to make changes in the traditional ways of presenting old masterpieces? They may believe that audiences are tired of seeing conventional interpretations and would enjoy something new and different. When these works were first presented, they surprised and delighted their audiences, but after years of traditional productions, many spectators know what to expect and are bored with these presentations. Modern directors try to interest theatregoers by showing how relevant the old pieces can be to present life.

Secondly, some directors may want to devise a new concept because they believe that today's professional singers, musicians and designers want to be challenged by new interpretations. They, too, are bored with presenting the works in the same way for years and would prefer to have a new perspective on the old pieces. A third reason for reinterpretation may be that some directors like to shock audiences with a radical new version because it attracts publicity to the director as well as the producing company.

As you may imagine, the traditionalists among music lovers are not happy with these new interpretations. They believe that the new versions are contrary to the intentions of the composers and librettists. They contend that the authors' ideas, messages and meanings are changed and are, therefore, not to be condoned. Others, who support the new renditions, think that to make theatre attractive to younger audiences, productions must be interesting, exciting and meaningful to them. They believe that if the new versions entertain or make an audience think, they should be presented.

We recommend that the stage director research and analyze the work, the expression of theme and thoughts, the authors' intentions and previous productions. The stage director, however, should look at the piece as though it were being presented for the first time. It is permissible to study previous productions so that you are aware of various options, but there is no one interpretation that must be used for any musical. Be original and present a version that will bring entertainment and intellectual value to your audience.

So how many changes in the script and score can you make in your interpretation? It depends on whether your musical is under copyright. Most modern musicals are, and as noted in chapter two, your contract with the licensor will probably stipulate that you cannot make any changes to the music, lyrics or dialogue. On the other hand, many old operas and operettas are in the public domain and can be altered to suit your purposes.

COMMUNICATING WITH THE TEAM

At meetings with the musical director, choreographer and designers, the stage director should pre-

Look at your available space. How can you best use your playing areas to express your concept? The musicians do not have to be in an orchestra pit. Perhaps they can better serve your ideas by being onstage, backstage or in a theatre box. Would some scenes play better in the aisles, a box or a balcony? Are there ways to involve some audience members in the action?

sent for discussion the production analysis and costume list described in the previous chapter and talk about style, interpretation and staging. The stage director should state how he or she sees and hears each scene: time period, place, mood, atmosphere, and concept for the production. If he or she has a preference for colors, lines, shapes, spaces or textures onstage, this should be pointed out.

The choreographer should present any particular needs that the dancers will have in costuming (dance costumes are different from regular costumes in that they have to be strong and well-made to permit exceptional movement), wigs, makeup and lighting. The choreographer will also need to investigate plans for scenery and properties to know how much space is available for dance numbers.

The musical director should list potential problems with regard to the music and singing. One may be the amplification of singers and orchestra: What types of microphones (body, overhead, floor and so forth) should be used and where should speakers be placed?

The stage director, costume designer and choreographer should arrive at a final list of costumes and wigs to make, buy, rent or borrow and should decide how to handle unusual makeups.

As soon as the designers have time to research and formulate their ideas, the stage and musical directors and choreographer should listen to them as they show plans to achieve the effect wanted. The scene designer should present color renderings, models and ground plans; the costume designer should exhibit sketches of costumes, wigs and unusual makeups; and the sound designer may submit ideas for sound amplification and recorded sound effects. These plans should be discussed and revised until the stage director thinks they are satisfactory.

After the scene designer's ideas have been approved, the lighting designer can begin to plan how to implement the stage director's vision as well as his or her own thoughts on the subject. During the rehearsal period, there should be more discussions by the stage director, choreographer and lighting designer until the plans for lighting are finalized.

PREBLOCKING THE MUSICAL BY THE STAGE DIRECTOR

After approval of the scene designer's work, the stage director can begin to plan the blocking. This is the arrangement of performers onstage and their movements. Some directors do not like to work on blocking before rehearsals, preferring to rely on the inspiration of the moment and the spontaneous movements of actors. Peter Brook wrote in *The Empty Space* that any director who arrives at a first rehearsal with his script prepared with movements and business is a real deadly theatre man.

If you are working with only a few experienced performers, you too may prefer not to preblock, but if you are directing a large number of inexperienced amateurs, you may have chaos if you allow ten or more of them to wander around the stage. For people on a short rehearsal schedule, it will probably save valuable time if the stage director figures out before rehearsals where performers will enter and exit and their major movements. After rehearsals start, if actors are uncomfortable with these movements or suggest better ones, the blocking can and should be changed. Performers' input may give the stage director new insights into the script.

From the ground plans, models, renderings, and discussions with the scene designer, the stage director should be able to visualize how the stage will look in each scene. Now imagine your performers in the first set and draw a diagram showing their positions. Next, decide when they will move and where they will move to. Write in the directions or make another drawing showing these movements. Continue this way throughout the script, writing in pencil. Because your ideas about blocking may change frequently from prerehearsal to dress re-

hearsals, you should write in pencil so that your notes can be easily altered. If you cannot purchase a script and must use a rented one that has to be returned clean after the last performance, insert blank paper for your notes between pages or write on self-sticking notepaper that can be removed.

You will find stage directions in your script that usually indicate the blocking done in a Broadway production. Some of these directions can be used, but others cannot because your floor plan or scenery or interpretation is different. So use the stage directions in the script or ignore them. (See Figure 4-1 for a sample page from a script of *The Mikado* marked by a director in prerehearsal blocking.)

To save time in writing, abbreviations and symbols such as the following are commonly used:

- Refer to characters by the first letter or two of their name.
- Indicate a "cross" by X; for example, "Nan crosses down right to John" may be written "N X DR to J;" for cross two steps left," write "X 2 L."
- Use an upward arrow ↑ to show that a character rises and a downward arrow ↓ when the actor sits.
- Draw ∨s to signify in what direction a performer is facing, such as ∨, ∧, <, or >.
- Write | to suggest a short pause and || for a longer pause.

All directors make up their own marks, so use whatever works for you. For more information about blocking, see chapter eleven.

PLANNING BY THE MUSICAL DIRECTOR/CONDUCTOR

To prepare for auditions and rehearsals, the musical director/conductor must understand and accept the stage director's concept for interpreting the work. He or she should then decide how each musical number should sound.

Before going into auditions, the musical director must not only analyze the number and types of voices and singing ranges needed for soloists and singing chorus but he or she must also consider how these characters should look—their age, height, build and appearance. After all, the chorus line for The Hot Box nightclub in *Guys and Dolls* demands different women from the Shark Girls in

FIGURE 4-1 **STAGE DIRECTOR'S PREBLOCKING OF EXCERPT FROM ACT I OF *THE MIKADO***

NANKI-POO If it were not for the law, we should now be sitting side by side, like that.
(Sits by her) on L bench

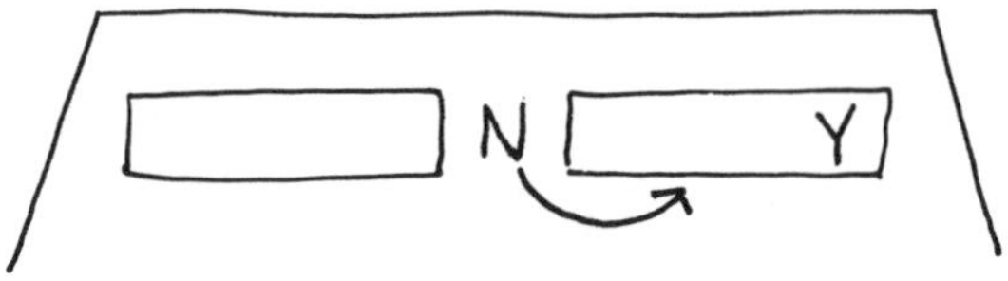

YUM-YUM Instead of being obliged to sit half a mile off, like that.
(Crosses and sits ~~at other side of stage.~~)
R bench

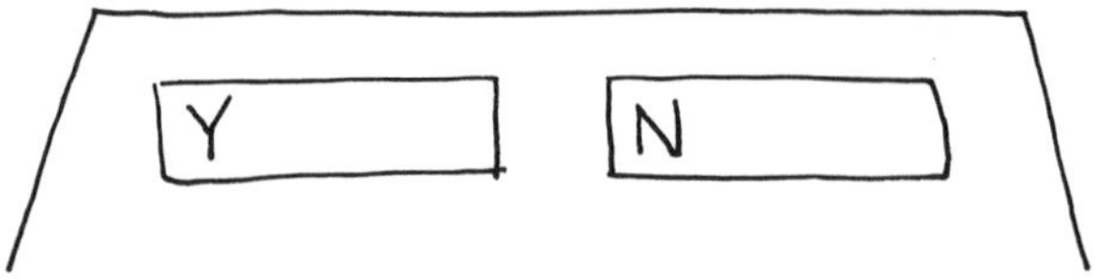

(X to Y↓ R bench)
NANKI-POO We should be gazing into each other's eyes, like that.
(Gazing at her sentimentally)

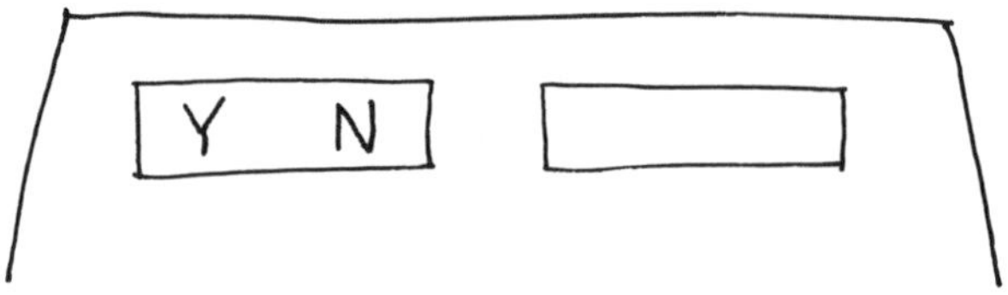

YUM-YUM Breathing sighs of unutterable love—like that.
(Sighing and gazing lovingly at him)

NANKI-POO With our arms round each other's waists, like that.
(Embracing her)
(removing N's arms)
YUM-YUM Yes, if it wasn't for the law.

(dejected, turns >)
NANKI-POO If it wasn't for the law.

(↑ XC)
YUM-YUM As it is, of course we couldn't do anything of the kind. (>)

(↑ X to Y)
NANKI-POO Not for worlds!

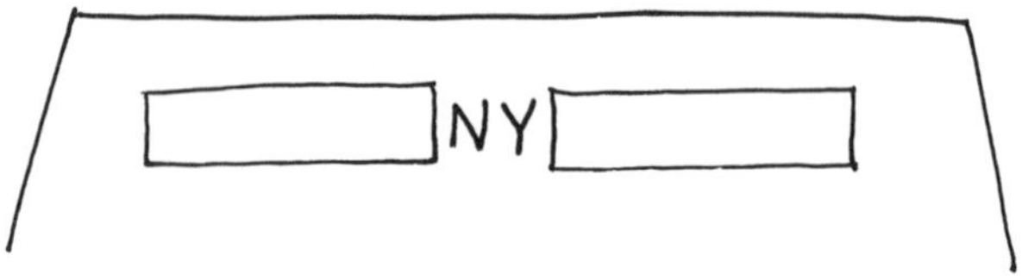

(turns to N)
YUM-YUM Being engaged to Ko Ko, you know!

(nodding head ∨)
NANKI-POO Being engaged to Ko Ko!

West Side Story.

Decisions must also be made about how to handle auditions. For specific auditions, the musical director will often request the publicity director to publicize that all singers should bring to auditions their own music and be prepared to sing one minute of any song. If the musical director wants to hear candidates for leading roles sing particular selections, these stipulations should be well-publicized several weeks before auditions.

As for acquiring an orchestra, the musical director/conductor should determine the instruments needed and where the players may "double" (that is, one musician playing two instruments). Then the conductor may begin making inquiries to musicians in your school or community. It may be helpful for the conductor to prepare a rehearsal and performance schedule early so that prospective musicians will know exactly what they are committing themselves to.

PLANNING BY THE CHOREOGRAPHER

As soon as the stage director sets the concept for the show and the scene and costume designers' plans become available, the choreographer can begin to choreograph the routines. As mentioned in the last chapter, the choreographer should request that the musical director and rehearsal pianist make a tape of the dance music. Tempos, cuts or additions to the dances should be decided upon by the directors and choreographer as early as possible.

As you listen to the tape of the dance music, visualize the characters who are onstage at that time, the place, the situation, and the reason for the dance. Then examine the score and ask yourself:

- Is the music dissonant or consonant?
- Does it have a steady or uneven rhythm?
- What instruments carry the orchestration?

- If a dance bridge occurs within a song, consider the lyrics: Do they suggest movement?

As you listen, try to think of an overall pattern that will tell the story of this dance.

- Is it symmetrical or asymmetrical?
- Are there different types of movement happening all over the stage or do people move in unison?
- Who should have the focus in this dance?
- What are the dynamics? Are there moments of energetic movement alternating with soft and subtle motions?

Then proceed to create actual steps that are set to musical counts. Envision them on the stage; then using your own notation, write the dance down on paper in a way that you can read it. Can you incorporate the set into your dance? What about props? What lighting would be appropriate? Can you create movement that will use the costumes in a creative way? What sort of shoes will the dancers wear?

Remember that your dances must be relevant to the production's plot and overall style. Do not, for example, stick a classical ballet interlude into *Grease.* Modern theatrical dances are integral parts of the plot and should never be treated as a separate entity.

To prepare for auditions, the choreographer must determine the number and qualifications needed for solo and chorus dancers. The choreographer should decide on the types of dancing they must do and what they should look like—how old, how tall, what build? What sort of characters are the dancers? Are they showgirls? Businessmen? Village lads and lasses? Do they also sing?

If specific auditions are to be held, the choreographer should devise a short combination of dance steps that are representative of those to be done in the musical. This combination will be taught to the aspirants who will then demonstrate how quickly they are able to learn and how well they perform.

CHAPTER FIVE

Planning the Technical Elements

In the theatre, the word *technical* covers the scenery, special effects, properties, lighting, sound, costumes, makeup and hairstyles. As mentioned in chapter four, preproduction planning should include conferences with the stage director and designers in which the stage director communicates ideas about the style, interpretation and effects desired. Later, when the designers present their plans, the stage director should consider, discuss and either approve them or ask for revisions.

A major concern for the designers and stage director is that all of the technical elements work together harmoniously to contribute to:

- style (selective realism, theatricalism, formalism, etc.)
- genre (comedy, farce, melodrama, drama, etc.)
- stage director's interpretation of production
- helping the audience understand the plot, characters and theme
- establishing mood and atmosphere
- adding variety and excitement

It is important that there be agreement on the colors to be used throughout the show in the settings, props, lighting, costumes and makeup. If there is any disagreement among the designers, technical director and crews about colors or anything else, the stage director should try to settle the problem. The stage director is responsible for bringing all elements together into a cohesive whole and, therefore, must maintain his or her authority as the artistic head of the show. The stage director's chief assistant,

the stage manager, should aid in the coordination of the technical elements and should have all cues regarding scenery, special effects, props, curtains, lighting and sound written in the stage manager's promptscript. The technical director should also assist in coordinating the technical work.

SCENERY AND SPECIAL EFFECTS

In designing the settings, the scene designer tries to provide a visual environment that is suitable for each scene and the play as a whole. This designer helps the audience understand the style, genre, mood, atmosphere and the following:

- Time period
- Place
- The performing area
- Socioeconomic level of people who inhabit the environment

The scene designer also helps the stage director obtain interesting stage pictures by adding performers to effective sets. In addition, this designer is responsible for dressing the set with *set (or trim) properties* (like furniture, pictures and plants) and creating *special effects* (such as fog, smoke or snow).

The scene designer should provide the stage director with *floor plans* (also termed *ground plans*), which are line drawings of each set as seen from above (see Figure 5-1). The scene designer may also prepare renderings or models of the sets. *Renderings* are perspective drawings of the sets that will give the stage director and others a good idea of what

FIGURE 5-1 **SCENE DESIGNER'S GROUND PLAN OF SET FOR ACT I, SCENE 1 OF *BRIGADOON*
(DESIGNER: JAMES MORRIS-SMITH, MARSHALL UNIVERSITY)**

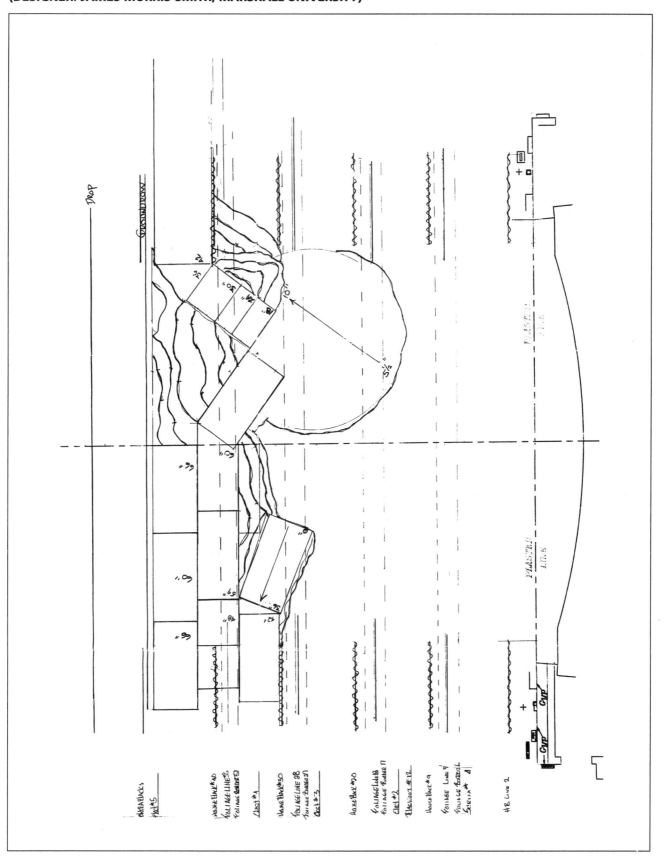

FIGURE 5-2 **SCENE DESIGNER'S RENDERING OF SET FOR** *LITTLE SHOP OF HORRORS*
(DESIGNER: MIKE MURPHY, MARSHALL UNIVERSITY)

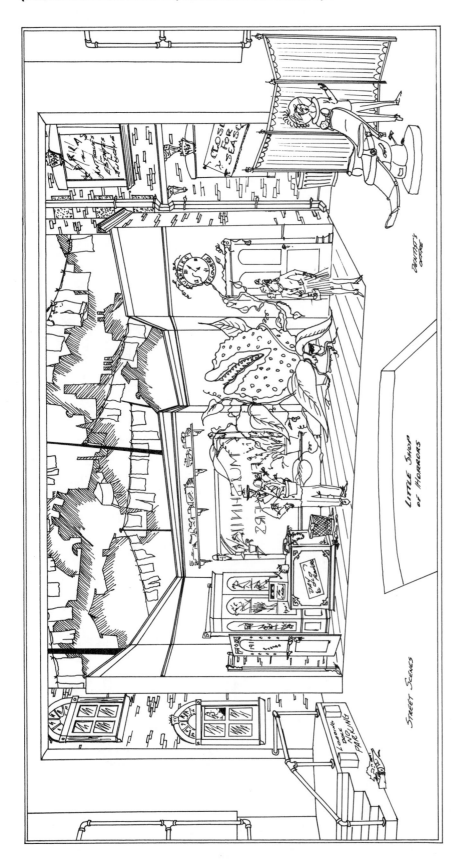

the audience will see onstage (see Figure 5-2). *Models* are three-dimensional representations of the sets made with cardboard, cloth, modeling clay and other materials.

After the stage director approves the plans, this designer makes working drawings that are given to the technical director and those who will do the construction and painting of the sets. Later, before technical rehearsals, this designer will supervise the erection and shifting of sets by the stage crew.

Scenery and properties in large Broadway musicals are likely to be elaborate and expensive, but a school/community production does not have to copy what was done in New York. Although their budget is much smaller, amateurs can provide an environment for each scene that is appropriate, tasteful and practical.

For a multiscene show, one of the most important considerations is that the settings be constructed so that they can be changed quickly. To have a fast production, there must be no waiting for scene changes. For this reason, wing-drop-border sets, such as the one depicted in Figure 5-1, are often used for musicals. By flying in a new backdrop from the fly loft, you can have the next set in place in a few seconds. If you do not have a fly loft in your theatre, however, consider using some of the other suggestions from chapter three, especially the following:

- Architectural set
- Unit set
- Simultaneous set
- Space stage with projected scenery
- Revolving stage sets
- Wagon sets
- Elevator sets
- Partial sets or screens in front of curtains or draperies

If your organization has a scene designer who can prepare plans for the scenery and properties and a technical director and technicians who can execute the plans, you will probably prefer to build your sets and some of the props. If, however, your group does not have the personnel or facilities for designing, constructing and painting scenery and props, you may have to buy, rent or borrow them.

If you know of another organization that has produced this musical, ask if they have settings, special effects or props available to buy, rent or borrow. Also, furniture, lamps and chandeliers can sometimes be borrowed from local merchants who may ask for nothing in return other than credit on the program. There are theatrical supply houses who rent or sell painted backdrops, special effects and some props. The best way to make your selections is to go to the supply house to look at them, but if that is impossible, you may select from a catalog. Try to make sure, though, that all drops are painted in the same style and look as though they belong to the same show. For help, consult theatrical supply houses, whose names and addresses may be found in the directories listed near the end of chapter two.

PROPERTIES

The stage director or stage manager should prepare an accurate list and oversee the acquisition or construction of hand props (like a magazine, drink or coins) by the property crew (see Figure 5-3). The scene designer supervises set (or trim) props, and the costume designer selects props that are part of a costume (such as a purse or handkerchief).

The stage director will probably want to use props in rehearsals as soon as the actors have learned their parts and no longer need to carry scripts. If the actual props are not yet available, substitute props should be used until they are.

LIGHTING

Stage lighting makes visible what the audience has to see to understand the musical, and it adds color, light and shade to the scenery and properties. The lighting designer can help to establish the following:

- Mood and atmosphere (lights can and probably should change as music and situations onstage do)
- Style and genre
- Time of day
- Time of year

FIGURE 5-3 **STAGE DIRECTOR'S PROP LIST FOR FIRST TWO SCENES AND INTERLUDE OF *BRIGADOON***

ACT I, SC. 1 A forest in the Scottish Highlands. 5 A.M. in May.

Road map of Scotland (Jeff)

2 rifles

2 rucksacks

Flask with liquid inside (Jeff)

INTERLUDE A road in the town of Brigadoon. Few minutes later.

Cart with milk and cream, cups, jugs, 1 stool, jug of claret (Angus)

Cart with woolens, plaids and 1 stool (Archie)

Cart with candy and 1 stool (Sandy)

Other people carry baskets for their purchases

Some in chorus have trays of flowers or vegetables to sell

Two have jugs of ale to sell

Two have long sticks with meat and/or fish hanging from them to sell

One has woolen clothes (caps, scarves, hose) to sell

ACT I, SC. 2 The square of Brigadoon—MacConnachy Square. Later that morning.

Above carts and props are onstage.

Book (Harry)

Basket (Fiona)

Large piece of parchment with writing on it (Andrew)

Coins (Fiona and Tommy)

Loaf of bread—Offstage L for Fiona

Handkerchief (Jean)

Black old-fashioned-looking umbrellas for some in chorus

Many in chorus have loaded baskets

- Time of year
- Weather conditions
- The important area onstage
- Performers, props or scenery that should be emphasized
- Some special effects (such as lightning)
- Moving from one scene to the next (through fade outs, fade ins, cross-fades, blackouts and bump ups).

Follow spotlighting from the house or the stage is often used for musicals. While seldom used in lighting stage plays, you will find follow spots called for frequently in musical scripts. These are strong lights that can be moved by an operator to follow leading performers as they move around the stage. The stage director should provide instructions for the lighting designer stating where and when a person or persons are to be lighted by one or more follow spots. The stage director should also describe other lighting for each scene and the cues for changes (see Figure 5-4).

After the lighting designer receives floor plans from the scene designer, he or she then makes for each set a *light plot*, which shows the type, size and location of each lighting instrument, the area that each will light, the filter's color (which may be influenced by the colors of the scenery, costumes and makeup onstage) and the needed circuitry.

FIGURE 5-4 **STAGE DIRECTOR'S INSTRUCTIONS FOR LIGHTING THE PROLOGUE AND FIRST THREE SCENES OF** *FIDDLER ON THE ROOF*

Spot Conductor as he enters pit. After his bow, blackout spot.

As music starts, spot Fiddler on the roof as noted below.

PROLOGUE Exterior of Tevye's house.

Spot Fiddler on the roof.

When Tevye enters at R, spot him and start to bring up stage lights

Keep follow spot on Tevye until he joins Papas at R to sing with them, then broaden to cover all Papas.

Next spot Mamas at L. Then spot Sons at RC. Next spot Daughters at LC.

Then bring up lights to cover all center stage.

After "horse-mule" argument, spot Tevye and follow him.

Fade out stage lights as chorus exits.

Fade out Tevye's spot at end of scene.

ACT I, SC. 1 Daytime: kitchen of Tevye's house.

When "Matchmaker" starts, concentrate on three girls and darken other areas.

Blackout at end of scene.

ACT I SC. 2 Late afternoon (the sun is setting): exterior of Tevye's house.

Spot Tevye on solo and darken stage lights.

After solo, bring up stage lights.

Fade out at end of scene.

ACT I, SC. 3 Evening: interior of Tevye's house.

When "Sabbath Prayer" starts, fade out stage lights so that most of the lighting comes from candles. The chorus with candles is standing around the sides of the stage.

When everyone blows out candles at end, the stage should be dark.

When light plots are completed, an *instrument schedule* should be made that lists every lighting instrument with all pertinent information about it. This designer also sees that lighting instruments are hung and focused, that color filters are installed, and that the control board is operated properly.

One problem to be discussed by the lighting designer, stage director and conductor is turning off the lights on the orchestra's music stands during blackouts. Rather than ask the musicians to do this, it is better to have the lighting technicians or the conductor control these lights. Of course, lights cannot be turned off or dimmed too much if the orchestra has to play during the blackout.

Lighting equipment may be rented or bought from theatrical supply houses. Examine their cata-

logs to find everything you need from spotlights to control boards.

SOUND

The sound designer makes audible what the audience needs to hear by amplifying voices and instruments and by playing recorded sound effects and music. Sound may help to establish the following:

• Time of day (a clock strikes the hour)
• Place of a scene (street sounds)
• Mood and atmosphere (birds chirping)
• Weather conditions (thunder)
• Offstage occurrences (a car wreck)

The stage director should also give the sound designer instructions for recorded sound effects and music (see Figure 5-5). A recording of almost any

FIGURE 5-5 **STAGE DIRECTOR'S INSTRUCTIONS FOR SOUND IN *SOUTH PACIFIC***

ACT I, SC. 1 (P. 4)—Six bars after curtain goes up, bird caw sounds begin. Fade out sound when children begin to sing.

ACT I, SC. 9 (P. 47)—On blackout of scene, ship's bell rings 8 times in groups in two.

ACT I, SC. 11 (P. 52)—As Cable starts to kiss Liat, ship's bell rings 8 times in groups of two.

(P. 53)—On blackout of scene, ship's bell rings 8 times in groups of two.

ACT I, SC. 12 (P. 54)—After Billis asks for the second time for the bell to ring, ship's bell rings 8 times in groups of two.

ACT II, SC. 1 (P. 62)—Nellie brings practical mike onto ramp from L.

ACT II, SC. 4 (P. 79)—On blackout of scene, begin aircraft take-off.

ACT II, SC. 5 (P. 80)—One aircraft takes off during scene. At end of take-off, begin static.

ACT II, SC. 6 (P.81)—After first line of scene, static is out.

(P. 84)—Static with microphone used by actors off L. Near end of this page, sound volume is lowered to half.

(P. 85)—On blackout of scene, continue static.

ACT II, SC. 7 (P. 86)—Continue static with Emile on microphone. On Quale's last word, cut sound.

ACT II, SC. 8 (P. 87)— Static with Emile on microphone. At bottom of page, aircraft sound starts low and builds.

(P.88)—Sound is out.

ACT II, SC. 11 (P.92)—Steeves speaks on microphone off L.

(P. 94)—At end of scene, start drone of airplanes in distance.

ACT II, SC. 12 (P. 95)—At end of page, take volume to high then gradually fade out sound of airplanes.

sound effect (such as an offstage explosion, rain or a train) can be bought, and if it cannot be purchased, a resourceful sound designer should be able to create it. The sound designer also takes care of the sound equipment, provides instructions to all concerned about the use and care of microphones and speakers, and supervises the audio technicians at the control console.

Equipment and sound effects records may be rented or bought from theatrical supply houses. Place your order early!

COSTUMES

Costumes can help the audience understand the following about the characters and the musical:

- Gender of character
- Personality
- Age
- Socioeconomic status
- Occupation
- Importance of character
- Character relationships (for example, members of a family may wear the same colors)
- Style and genre of musical
- Mood and atmosphere of scene
- Time period
- Time of day
- Place
- Occasion (such as a formal dance, wedding or funeral)

Costumes may be designed by a costume designer and made locally, or they may be bought, rented or borrowed. If you have a costume designer and a crew to execute the plans, your group may prefer to make its own costumes. Then, after the last performance, the costumes can be cleaned and stored for use in another show or, perhaps, rented or sold to another producing group.

If you know of another producing organization that has performed the same musical, call them to ask if they have any costumes to rent or purchase. To buy inexpensive contemporary suits and dresses, try your local Goodwill, Salvation Army or secondhand store.

some or all of the clothes from a costume rental company. In this procedure, you do not need a costume designer because the designing is done by the costume house. What you need is a costume coordinator. The producer, stage director or a coordinator should write or telephone early to costume rental companies (addresses may be found in directories listed near the end of chapter two or in the yellow pages of your telephone directory). In your inquiry, request a costume plot for the musical, rental prices for the number and dates of performances and forms on which to record performers' measurements.

Visiting the costume house to see the garments is the best way to choose them, but if that is not feasible, you will have to provide good information about what you want with your order. Be specific about each character's age, personality and occupation; use descriptive adjectives to show your interpretations of the roles (evil, heroic, angelic and so forth); state color preferences and colors of the sets; and give complete measurements, as requested by the costume house, for everyone, including children—don't just list a dress or suit size.

As soon as casting is completed, the costume designer or coordinator should take accurate measurements of the performers and send the order off as early as possible. If there are other clothes to be made, bought or borrowed locally, the costume personnel should begin immediately to acquire them.

The costume crew is also responsible for obtaining costume accessories, which are those articles worn (such as wigs, hats, jewelry, gloves, shoes, swords) or carried in the hands (like fans, handkerchiefs, handbags, canes). Rental companies will of-

ten provide these accessories if you ask for them, but you may have to pay extra for some (like wigs, swords and canes), and others may not be available.

One problem to be considered is fast changes of costumes. These can be speeded up with breakaway clothes that are held together with velcro or a zipper and can be quickly pulled apart offstage. Another way is to wear one costume over another. Offstage the top garment can be removed and the actor is ready to return to the stage in the underneath clothes. These changes require one or two dressers for each performer and enough space close to the stage for these maneuvers.

The costume designer or coordinator and chief assistant, the wardrobe supervisor, should unpack the costumes when they arrive, supervise fittings and the dress parade, do alterations, repairs and laundering, and after the final performance pack the costumes for return to their owners. The costume crew should also clean and store costumes that belong to the organization.

MAKEUP AND HAIRSTYLES

Stage makeup and hairstyles must be right for the character, the costume and the style, genre, time period and place of the musical. If done well, makeup and hairstyle can communicate a lot about a character to an audience:

- Age
- Health
- Personality
- Occupation
- Environment
- Race

One important function of stage makeup is to bring out the actors' features that may not be distinct to the audience because of stage lighting and distance. If you are playing in a small theatre, some men and children may not need makeup, but if you are in a large theatre, everyone will probably need some.

At the dress parade, the stage director and/or costume designer should talk to each actor about any special makeup and hair concerns. At the first dress rehearsal, the stage director must check each performer to be sure that his or her appearance is appropriate. If there are children, men or women in the cast who are not supposed to be wearing makeup, be conservative. Do not allow these actors to wear noticeable eye makeup, rouge or lipstick. Be sure that the closest members of the audience will believe that these characters do *not* have on makeup.

Because infections can be spread through sharing makeup, performers should provide their own cosmetics and be responsible for doing their makeup and hair. For *straight makeups* in which the actors' features and skin colors are merely enhanced, the children, men and women who are playing characters who do not wear makeup will need to buy, at a minimum, the following:

- Foundation
- Eyebrow pencil (to shape the eyebrows and, if needed, line the eyes)
- Powder and puff
- Cleansing cream
- Tissues

These actors will not usually need lipstick if they will remove any foundation that may be on their lips.

Women who are playing characters that wear makeup will probably want to add the following to the above list:

- Lipstick
- Rouge
- Eyeliner

Local hairstylists and cosmeticians may be willing to help the cast for program credit. In this case, the organization should purchase the makeup and other supplies that the experts require.

- Eye shadow
- Mascara

Other cosmetics will be needed for *corrective makeups*, in which actors' faces are changed to make them seem more beautiful or handsome, and *character makeups*, in which faces are altered considerably to suggest old age, disfigurements, animals and so forth. For instruction in what cosmetics to buy and how to apply them, refer to the makeup books listed in the bibliography.

If you have beginning actors, you will probably need some experienced hairstyling and makeup people to supervise the performers—especially if they must apply difficult character makeups.

If wigs are to be worn, the organization should purchase or rent them. Makeup and modern wigs should be available at local stores; period wigs may be found at some costume and theatrical supply houses.

CHAPTER SIX

Organizing the Managers

Before auditions are held, the producer should complete the team needed to produce the musical: the managers of publicity, business, tickets, refreshments/souvenirs, programs, house and stage. These jobs are described in this chapter.

PUBLICITY MANAGER

This person supervises all publicity and promotion for the show, which may include these tasks:

• Preparing posters, flyers, postcards, billboards, newspaper and radio-TV ads with the following information (see Figure 6-1 for an example of a flyer):

☐ Producing organization
☐ Title and authors
☐ Performance dates and times
☐ Theatre and address
☐ Ticket information with box office hours and telephone

• Writing press releases for newspapers. The above information may also be given in the first press release along with the following:

☐ Names of producer, stage director, choreographer, musical director/conductor and designers
☐ Information about the time and place of auditions

The second release may repeat some of the above and add these:

☐ Cast and orchestra lists

☐ Synopsis of plot
☐ Information about previous Broadway and film productions
☐ Awards that the musical has won

The third may be timed for release the week before opening, stressing the following:

☐ Dates and times of performances
☐ Where and when to buy tickets or make phone reservations

• Arranging for signs and displays of photos in front of the theatre or in the lobby

• Arranging personal appearances of performers at club meetings, senior citizens' centers, malls and other places that have crowds

• Making contacts with the media:

☐ Sending them press releases
☐ Arranging interviews and photographs of the cast and directors
☐ Requesting free listings in "Coming Events" newspaper columns
☐ Asking for free public service announcements and interviews with performers and directors on radio and TV
☐ Inviting critics to attend opening night

BUSINESS MANAGER

The business manager assists the producer with financial responsibilities. The chief qualification for this person is that he be competent in the handling of money because the duties include taking care of

FIGURE 6-1 **FLYER FOR *BRIGADOON***
(DESIGNED AND PRINTED BY MARSHALL UNIVERSITY PRINTING SERVICES)

MARSHALL UNIVERSITY DEPARTMENTS OF THEATRE/DANCE AND MUSIC PRESENT

BRIGaDOON

Music by Frederick Loewe
Book and Lyrics by Alan Jay Lerner

November 11-14, 1992 at 8:00 p.m.
November 15 at 2:00 p.m.
in the
JOAN C. EDWARDS PLAYHOUSE

Ticket sales begin
October 28
$8.00 general admission - $5.00 for faculty, staff, and students
with MUID and activity card.
For more information call 696-ARTS

receipts from the sales of tickets, program ads, refreshments and souvenirs and from grants, gifts and other sources of income.

He or she should watch the budget carefully. To keep expenditures under control, the producer or business manager should approve all purchases before they are made. This manager is responsible for the expenditure of funds (paying bills, salaries, taxes and other expenses) and keeping accurate financial records so that a final accounting can be prepared after the show closes.

Policies to be set by the producer and/or business manager involving tickets include these:

- Will there be reserved seats, general admission or both?
- Will all reserved seats be the same price, or will some seats be less because the view of the stage from these locations is not as good as from full-priced seats?
- Will you offer a discount for tickets bought in advance?
- Will there be a special price for children, students, senior citizens, large groups and others?
- What days and hours will the box office be open?
- Will you accept phone and mail reservations?
- May tickets be exchanged?
- May tickets be bought with a credit card or check?
- How long will unpaid reservations be held at the box office?
- Will you offer complimentary tickets to merchants and others who donate or lend properties, costumes and materials or provide services?
- Will you offer complimentary tickets to directors, cast, orchestra, production staff and crews?

TICKET MANAGER

The ticket manager, who reports to the business manager, is responsible for these tasks:

- Ordering or making tickets
- Training the ticket-sellers
- Setting up a schedule for staffing the box office
- Taking reservations and selling tickets at the box office and by mail and telephone

Sometimes a local restaurant or store may pay for the tickets in exchange for putting its name on their backs or on the ticket envelopes.

- Maintaining accurate records for each performance of the number of tickets sold at each price and audience attendance
- Promoting theatre parties (which may involve a discount to large groups)
- Banking or delivering the receipts to the business manager

The cost to prepare tickets varies: Cheap ones can be made on a computer printer or duplicating machine; more expensive ones can be printed locally or bought from a ticket supplier. (For names of suppliers, consult *The New York Theatrical Sourcebook, TCI Buyers Guide,* or *Regional Theatre Directory* listed in chapter two.

Information that should be on the ticket includes the following (see Figure 6-2):

- Name of producing organization
- Name of show
- Date of performance
- Time of performance
- Place of performance
- Location of seat (if it is a reserved seat) or "General Admission" (if it is for an unreserved area)
- Price of ticket
- Ticket number

The ticket may be perforated near one end so that it can be torn easily at the door by the ticket-taker. The smaller part should be retained by the ticket-taker (and given later to the ticket manager), and the larger part given back to the customer.

REFRESHMENTS/SOUVENIRS MANAGER

Selling refreshments before and after performances and at intermissions should be managed by a capable individual, whose responsibilities include:

- Purchasing supplies

FIGURE 6-2 **TICKET FOR *THE BOY FRIEND***

- Maintaining proper standards of cleanliness
- Obtaining city or state permits (if needed)
- Training the sellers

If you wish to sell souvenirs, such as T-shirts, caps and coffee mugs with the musical's logo, ask the licensor where you can get this merchandise.

PROGRAM MANAGER

This person is responsible for selling ads for the program and may also oversee the preparation of the entire program. Traditionally in the U.S. a free program that gives essential information about the musical presentation is offered to customers.

A typical four-page program may include the following (see Figures 6-3 and 6-4 for an example):

On the *front cover*:
- Producing organization
- Title, authors, and other credits stipulated by licensor
- Dates, times and places of performances

On the *inside pages* and *back cover*:
- Names of producer, stage director, choreographer, musical director/conductor
- Designers of scenery, lighting, sound, costumes, makeup, hairstyles and technical director
- Cast
- Orchestra
- Place and time of musical
- List of scenes and musical numbers with indication of length of intermission
- Production staff: Stage manager, assistant director, rehearsal pianist, master electrician, audio technician, master carpenter, properties master, and managers of publicity, business, tickets, refreshments/souvenirs, programs and house
- Crews (Be sure to include the names of everyone who works on the production)
- Acknowledgments (List those who supplied materials or services)
- Credit for licensor of musical (Check your contract with the licensor to see how the credit should be worded; for example, "*South Pacific* is presented through special arrangement with The Rodgers & Hammerstein Theatre Library, 1633 Broadway, Suite 3801, New York, NY 10019.")

FIGURE 6-3 **OUTSIDE OF PROGRAM FOR** *1776*
(DESIGNED AND PRINTED BY MARSHALL UNIVERSITY PRINTING SERVICES)

MU THEATRE/DANCE AND MUSIC DEPARTMENTS PRESENT

1776
a musical
book by Peter Stone
music by Sherman Edwards

OCTOBER 14-17, 1987 • 8:00 p.m.
OCTOBER 18 • SUNDAY MATINEE • 2:00 p.m.
Old Main Auditorium

PRODUCTION STAFF

Stage Manager . . . . Shane Ross
Assistant Director . . . . W. Daniel Ray II
Assistant Stage Manager . . . . Kevin Bannon
Rehearsal Pianist . . . . Wendy Keeney
Master Electrician . . . . Samuel Kincaid
Electricians . . . . Carrie Bickelmeier, Erick Lane, Randy Childers
Audio . . . . Sean Buckingham
Audio Assistant . . . . Paul Willard
Rigger . . . . Chris Urbanic
Property Mistress . . . . Wendy Smith
Property Assistants . . . . Terri Ball, Stephanie Robertson, Miriam Young
Key Grip . . . . Julie Marks
Grips . . . . Charles Dent, John Teter, Scott Tigno, Lane Marshall
Booth Coordinator . . . . Jane Ann Modlin, Kevin Bannon
Costumes . . . . Mary Racer, Lisa Prichard, Sonya McMillion
Costumes by . . . . Krause Costume Co., Cleveland, OH
Hair Stylist . . . . Billie Patton
Construction . . . . All of the above and John Jozwick, Julie Moore,
                                    Lisa Scites, Cynthia Walker, Thomas White
Box Office . . . . Susie Dolen
Box Office Assistant . . . . Brian Moore
Poster, Flyer and Program . . . . Rhonda Stennett
Head Usher . . . . Earl Strohmeyer

ACKNOWLEDGEMENTS

1776 is presented through special arrangement with Music Theatre International,
810 Seventh Avenue, New York, NY 10019-5818.

Stephen L. Christian for Hancock's desk and chair.
Stephen Christian, Jr. for staging cane fight.

West Virginia Electric Supply Co.
Ralph Carrico and the firm he represents
Mr. Nelson Smith

FIGURE 6-4 **INSIDE OF PROGRAM FOR *1776***
(DESIGNED AND PRINTED BY MARSHALL UNIVERSITY PRINTING SERVICES)

The Marshall University Departments of Theatre/Dance and Music present

"1776"

America's Prize-Winning Musical

Music and Lyrics by SHERMAN EDWARDS
Book by PETER STONE
Based on a concept by SHERMAN EDWARDS
Original Production Directed by PETER HUNT
Originally Produced on the Broadway Stage by STUART OSTROW

Producers .... N.B. East and Donald A. Williams
Stage Director .... Elaine Adams Novak
Musical Director/Conductor .... J.D. Folsom
Lighting and Scenic Designer .... Bruce Greenwood
Technical Director .... James Morris-Smith

CAST

Members of the Continental Congress

President: John Hancock .... Stephen L. Christian
Massachusetts: John Adams .... Bil Neal
New Hampshire: Dr. Josiah Bartlett .... Tim Lively
Rhode Island: Stephen Hopkins .... Aaron Searls
Connecticut: Roger Sherman .... Ron Short
New York: Lewis Morris .... George Fleshman
New York: Robert Livingston .... L. Scott Tignor
New Jersey: Rev. John Witherspoon .... John Page Spears
Pennsylvania: Benjamin Franklin .... Gregory A. Rinaldi
Pennsylvania: John Dickinson .... Wes Ramsey
Pennsylvania: James Wilson .... Eddie Harbert
Delaware: Caesar Rodney .... C. Robert Shank
Delaware: Col. Thomas McKean .... Charles E. Cummings
Delaware: George Read .... W. Daniel Ray II
Maryland: Samuel Chase .... Harold Frye
Virginia: Richard Henry Lee .... George R. Snider III
Virginia: Thomas Jefferson .... Stephen Christian Jr.
North Carolina: Joseph Hewes .... Charles R. Dent
South Carolina: Edward Rutledge .... Mark Smith
Georgia: Dr. Lyman Hall .... James A. Plyburn
Congressional Secretary: Charles Thomson .... Ed Heaberlin
Congressional Custodian: Andrew McNair .... John Michael Teter

Others:
A Leather Apron .... Dwayne Williamson
Courier .... Michael D. Musa
Abigail Adams .... Mechiele Shawver
Martha Jefferson .... Yvea Duncan

PLEASE DO NOT EAT, DRINK, SMOKE, OR USE A CAMERA OR
RECORDING DEVICE IN OLD MAIN THEATRE.

PLACE: A single setting representing the Chamber and an Anteroom of the Continental Congress, a Mall, High Street, and Thomas Jefferson's Room, in Philadelphia: and certain reaches of John Adams' mind.

TIME: May, June, and July, 1776.

MUSICAL NUMBERS

Scene 1: The Chamber of the Continental Congress
"Sit Down, John" .... John Adams and the Congress
"Piddle, Twiddle and Resolve" .... Adams
"Till Then" .... John and Abigail Adams
The Mall
Scene 2: "The Lees of Old Virginia" .... Lee, Franklin, and Adams
Scene 3: The Chamber
"But, Mr. Adams" .... Adams, Franklin, Jefferson, Sherman, and Livingston
Scene 4: Jefferson's Room and Outside on High Street
"Yours, Yours, Yours" .... John and Abigail Adams
"He Plays the Violin" .... Martha Jefferson, Franklin, and Adams
Scene 5: The Chamber
"Cool, Cool, Considerate Men" .... Dickinson, the Conservatives, Hancock and Thomson
"Mamma Look Sharp" .... Courier, Congressional Custodian and Leather Apron

INTERMISSION (TEN MINUTES)

Scene 6: The Congressional Anteroom
"The Egg" .... Franklin, Adams, and Jefferson
Scene 7: The Chamber
"Molasses to Rum" .... Rutledge
"Yours, Yours, Yours" (Reprise) .... Abigail
"Is Anybody There?" .... Adams, Franklin, Jefferson, and Thomson

ORCHESTRA

VIOLIN
William Wassum
Louisa Ritter
Connie Waterman
Sam Bauserman
John Gilmore

Viola
Julia Smith
Chrystalle Crabtree

CELLO
Lois Hahn
Ann Chaffin

CONTRABASS
Ronald Caviani

PERCUSSION
Kenneth Bond
Russell Davis

KEYBOARDS
Wendy Keeney
Joy Wilkes

WOODWINDS
Tony Dean
Steve Slater
Kevin Turley
Tami Neal
Jacquelyn Harlow
Julie Meadows

BRASSWINDS
Steve Riley
Christopher Gibson
Okey Napier
Thomas Bias
Tom Waybright
Brenda Graves
Kirk Hickle
Chase Bryant

- House rules (For example, "Please do not smoke, eat, drink or use a camera, recording device or personal telephone in this theatre.")
- Sponsors and patrons
- Coming events

If you wish to include in the program photographs, short biographies of the directors and cast, and ads bought by local stores and restaurants, you will have to add more pages.

In addition to the free program, some organizations prepare and sell a souvenir book that has the same information plus more and bigger photographs, biographies of performers and directors, and stories about the musical and its writers. To sell ads and prepare a program and souvenir book, the program manager will need several assistants.

HOUSE MANAGER

The house manager is in charge of the house and all that goes on within the audience's space. This person should know how to contact quickly the police and fire departments, ambulances, technicians to repair the heating-cooling equipment and custodians. He should also know where to locate a first-aid kit.

The ticket-takers and ushers, who should have small flashlights and wear some identification (such as a badge or stick-on label reading "Usher"), should arrive at least fifteen minutes before the house is opened to the audience. In that time, the house manager instructs them in the following:

- The ticket system
- The seating plan
- The location of rest rooms, water fountains, and telephones
- How to escort customers to their seats and give one program to each with courtesy and a smile
- How to assist those who are disabled
- How to handle latecomers

The house manager also oversees the following:

- Checking on the temperature and cleanliness of the house, lobby, rest rooms and water fountains
- Stopping audience members with food or drinks from entering the house
- Reminding spectators with cameras, tape recorders, personal phones and beepers that they may not be used in the theatre (Your policy may be that they must be left at the door with the house manager.)
- Closing the doors to the house when the musical begins; opening them for intermission; warning the audience through flashing lights, ringing a bell, or announcement that the second act will begin in a few minutes; closing the doors to the house as the second act begins; and opening them at the end of the musical.
- Keeping latecomers in the lobby until there is a break in the onstage action. They may then be ushered to vacant seats near the door. During intermission they can be taken to their correct seats.
- Taking care of lost-and-found articles
- Obeying fire and smoking regulations
- Maintaining order in the house, which may involve insisting that noisy spectators (including crying children) be quiet or leave
- Handling emergencies in the house, such as illness or a fire alarm (Doctors expecting emergency calls to the box office phone may tell their seat locations to the house manager, who will discreetly notify them when the calls come.)

(For more information about the work of the house manager, see chapter twelve.)

STAGE MANAGER

The stage manager has many duties, which may include the following:

- Assisting the stage director in preproduction planning, auditions and rehearsals
- Keeping an up-to-date list of addresses and phone numbers of everyone in the company
- Helping the stage director plan rehearsal schedules and inform all concerned
- Posting sign-in sheets, telephoning those who are absent, and asking for excuses from those who are tardy
- Notifying those involved of special promotions, photo sessions, publicity interviews, fittings for costumes and so forth
- Checking to be sure that fire, police and theatre regulations are observed

- Helping the stage director, musical director and choreographer in rehearsals by opening and closing rehearsal rooms and seeing that rooms are lighted, properly heated or cooled, and equipped with pianos and other necessary items
- Marking rehearsal floors with chalk or tape to indicate where scenery will be and placing rehearsal chairs where furniture and props will be located
- Knowing the location of a first-aid kit and being prepared to handle emergencies that may occur in rehearsals or performances
- Acting as liaison between the stage director and designers and crews
- Prompting and keeping the promptscript up-to-date by recording blocking, stage business and line changes; cues for lights, sound, music, curtains, and shifts of sets and props; floor plans of sets; plots for lights, sound, costumes and properties; and all other information needed to produce the musical
- Assigning dressing rooms
- Helping to organize set and property shifts and determine technical cues
- Preparing a list of acknowledgments for the program
- Rehearsing understudies

During final run-throughs, technical and dress rehearsals, and performances, the stage manager is in charge backstage and is responsible for maintaining the caliber of the show. The stage manager has these responsibilities:

- Opening and closing the theatre
- Checking on the attendance of performers and crews, telephoning absentees, and making arrangements to cover for them
- Keeping in a safe place performers' valuables (such as money, watches and jewelry) that they do not wish to leave in the dressing rooms while they are onstage
- Checking on all technical elements to be certain that they are ready for performance
- Notifying performers, crews, orchestra and conductor of the time by calling "half hour, please," "fifteen minutes, please," "five minutes, please," and "places, please," before the

first act begins. At intermission(s), the stage manager calls "five minutes, please," and "places, please."

- Notifying the house manager when the house may be opened to the public. This is usually at thirty minutes before curtain.
- Checking to see that performers are properly costumed and made up
- Starting the first act and subsequent acts after the house manager informs the stage manager that the audience is seated. If an understudy is to play a role, the stage manager may use a backstage microphone to announce to the audience as the houselights are dimming: "At tonight's performance the role of (name of character) will be played by (name of understudy)." Also, if there is time to prepare it, a slip of paper with this information should be inserted in all programs.
- Calling performers to the stage for their entrances (This is not necessary if the theatre is equipped with a stage-monitoring system so that performers may follow the progress of the show in their dressing and makeup rooms and greenroom.)
- Prompting and giving cues for technical changes
- Ordering scene shifts and instructing performers when they may go onstage
- Maintaining order and quiet backstage
- Calling for an encore to be played, if the music is in the score, the encore has been rehearsed, and the audience demands it by enthusiastic applause
- Stopping the show if an emergency arises and explaining to the audience what happened
- Deciding at curtain call when to close the curtains for the last time and bring up the houselights
- Keeping an accurate record of the playing time of acts and the length of intermissions
- Returning after the performance all valuables belonging to performers
- Having scenery, props, costumes, and lighting and sound equipment cleaned, repaired or replaced as required
- Rehearsing cast replacements and calling for

brush-up rehearsals of the company, if they are needed

After the final performance, the stage manager may help to strike the sets and assist in returning rented and borrowed items, such as scripts, scores, orchestrations, dialogue and vocal parts, costumes and props.

Because the stage manager has many responsibilities, he or she will probably want one or two assistants. (See chapters four, five, seven, eight, nine, ten, eleven, twelve and thirteen for more information about the work of the stage manager.)

CHAPTER SEVEN

Holding Auditions and Casting Musicals

Many directors say that casting is the most important part of directing. Here is where directors make or break the show, so give auditions and casting a great deal of thought.

The stage and musical directors and choreographer should decide on the date, time and place of auditions for performers, the type of tryouts (open or closed, general or specific), and whether a callback will be held. The musical director should acquire pianists to accompany auditions and rehearsals and other musicians to play for performances. The procedures for these kinds of auditions and casting are described in this chapter.

AUDITIONING PERFORMERS

The producer and stage director should see that an efficient operation is set up for auditions and that publicity is obtained in newspapers, posters, flyers, announcements in classes, and on television and radio stating the title of the musical, the name of the producing organization, and the dates, times and place of auditions. If you want aspirants to arrive with a prepared one-minute excerpt from a song, a monologue, or dressed in dance clothes, be sure to notify the publicity manager to mention these requirements. You may also want to publicize a list of characters with their ages, descriptions, singing ranges and types of dancing that they do (see Figure 7-1 on page 53).

Audition Form

Before tryouts, the stage director should prepare an audition form for candidates to complete (see Figure 7-2). The stage director may ask for some or all of the following information:

- Name (or name to be used on the program and in publicity)
- Address (with zip code)
- Telephone (with area code)
- Agent (if applicable)
- Union affiliations (if you are likely to have members of the performers' unions present)
- Height (without shoes)
- Weight
- Age (or age range)
- Color of hair
- Vocal range (soprano, mezzo-soprano, alto,

Some theatrical organizations have a nontraditional casting policy. These groups believe in casting female and ethnic actors in roles where race, ethnicity or gender is not germane to the character's or the play's development. This policy, which gives women and minority groups the opportunity to play many parts that would not otherwise be open to them, should be discussed by your staff and decided upon before auditions, as it will affect your description of the characters.

FIGURE 7-1 **ANNOUNCEMENT OF AUDITIONS FOR** *1776*

M. U. THEATRE AND MUSIC DEPARTMENTS

NEED YOU TO PLAY THE ROLES OF THE CREATORS OF THE DECLARATION OF INDEPENDENCE.

AUDITIONS FOR THE MUSICAL "1776" WILL BE ON TUES., SEPT. 1 AT 3 AND AT 7 P.M. IN OLD MAIN THEATRE

NEEDED: 24 MEN, 2 WOMEN

AUDITIONS ARE OPEN TO EVERYONE: STUDENTS, FACULTY, STAFF, AND TOWNSPEOPLE: To try out for a character who sings solo, please bring music and be prepared to sing one minute of any song--it does not have to be from 1776. An accompanist will be provided. Everyone will be asked to read with other actors an excerpt from the script.

THE FOLLOWING SPEAK AND SING SOLOS:

JOHN ADAMS from Mass.; age 40; 5'8" tall. Has piercing speaking voice. Has 9 solos, must waltz. Singing range: C to E.
BENJAMIN FRANKLIN from Pa.; age 70. Limps, uses a cane. Bawdy, witty. B to F.
THOMAS JEFFERSON from Va.; age 33; 6'3" tall. Primary writer of declaration. E to G.
ABIGAIL ADAMS: John's wife; age 32. Attractive, intelligent, has sense of humor. D to F.
MARTHA JEFFERSON: Thomas's wife; 27. Lovely, well-built lady. Dances. B to D.
JOHN HANCOCK from Mass.; 40. President of Continental Congress. G to E.
CHARLES THOMSON: Secretary of Congress; age 47. Prissy, pedantic. E to E.
RICHARD HENRY LEE from Va.; 45. Large, ambling, gregarious aristocrat. C to F.
JOHN DICKINSON from Pa.; 44. Large, theatrical, stylish, playful man. B to E.
EDWARD RUTLEDGE from S.C.; 26. Handsome, well-dressed dandy. C to A.
ROGER SHERMAN from Conn.; 55. Serious, self-righteous ex-cobbler. E to B.
ROBERT LIVINGSTON from N.Y.; 30. Gentleman from cosmopolitan city. B to F.
COURIER: Dusty, bedraggled youth. Singing range: B to D.

THE FOLLOWING SPEAK AND SING WITH GROUPS:

JAMES WILSON from Pa.; 33. Small, pompous, flatterer; wears glasses.
STEPHEN HOPKINS from R.I.; 70. Gnarled, grizzled, wears black, drinks rum.
SAMUEL CHASE from Md.; 35. Obese, ungainly man who leans backwards when he walks.
COL. THOMAS McKEAN from Del; 42. Large Scotsman with Scottish dialect.
GEORGE READ from Del.; 43. Small, brightly dressed prig.
DR. LYMAN HALL from Ga.; 55. Tall, distinguished, well-dressed gentleman.
LEWIS MORRIS from N.Y.; 50. Proper, formal, well-dressed man.
JOSEPH HEWES from N.C.; 46. Southern aristocrat, dressed brightly.
DR. JOSIAH BARTLETT from N.H.; 48. Dry, taciturn New Englander.
CAESAR RODNEY from Del.; 48. Gaunt, bony, in bad health.
ANDREW McNAIR: Custodian; gnomish little man of indeterminate age.
A LEATHER APRON: Strongbacked, bland youth.
REV. JOHN WITHERSPOON from N.J.; 54. Soft-spoken, pious.

SCRIPTS ARE AVAILABLE FOR PERUSAL IN THE THEATRE OFFICE.
FOR MORE INFORMATION, SEE DR. E. A. NOVAK IN THEATRE OFFICE.

FIGURE 7-2 **AUDITION FORM**

Name as you want it on the program: _____

Address (give zip code): _____

Height (without shoes): _____ Weight: _____ Age: _____

Telephone (give area code): _____

Hometown (needed for publicity): _____

Vocal range (soprano, tenor, etc.) _____

Types of dancing you do well (ballet, tap, etc.): _____

Rehearsals will normally be from 6:30 P.M. to 9:30 P.M. on Mon. through Fri. but there may be some rehearsals in the afternoons or on weekends. Put an X in the squares below to indicate the times that you CANNOT rehearse.

	MON	TUE	WED	THU	FRI	SAT	SUN
1:30-2:30 P.M.							
2:30-3:30							
3:30-4:30							
6:30-7:30							
7:30-8:30							
8:30-9:30							

Commitments that will interfere with rehearsals: _____

_____

Acting training and experience: _____

_____

Singing training and experience: _____

Dance training and experience: _____

_____

I will accept any role in this production: ☐ Yes ☐ No

tenor, baritone, bass)
- Types of dancing done well (ballet, tap, jazz and so forth)
- Hometown (if needed for publicity)
- Class or grade (if in a school situation)
- Social security or student numbers
- Training and experience in acting, singing and dancing
- Commitments that will interfere with rehearsals (Indicate when rehearsals will be held so

that they can tell you which ones they cannot attend. See Figure 7-2.)
- I will accept any role in this production.
  ☐ Yes ☐ No
- If not cast, I would like to work in the jobs checked below:

☐ Props ☐ Makeup
☐ Building sets ☐ Costumes
☐ Stage crew ☐ Ushering

It is all right for directors to speak to possible performers about attending auditions, but it is *not* a good idea to promise a part to anyone before auditions take place.

☆ ☆ ☆

☐ Lighting   ☐ Selling refreshments
☐ Sound

Now let's look at the different types of auditions: open or closed, general or specific, and callbacks.

Open Auditions

In open general or specific auditions, aspirants gather in a large room or theatre to try out and to watch others audition. If you say that auditions are open, it implies that everyone is eligible to try out. If you wish to open auditions only to, for example, the members of a certain organization or to students who study fine arts, you should stipulate this in your publicity and also put it in a prominent place on your audition form.

Advantages and Disadvantages

One advantage of open auditions over closed is that the directors can see all of the candidates together in one place and are, therefore, less likely to forget about a talented prospect. Also, you are more apt to determine how the contestants look and work together. Another advantage is that everyone has the opportunity to see others try out. Sometimes inexperienced performers can learn by watching an outstanding audition. Also, they may understand better why they were not cast and how hard they will have to work before the next production in order to be castable.

A disadvantage is that some may think that, as the stage director, you are being unfair if you let some people read for three minutes and cut others off after one minute. It is important that actors believe that everyone has an equal opportunity to demonstrate his or her abilities, so be fair to all. An-

other disadvantage is that some may become very nervous about trying out before a large group; however, if working before many people makes a performer anxious, the directors should be aware of this before casting. After all, those cast will (hopefully) have to perform before big audiences.

Private, Personal or Closed Auditions

If you state in publicity that your auditions will be private, personal or closed, this means that the only people in the audition area will be the directors, their assistants and a rehearsal pianist. Performers can sign up in advance for an appointment. On arrival, they can fill out the audition form as they wait in another room. When it is their turn, one or two may then be admitted into the audition area. After the audition, they may leave.

Personal auditions, which are used professionally but less often in the amateur theatre, may begin with an interview so that the directors can become better acquainted with the performer and find out more about his or her training, experience and aspirations. For a general audition, the aspirant may then be asked to do a prepared song, dance and a monologue of his or her choice. For a specific audition, the candidate may sing, dance and read for the particular show to be produced. The reading may be done with another prospect or with the stage manager.

Advantages and Disadvantages

The advantages to the private audition are that if the performers have an appointment, they do not have to wait long to try out, and they may be more relaxed because only a few people are in the room. Also, a large room or theatre is not needed since closed auditions can be done in a small room, office or studio. In addition, directors can talk personally with the applicants and, perhaps, get to know them better than in an open audition.

The disadvantages are the following: Private auditions take a lot of time; directors may not have the chance to see how the candidate looks with and reacts to other performers; once an actor is out of sight the directors may forget about the person; and newcomers do not get to watch and learn from those who are good at auditioning.

General Auditions

If you are expecting several hundred to audition, you may want to hold general auditions first (either open or closed) to select the best to come back for specific auditions. How many should you choose for specific auditions? About twice the number in the cast; for example, if you need forty performers, pick about eighty for specific auditions.

General auditions are often used too when you (and perhaps other directors) are casting several productions at one time. This may occur at the beginning of a school year or the start of a summer season of shows.

Procedure

For a general audition, performers can obtain from a central office an audition form. After they complete it and return it to the office, they may be given a number. Numbers 1 to 15 may be asked to report at 6:30 P.M. to try out, Numbers 16 to 30 may be asked to report at 7:30 P.M., and so forth. The candidates may be asked to prepare a one-minute memorized monologue from any play or musical and to bring music and be ready to sing one-minute from any song, accompanied by the show's pianist or their own pianist or tape recording. If they want to do a dance audition, they may then do their own routine for one minute.

The stage manager should keep this procedure on time by stopping contestants who go over one minute in each category. He or she should also get the candidates on in the right order and off as quickly as possible.

After the general audition is finished, the three directors can then decide on those to call back for specific auditions. Some directors can cast a musical from just a general audition or from a general audition and a callback, but many will want to have a general audition, a specific audition and then a callback audition.

Specific Auditions

If you are not expecting a large number of people to audition for your musical, you will probably want to use two specific auditions (either open or closed) of two to three hours each on one day or successive days. This may or may not be followed by a callback.

For specific auditions, singers are often asked to bring their own music and be prepared to sing one minute of any song. Sometimes they are asked to be ready to sing parts of two different types of songs (for instance, a ballad and an up-tempo song). Occasionally, the musical director may want to hear all candidates for a certain part sing a portion of a well-known song (for example, all men wanting to play Emile in *South Pacific* may be asked to prepare "Some Enchanted Evening"). This requirement should, of course, be well-publicized in advance.

For the auditions, the stage director should select from the musical's dialogue short excerpts for one to three actors that will take about three to four minutes to read orally. If the stage director plans to use improvisations at auditions, he or she may select several situations in the script for this purpose. If possible, scripts should be left in a central place for performers to borrow for a day or two in order to familiarize themselves with the plot, characters and dialogue. An alternative is to prepare copies of several excerpts from the musical that involve all of the major characters. Actors can then pick up a copy and practice reading the cuttings before auditions.

The choreographer should get ready for tryouts by devising a combination of dance steps that may be used in the show.

Opening Speech

Usually, at open specific auditions, the stage director begins by talking briefly to the candidates. This may include the following:

• Ask the contenders to move into one section of the room or theatre so that you can identify who they are. Relegate onlookers to the back, or ask them to leave if you do not want them there.

• Announce the performance dates so that those who have commitments for those days will not try out.

• If you have already cast any role, be sure to state this; for example, if you have contracted with a guest artist to star in the production, be sure the performers know that this part is not available.

• Remind them to fill out the audition form carefully and note any possible conflicts with the rehearsal schedule.

• Introduce members of the production team

who are present: the producer, musical director, choreographer, rehearsal pianists, stage manager and so forth. Name the ones who are responsible for the casting.

• Tell them briefly what the musical is about and the qualifications needed to play the leads. For instance, if you are presenting *Gypsy*, you might point out that the actress who plays Baby June should be petite and be able to tap dance on pointe and do a split while twirling a baton in each hand.

• When you have people who seem to be very nervous, you may want to try to relax them with exercises or by singing together a well-known song. If you have a small number, you might try aerobic exercises, improvisations or children's games.

• Let them know the procedure for auditions. If everyone is to be tested for singing, dancing and acting, tell them how you are going to accomplish this.

• If you think now that you will hold a callback session, inform them when and where the callback list will be posted. Also announce when and where the cast list will be posted and rehearsals will begin.

• Give the candidates the opportunity to ask questions.

Procedure

If the three directors want to see all auditions for acting, singing and dancing, only one room is needed; however, often the choreographer or musical director is not interested in seeing the other auditions and, thus, two rooms may be the answer. Sometimes, however, there are so many contenders that three rooms are desirable. After the opening speech, the candidates are divided into three sections. Then, the musical director listens to the singing of a section in one room while the choreographer evaluates the dancing of another group in a second room, and the stage director hears readings by the third section in another room. It helps the directors if there are assistants to handle the audition forms as they move the groups from room to room until all have had an opportunity to act, sing and dance.

The musical director should ask each performer to stand in front of the group as he or she sings a prepared selection, accompanied by the show's or the candidate's accompanist or recording. The musical director may also wish to test for sight-reading ability by asking the prospect to sing part of another song without preparation. The musical director should then write a grade or comment on the back of the audition form, especially noting if the person is worthy of being called back or cast.

In another room, the choreographer may teach the group a short combination of dance steps. Then a few dancers at a time will perform the combination while the choreographer writes a grade or comment on each audition form and marks those who should be called back or cast.

In a third room, the stage director may ask one to three people to stand in front of the room and read a short excerpt from the musical's dialogue. The stage director will probably want to hear the best contenders read additional excerpts with different persons, as it is important to see how actors work and respond to others. If there is enough time available, the stage director may also have candidates improvise on a situation in the script to see how creative and imaginative they are. To set up an improvisation, tell two or three actors what characters they are and what the situation is. Give each group a few minutes to think about their characters, what happens, when and where the scene takes place, and why it occurs. Then they may present their improvisation, making up their own dialogue and movements. Following the improvisations and readings, the stage director should make notes on the audition forms as to who should be called back or cast.

After auditions are finished, the directors should meet to discuss the auditions. *If you can cast the musical now, do so.* If you can cast certain roles now, but not all, you may want to hold a callback to see once again the candidates for uncast parts. If you do this, however, be sure to state in the callback announcement that you have already cast some performers who are *not* being called back; otherwise people you want may think that you do not want them. Advise everyone to check the cast list and state where and when it will be posted and when rehearsals will start.

Instead of a partial callback, however, we recommend that you *call back everyone whom you are considering for the cast.* Eliminate the ones that you know you do not want, and call back the good ones to determine how they work with other performers. Try to hold the list down to the number that you need to cast the show plus several more possible choices. After hearing and seeing them again, you may change your mind about some of your tentative selections.

Callback List

The announcement of callbacks may be headed "Callback List." Then list the names in alphabetical order of those whom you want to sing, dance and read again. Be sure to indicate the day, time and place that callbacks will be held and whether they should bring music and dance clothes and shoes.

Callbacks

At a callback all three directors should see every audition as the applicants are tested again for acting, singing and dancing. Now the directors have the opportunity to determine how the aspirants respond to others as they are asked to read various roles with different actors. Applicants may also be asked to sing part of their prepared song again or to sing portions of other songs from the show. In addition, they may be requested to do dance steps that will be used in the musical.

All should sing so that the musical director may judge their ability to handle the score; all should dance so that the choreographer may determine their physical capabilities; and all should read an excerpt so that the stage director may evaluate their acting abilities.

After everyone you called back has had an opportunity to audition, the three directors should meet to decide on the cast.

CASTING PERFORMERS

In casting, the directors must try to be objective, fair, and willing to give new people a chance. You may, at times, be tempted to cast good friends or members of your family, but this should be done only if they are the best for the parts.

To cast your musical well, you should consider everything you know about the person in addition to what she does at the audition. You must evaluate the candidate's education, training and experience in acting, singing and dancing. You must also recall how this person performed in other productions and the reputation she has for reliability, punctuality,

There are people who audition badly but who grow in rehearsals and eventually give a magnificent performance. There are also those who give a brilliant audition but who never get any better. If a person is a stranger to you, you have no way of knowing if he or she fits into one of these categories. If possible, ask other directors what their experiences have been with these candidates.

good health, congeniality and other traits you consider important.

Procedure

When the three directors meet to decide on casting, start with the largest roles and work down to the extras. For each character, you must have an image in your mind of how that person should look and sound. Consider the applicants who have the physical characteristics for the part (tall, short, heavy, middle-aged, young, handsome, booming voice, southern dialect and so forth) and can handle the singing, dancing and acting required. The directors should discuss the top candidates for each part and decide who best fits the role.

In casting leading parts, the stage director should have the final decision, but if the character sings and dances, the stage director should be willing to listen to the advice of the musical director on the aspirant's singing abilities and to the choreographer on dancing skills. The stage director should also cast speaking roles and walk-ons who do not sing or dance.

As for choral parts, the musical director should have the most to say about casting the singing chorus, and the choreographer should select the dancing chorus. Difficulty comes when the musical has a chorus that sings and dances; then the musical director and choreographer must compromise. If they cannot, the stage director will have to make the final decision.

FIGURE 7-3 **ANNOUNCEMENT OF CAST**

Cast List for *Hello, Dolly!* (In Order of Speaking)

Dolly Gallagher Levi . . . . (Name of actor)

Ernestina . . . . "

Ambrose Kemper . . . . "

Horace Vandergelder . . . . We are unable to cast this role. If you would like to audition for this part, please see the stage director immediately.

Ermengarde . . . . (Name of actor)

Cornelius Hackl . . . . "

Barnaby Tucker . . . . "

Minnie Fay . . . . "

Irene Molloy . . . . "

Mrs. Rose . . . . "

Rudolph . . . . "

Stanley . . . . "

Cook #1 . . . . "

Cook #2 . . . . "

Judge . . . . "

Court Clerk . . . . "

Policeman . . . . "

Chorus   (Names in alphabetical order of singers-dancers)

                                                                    "

                                                                    "

                                                                    "

                                                                    "

                                                                    "

                                                                    "

                                                                    "

                                                                    "

                                                                    "

Cast: Please initial by your name to indicate that you accept the role. You may get scripts and music in the theatre office.

First Rehearsal: Wednesday, Sept. 6, 6:30 P.M., Old Main Auditorium. Everyone in the cast is needed. Bring script, music, and a pencil.

Our thanks to all who auditioned.

(Name of stage director)   (Name of musical director)   (Name of choreographer)

Cast List

The stage director should prepare the cast list and post it at the time and place stated at auditions (see Figure 7-3). This announcement may contain:

- A list of all characters (in the order of speaking or in the order of appearance in the musical) with the names of the performers who will play the roles.
- If a part is uncast, write by the name of the character: "We are unable to cast this role. If you would like to audition for this part, please see the stage director immediately."
- A request for each person listed to initial by his or her name to indicate acceptance of the role.
- The place where the cast may obtain scripts and music.
- The date, time, place and names of performers who are needed at the first rehearsal.
- At the end of the page, thank all who tried out and sign it with the names of the auditioners.

If you are sure that your casting is good, the title at the top of the page may be "Cast List." If you are not certain, title it "Tentative Cast List." This will warn the performers that you may make changes for about the first week or two of rehearsals. If you find that a performer is not meeting your expectations, is often late or absent, or has a bad attitude about taking direction, the directors should consider replacing this person with someone who is more responsible and easier to work with.

For organizations who do not have an office or central place to post the callback and cast lists, the stage director or stage manager may telephone each performer. An alternative is to announce at auditions and callbacks a telephone number that the candidates may use to find out if they are on the lists.

Understudies

In the amateur theatre, understudies are seldom designated unless the show will run for a long time or there is doubt that some cast members will be able to

If your community cannot provide expert musicians, contact the nearest college or university that has a music department. Hiring musicians, though, means that the producer must be consulted since he or she should approve all contracts and expenditures of money.

make all performances. If understudies are selected, they should be encouraged to watch rehearsals and should be rehearsed by the directors or the stage manager. A common practice is to put the stage manager in charge of understudy rehearsals.

ACQUIRING REHEARSAL PIANISTS AND ORCHESTRA

The musical director is in charge of obtaining capable pianists to accompany auditions and rehearsals. These should be skillful musicians who sight-read well.

The number of musicians needed to accompany performances should be decided by the producer and musical and stage directors. It is the musical director, however, who must acquire the accompaniment, which may consist of any number of instruments from one piano or synthesizer to a large orchestra. One way of finding musicians is to hold a well-publicized audition at which those wishing to try out may play two or three minutes of a selection of their choice. The musical director may also want to test them for sight-reading ability.

If enough experienced musicians cannot be found through auditions, the musical director may have to recruit or employ accomplished instrumentalists as the conductor will probably want at least one expert with three or four novices.

CHAPTER EIGHT

Beginning Rehearsals

Chapters eight through twelve deal with rehearsing and performing musicals; chapters thirteen and fourteen are concerned with revues and operas. This chapter takes up coordinating the work of the stage director, choreographer and musical director/conductor, devising a rehearsal schedule and starting rehearsals.

COORDINATING THE WORK OF THE DIRECTORS

The stage director, with the help of the stage manager, plans the cast's rehearsal schedule. But before writing it, the stage director must consult with the musical director and choreographer for preferred times and days to rehearse, choices of rooms, the order in which they want to rehearse their numbers, and how much time should be allotted to each. The orchestra's rehearsal schedule is set by the conductor until the musicians begin to accompany the performers at which time the orchestra follows the cast's schedule.

The stage director should provide the musical director and choreographer with a list of the numbers to rehearse, noting who is in each one, what the scenery, properties and lighting will look like, and what costumes, makeup and wigs will be worn.

Cast rehearsals usually begin with all directors and cast members present at a reading and discussion of the musical. Next, rehearsals are held separately, as follows:

- The musical director rehearses singers.
- The choreographer instructs dancers.
- The stage director coaches actors and blocks everything that does not involve dancing.
- The conductor works with the orchestra.

At the beginning, the musical director needs time to rehearse each song. Before movement is blocked, the musical director should have several rehearsals with the singers to work on pitch, dynamics, rhythm and tempo. He or she must be sure that they are pronouncing the words, phrasing and building to climaxes well with an appropriate quality of voice.

After the singers have memorized the words and music of the songs, the stage director will usually block the movement for a song until the performers start to dance; then the choreographer takes over. If the stage director is not comfortable with blocking movement of singers, he or she may want the choreographer to block the whole number.

When the cast has learned the songs, dances, dialogue and blocking, these elements are put together in integration rehearsals. Now is the time for concentrated work on developing characterizations, line interpretations, projection, articulation, stage business and listening.

In run-throughs, the show is polished until it is running smoothly. Then some technical elements are introduced: Properties, scenery and curtains may be added. A dress parade may be held before a run-through so that performers can try on costumes and model them onstage for the stage director, choreographer and costume designer (or coordinator) to see

Sometimes during the rehearsal period creative differences erupt: The conductor and choreographer may argue about tempos; the musical director may complain that the movement devised by the stage director or choreographer prevents singers from singing well or from seeing the conductor; the stage director may yell that performers cannot be heard because the orchestra is too loud; and so forth. When there are differences of opinion, it is up to the stage director to solve the problem. As the artistic head of the production, the stage director has the final word. The only exception would be if the "final word" involves the expenditure of more money; then the producer has it.

how it fits and if alterations are needed before dress rehearsals. The dress parade is also a good time for the stage director and costume designer to talk with the cast about their makeup and hairstyles.

About this time, a special rehearsal is often held to coordinate the orchestra with the performers: All music is rehearsed, songs are sung, and dances may be performed, but dialogue is omitted, unless there is musical underscoring. After this concentrated rehearsal, the orchestra is usually called to accompany the remaining cast rehearsals.

At least one rehearsal (without performers and orchestra) should be scheduled for scenery, curtains, properties, lighting and sound. After this special rehearsal, costumes and makeup are added to the show for several dress rehearsals before the performances.

DEVISING A REHEARSAL SCHEDULE

The number of rehearsals can vary greatly depending on the difficulty of the musical and the competency of the personnel. Most school/community groups who rehearse four or five times a week for three to four hours each will need from six to eight weeks for a large musical. The stage director, along with the stage manager, must plan the cast's schedule based on his or her knowledge of the show and the people involved and a guess of how many rehearsals it will take to achieve a good performance.

If you have seven weeks for rehearsals and if

the singing, dancing and acting are about equally important in the show, the schedule for auditions and rehearsals may look something like this:

1ST WEEK Mon. Open specific audition.

Tue. Open specific audition.

Wed. Reading of dialogue, listening to music, analysis of musical and discussion with complete cast and all directors. Measure for costumes.

Thu. Musical director's first singing rehearsal.

Fri. Choreographer's first dancing rehearsal.

2ND WEEK Mon. Stage director's rehearsal to block dialogue for half of Act I with principals.

Tue. Musical director's second singing rehearsal.

Wed. Stage director's rehearsal to block dialogue for second half of Act I with principals.

Thu. Choreographer's second dancing rehearsal.

Fri. Musical director's third singing rehearsal.

3RD WEEK Mon. Stage director's rehearsal to review blocking of dialogue in Act I with everyone in these scenes.

Tue. Choreographer's third dancing rehearsal.

Wed. Stage director's rehearsal to block dialogue of Act II with principals.

Thu. Musical director's fourth singing rehearsal.

Fri. Choreographer's fourth dancing rehearsal.

4TH WEEK Mon. Stage director's rehearsal to review blocking of dialogue in Act II with everyone in these scenes.

Tue. Musical director's fifth singing rehearsal.

Wed. Choreographer's fifth dancing rehearsal.

Thu. Stage director's rehearsal to block songs in Act I.

Fri. Stage director's rehearsal to block

songs in Act II.

5TH WEEK Mon. Integration of all singing, dancing and acting for Act I. All three directors should be present at every rehearsal from here on.

Tue. Integration of all singing, dancing and acting for Act II.

Wed. Same for Act I. Everything must be memorized—no books onstage from here on.

Thu. Same for Act II.

Fri. Trouble spots (to be announced).

6TH WEEK Mon. Act I.

Tue. Act II and trouble spots from Act I.

Wed. Run-through of entire musical.

Thu. Same with props.

Fri. Same.

7TH WEEK Mon. Run-through of entire musical with scenery, props and curtains.

Tue. Same. Dress parade before the run-through.

Wed. Special rehearsal of orchestra with cast. (Note: The orchestra should have practiced separately with the conductor already.) At this time all music and musical numbers are rehearsed with the cast but not scenes of dialogue, unless there is musical underscoring.

Thu. Run-through of entire musical with scenery, props, curtains and orchestra.

Fri. Same.

Sat. Technical rehearsal for scenery, properties, lighting, sound designers, technical director, crews, stage manager, rehearsal pianist (no performers or orchestra).

8TH WEEK Sun. First dress rehearsal for all performers with costumes, makeup, all technical elements and orchestra. Block curtain call.

Mon. Second dress rehearsal. Production photographs taken during and/or after rehearsal.

Tue. Third dress rehearsal.

Wed. Performances begin.

You will probably find that your tentative schedule will have to be revised as unforeseen problems arise. If so, put in extra rehearsals as needed, perhaps on Saturday and Sunday of Weeks 1 through 6. Sometimes soloists and small groups of singers and dancers can be called for extra rehearsals at a time other than the hour scheduled for large groups. Also, singing, dancing and acting rehearsals can occur in three separate rooms at the same time, if rooms are available and the people involved are needed at only one of the three rehearsals.

If your musical plays more than one week, you should schedule a refresher rehearsal each week for the day prior to performances.

STARTING REHEARSALS

During the rehearsal period, the stage director and stage manager should prepare a rehearsal schedule for one or two weeks at a time and see that it is distributed or posted so that all concerned are aware of it. (For an example of a weekly rehearsal schedule, see Figure 8-1).

If a performer is absent from a rehearsal, the stage manager, as the enforcer of discipline, should telephone to find out the reason. The stage manager should also check to see that all directors have adequate rehearsal space, tuned pianos, rehearsal pianists, lighting, heating or cooling and other needs. As the liaison between the stage director and the designers and technical director, the stage manager must determine if all technical elements are progressing as planned. If there are any problems, he or she should report them to the stage director.

At rehearsals, the directors and stage manager should set an example for others by their behavior:

- Arriving early and starting the rehearsal on time
- Working diligently each minute of the rehearsal period (Many in the cast will appreciate it if you do not waste their time.)
- Following the rules of the organization or theatre about smoking, eating, drinking and keeping the place clean
- Having a goal for each rehearsal and achieving it

FIGURE 8-1 **WEEKLY REHEARSAL SCHEDULE**

Rehearsals for *Guys and Dolls*

All rehearsals are in the auditorium

Date	Time	Type	Needed
Wed. 10/1	6:30 P.M.	Reading of dialogue/Listening to music/ Analysis/Measuring for costumes	Entire cast
Thu. 10/2	6:30 P.M.	Singing rehearsal with musical director	Entire cast
Fri. 10/3	6:30 P.M.	Dancing rehearsal with choreographer	Adelaide, Hot Box Girls, Gamblers
Mon. 10/6	6:30 P.M.	Stage director's blocking of dialogue with principals only:	
		Act I, Sc. I	Rusty, Benny, Nicely, Arvide, Sarah, Harry, Brannigan, Nathan, Adelaide, Sky
	8:00 P.M.	Act 1, Sc. 2	Arvide, Sarah, Sky
	8:30 P.M.	Act 1, Sc. 3	Nathan, Joey
	8:45 P.M.	Act 1, Sc. 4	Nathan, Adelaide
Tue. 10/7	6:30 P.M.	Singing rehearsal with musical director	Entire cast

Next week's rehearsal schedule will be posted here on Tue., 10/7

Other goals may be these:

- Developing a good relationship with the cast
- Providing a nonthreatening space in which actors can work
- Encouraging performers to relax and enjoy the experience of working harmoniously together to their maximum abilities.

Reading

Traditionally rehearsals begin with assembling the cast, producer, directors, stage manager, rehearsal pianist and others who are interested to read the dialogue, listen to the music as played by the rehearsal pianist or a recording and talk about plans for the show.

At this rehearsal, the stage director should make clear the following:

- Genre, style and interpretation of the show
- Plans for the songs, dances, scenery, costumes, lighting and sound
- Time period of the musical

- Locale
- Customs of the day (For example, if you are directing *Fiddler on the Roof*, you might talk about what it was like to be a Jew in Anatevka, Russia, in 1905.)
- Theme and major ideas
- Plot
- Characters and their relationships
- Function of the major characters and their goals for the entire play

Each actor should be encouraged to read the script carefully, determining:

- Character's age and appearance
- Posture and movements
- Voice and speech
- Intellectual characteristics and education
- Economic status and occupation
- Emotional characteristics
- Personality
- Beliefs
- Attitudes

Konstantin Stanislavski, the famous Russian director, actor and teacher of acting, deplored intrigue, jealousy and selfish ambitions and said that he considered good manners to be part of an actor's creativity. You too should insist that actors be polite and civil to one another and to you. Your aim should be a happy, healthy atmosphere in which performers can create.

- Past life
- Objectives and motivations for each scene that the character is in, actions taken and obstacles encountered

It is imperative that everyone—even those who play the smallest parts—understand what this musical is about. When renting material, however, you may receive *sides* for performers instead of complete scripts. Sides only have the lines, lyrics, cues and stage directions for one character. In this case, the stage director may want to make several full scripts available for performers to read or the director may want to have more than one read-through so that the performers can become familiar with the plot, characters and theme.

While the entire cast is together, it may also be the best time to do the following:

- Measure for costumes.
- Answer the performers' questions, which can range from "What is this scene all about?" to personal problems like "Where can I park my car?"
- Talk about hairstyles for the musical, especially if you want actors to let their hair grow and not get it cut before performances.
- If any males are to have beards and/or mustaches, ask them if they want to grow these or wear fake ones.
- Mention any rules that performers are expected to follow, such as the following:

Always be present and on time for rehearsals.

Notify the stage manager if you cannot attend a rehearsal.

Check the rehearsal schedule carefully each week.

Do not bring food or cigarettes to rehearsal. A water bottle may be permitted, and mints, cough drops and lozenges may be allowed for singers who need help keeping their throats moist through singing rehearsals.

Be quiet during rehearsals.

Do not leave a rehearsal without notifying the stage manager.

Bring a pencil, script and music to rehearsals.

Use your time wisely by studying the script or music while you are waiting to rehearse.

Usually one reading rehearsal is sufficient, but some directors take longer to be sure that performers understand the interpretation to be given the musical's plot, characters and major ideas.

Exercises, Games and Improvisations

To get actors acquainted with each other and with the directors, build trust and friendship among them, relax and decrease inhibitions, try some exercises, games and improvisations, such as the following. Some of these may also serve as a warm-up for later rehearsals.

Exercises

1. Stand in a comfortably erect posture with feet about twelve inches apart and stretch your arms upward, reaching as high as you can. Go up on your toes and stretch higher. Then swing your arms in big circles, exercising your shoulders and arms. Next, facing front, bend to the left, stretching your right arm over your head; then bend to the right, stretching your left arm over your head.

2. To get rid of tension, tense and then relax various parts of your body: face, neck, shoulders, arms, hands, torso, legs, feet and the whole body.

3. Next, examine the flexibility of various parts of your body. Move the hands in circles from the wrists, then forward and backward and to the sides. Explore the movement that is possible with the arms, legs, feet, torso, shoulders and head.

4. Still standing, move the head slowly to look left, then to look right; repeat. Move the head to the center, relax the neck, and drop the head forward; then drop forward from the waist. Let the arms swing freely, without tension, from side to side. As you slowly stand upright, yawn as you raise your head to a good posture.

5. For breath control, put your hands on your hips and relax your throat and neck muscles. Inhale to a slow count of four, then exhale with a hissing sound to a slow count of eight.

6. Yawning is a good way to relax the throat and neck, so yawn before singing "mee, may, mah, moh, moo" on one breath. Vary this exercise by singing:

Nee, nay, nah, noh, noo
Tee, tay, tah, toh, too
Yee, yay, yah, yoh, yoo
Lee, lay, lah, loh, loo
Fee, fay, fah, foh, foo
Gee, gay, gah, goh, goo
Ree, ray, rah, roh, roo

7. Yawn before singing up the scale "do, re, mi, fa, sol, la, ti, do." Yawn and sing down the scale. Yawn and relax the jaw as you sing "yah" on each note up and down the scale.

8. Move your eyebrows up and down, wiggle the nose, move the lower jaw around, stick out the tongue and move it rapidly from side to side, pucker the lips and kiss the air, smile broadly, and make a "motor boat" sound by blowing through closed lips and vibrating them.

9. Repeat rapidly four times with distinct articulation the following tongue twisters:
a. Frank threw Fred three free throws.
b. Soldiers' shoulders shudder when shrill shells shriek.
c. Bob bought a black back bath brush.
d. Old oily Ollie oils old oily autos.
e. Around the rough and rugged rock the ragged rascal ran.
f. Peter Piper picked a peck of pickled peppers; where is the peck of pickled peppers Peter Piper picked?

10. Deliver the six sentences in Exercise 9 slowly with projection as though speaking to thousands of people. Keep your throat and neck muscles relaxed.

Theatre Games

1. Face a partner for the "mirror" exercise. Decide on who is the leader and who is the follower. When the leader moves, the follower imitates the movement as though he or she is the mirror image. After a few minutes, change roles. As a variation, the leader may add sounds to the movements that the follower must also mimic.

2. Imitate the following animals: wasp, butterfly, cat, dog, snake, rooster, octopus, goat, monkey, eagle, lion and elephant.

3. Walk as robots and then puppets with strings attached to the top of the head and both elbows, wrists, knees and feet.

4. Demonstrate what the following inanimate objects look like and how they work: a balloon, clock, telephone, spray can, book and an electric lightbulb.

5. With several people working together, demonstrate a roller coaster, clothes dryer, television, microwave oven with a turntable, and a merry-go-round.

6. Imagine that you are the following:
a. Children at the seashore in summertime
b. Teenagers having a snowball fight
c. Middle-aged folks working in a factory
d. Old people carrying heavy bags of groceries

7. Play children's games: Tag, Blind Man's Bluff, Simon Says, Charades, Hopscotch, or any game that requires you to move and work with others.

8. Act out the weirdest dream you ever had.

9. Demonstrate what you did in the happiest moment of your life or the saddest.

10. Interpret music by dancing as you wish to:
a. Contemporary popular music
b. Schubert, Tchaikovsky, Rimsky-Korsakov, Debussy or Stravinsky
c. Music from the score of the musical that you are rehearsing

Improvisations

1. Do improvisations of what your character was doing immediately before appearing in each scene of the musical. (This may help performers begin each scene with the right objectives, motivations, attitudes, thoughts, feelings and reactions to the stage environment.)

2. Do an improvisation of a scene that is difficult to comprehend. (To assist performers with a complex passage in the script, the stage director may discuss the ideas and emotions and then ask them to use their own words in an improvisation of the scene. After the actors appear to understand what the scene is about, the stage director should insist

that they return to the words in the script since these are the words that must be used in performance.)

3. Do improvisations of incidents that are spoken of in the musical but are not shown onstage. (If actors apparently do not understand what happened in these offstage occurrences, ask them to improvise them. Then, when they have to refer to them onstage, they may have a better idea of how the events affected their characters' lives.)

CHAPTER NINE

Musical Director/ Conductor's Rehearsals

The musical director is in charge of vocal rehearsals with choruses, smaller ensembles and soloists. In addition, this individual may serve as the conductor and lead rehearsals with the orchestra. The following chapter will take an in-depth look at how these rehearsals may be structured and the potential problems a musical director/conductor may encounter in school or community productions.

VOCAL REHEARSALS

Immediately after the show has been cast, the musical director begins by rehearsing choral groups.

Working With the Chorus

Normally, choruses are broken into four-part harmony: soprano, alto, tenor and bass. But there may be divisions within each group, such as first and second alto. Occasionally, you will find five-part or six-part harmony that may add mezzo-soprano and/or baritone.

Begin by reviewing your cast list and assign vocal parts to your choral singers. It is especially important that all singers work in a comfortable range. Nothing is more frustrating to a bass than to screech for high notes or to a soprano to reach down for low notes. Pay close attention to your singers during these initial rehearsals and, should problems occur, change parts within the first week.

In school productions, the musical director may have to be her own rehearsal pianist. If possible, however, try to obtain an accompanist so that you

may give your full attention to the singers.

Warm Them Up!

Taking the time to do a proper warm-up with your singers will save you valuable rehearsal time later on. By doing warm-ups, you achieve the following:

- Get your singers to think musically.
- Reawaken their ears to proper pitches.
- Get them into a "performance" mode.

It is always best to begin with simple stretching and breathing exercises, such as numbers 1 and 5 in the last chapter. Then use soft staccato exercises on major triads. Sing "ha-ha-ha-ha-ha" and repeat by ascending a half step.

Change the vowel to "he-he-he-he-he."

Proceed up the scale, changing the vowel to "hay," "hoh," and "hoo." Then connect the notes with a soft, easy legato on "ha."

Remember, start low and ease into the "head

voice." Never take your singers too high too fast—the voice is the most delicate instrument in the orchestra and it must be properly cared for.

Learning the Harmony

Accustomed to the melody, many untrained singers have trouble learning harmonic parts. A word to the wise: Be patient with musical newcomers. Before they attempt to sing, you should play each line on the piano and have them *hear* it and follow it in their vocal part. Then taking it slow and out of tempo, have them sing the line softly while they "read" it in their scores. In this way, they will develop a relational reading ability and will be able to practice at home.

Listen to Your Singers

As you teach harmonic parts to the chorus in these initial rehearsals, make sure they are

Singing the exact notes as written. Often, the printed notes in the vocal parts will be different from what your performers have heard on the cast album or a popular recording. Listen carefully and be sure your singers are singing what is printed—not what they have heard previously.

Keeping the exact rhythm. You may have to clap difficult measures before they attempt to sing it to ensure that they understand the rhythm.

Noting the marked dynamics. Inexperienced singers tend to belt everything triple forte. Even in the early stages of rehearsals, you should remind them of the marked dynamics in the score—and any others that you may want to insert.

Articulating the lyrics. Can you understand the words? Are they clearly enunciating consonants, particularly final *t*'s or *s*'s?

Inserting breath marks. Be sure to tell your singers where to breathe—don't leave it to their discretion. Many will not know that the proper place to breathe is after complete phrases. You should explain that gasping for air in the middle of a phrase

will give the overall choral sound a disjointed effect.

After all the individual parts have been mastered, it is a good idea to put them together and sing the whole number—even in early rehearsals. This is a good morale booster for the company, and it gives you an opportunity to hear the sounds that you will eventually blend into an ensemble. Though a proper balance will probably not take shape for a few more weeks, begin to think about the sound you want to achieve: Are your sopranos too loud? Are the tenors too weak? Make mental notes and during the course of rehearsals you may correct the balance.

Teaching harmonic choral parts is the most time-consuming task a musical director will face. This is why early choral rehearsals should begin immediately after casting. And, once they are learned, harmonic parts must be reviewed frequently. Even professional singers can forget their vocal parts, when they couple it with their blocking or choreography.

Working With Ensembles

Most musicals have numbers for small ensembles—the Barbershop Quartet in *The Music Man* or the Newsboys in *Gypsy*. After the choral work has begun, the musical director should start scheduling rehearsals with these smaller groups, which can be the toughest sessions you will have.

Since they are featured, your ensembles should be composed of the better choral singers—particularly those who can learn harmonic parts and sing them without support. The bass in the quartet of *The Music Man*, for, example, must sing his harmony by himself without the help of other basses. So be sure to choose singers who can handle harmonic parts confidently by themselves.

Even so, most ensembles need to be reviewed frequently, since they may be the first to be forgotten by the individual participants.

Working With the Soloists

After choral and ensemble rehearsals have begun, you should schedule individual appointments with your soloists. If you are also the conductor of the orchestra, these early rehearsals will help you establish an important relationship with your singers, who will rely upon you in performance.

As with the chorus and ensembles, you should

start by teaching the singer the precise melody as written. Once the music is learned, you should review it and set a tempo that is comfortable for the soloist and good for the overall show. You may want to use a metronome in early rehearsals so that the tempo will always be consistent.

You may also want to tape record the accompaniment for your singers, so that they may practice by themselves.

Make It Your Own

It is never too early to begin thinking about an original interpretation for a song. Many singers in school productions listen to cast albums and reproduce their songs the way professionals sang them in New York City many years ago.

Soloists can begin to make the song their own by relating the music and lyrics to the scene in which the song appears. Many young actors stop acting when they start singing. Instead, you should encourage your soloists to extend their character through the song by treating it like a musical monologue. Ask your singers these questions:

- What is your character doing in the course of this song?
- What does your character want to accomplish by singing it?

In this way, they will begin to create a complete throughline for the entire performance.

Also remind your singers that if they are using any character trait, such as a dialect, in their speeches, it should not change when they begin to sing. Maria in *West Side Story*, for example, speaks with a Puerto Rican accent, and she should sing with one as well.

Clues to Character: Lyrics

Too often singers will focus on the music and not realize that the lyrics communicate vital information about the character and the dramatic situation. Lyrics often expose the inner feelings of a character that cannot be divulged in naturalistic dialogue. Often solo songs in a musical express desires, as in *Gypsy*'s "All I Need Is the Girl." Or they delineate personality, as in Billy's "Soliloquy" from *Carousel*.

Clues to Character: The Musical Line

Since music is a language that communicates the dramatic situation, clues to an original interpretation of a character may also be found in the musical line itself. For example, does the song move by step or by leap? Does it progress at a steady rhythmic beat, such as "The Surrey With the Fringe on Top" from *Oklahoma!*, or is it filled with dotted notes that jump from phrase to phrase, as in "Anything You Can Do" from *Annie Get Your Gun*? Are notes heavily accented as in "Everything's Coming Up Roses" from *Gypsy*? Or are they to be softly delivered as in "Send in the Clowns" from *A Little Night Music*?

Moreover, a singer should listen to the accompaniment for clues to the character. Is this song accompanied with dissonance or consonance? If there is discord coming from the orchestra, clanging against the melody, there is tension and conflict in the scene. If there is a consonant and blended accompaniment to the song, then there is a unified feeling to the scene.

Integrating Music Into the Production

As the musical director/conductor, you must blend the music with the action onstage. To do this, you should attend as many non-singing rehearsals as you can. Listening to the spoken scenes will give you a sense of song cues, underscoring and the timing of musical bridges between scenes.

ORCHESTRA REHEARSALS

The conductor is in charge of rehearsing the orchestra. In a school production, you may need to work individually with players or hold sectional rehearsals for brass, percussion, and so forth, so that the music is learned properly. Besides correct pitches, rhythm and dynamics, make sure your players are phrasing the music correctly and producing clean attacks and releases.

Modifying the Score

High school and college musicians may have trouble reading music that was written for professionals. If available, you may want to consider a simplified score, or it may be necessary to modify the original. Difficult rhythmic passages, for example, may have to be cut or edited. Likewise, notes that are pushed to the edge of an instrument's range may be lowered or raised an octave. Remind your musicians to write lightly with pencil in their parts because all marks will have to be erased before returning the books to the licensor.

A Balancing Act

A major job of the conductor is to balance the sound coming from both the orchestra and the singers onstage. The primary purpose of a theatre orchestra is to accompany onstage action. At no time should the orchestra overpower the singers. A usual problem with school or community productions is that inexperienced players tend to play every note loudly, like a marching band, and singers complain that they cannot hear the sound of their own voices. Make sure your orchestra knows the dynamics of the score and knows how to accompany and work with—not against—a singer.

On the other hand, your orchestra should know when to step into the spotlight. During the overture, bridges, dance numbers, curtain calls and the audience's exit, your musicians may play louder than when they are accompanying a singer. You as the conductor must instill in your players a sense of the dynamics of the entire production.

A Style to Those Notes

In the course of rehearsing the orchestra, a conductor must go beyond the printed notes and establish a style for the music. Young trumpet players may not understand the musical idioms of a strip joint in *Gypsy*. To achieve a musical style, you might have your orchestra listen to other selections from the genre you are working in, so that they may begin to play music—not merely notes.

To develop your own interpretation of the music, you should think of the score as a character in the play. Find out where the music
- Supports the action onstage
- Conflicts with the action onstage
- Comments upon the action and individual characters

Answering the above questions will help you develop your own dynamics, tempos, and overall sound of the production.

And How Will the Orchestra Dress?

Traditionally, the performers onstage, who were costumed to match their roles, were distinct entities from the performers in the pit, who wore the black tuxedos of concert musicians. Over the years, some theatre people have questioned this costumed separation between performers *on* the stage and performers *before* the stage, and they have sought ways to integrate the production.

Consult with the stage director and costume designer. If the orchestra will be visible to the audience, how will you costume them? Should they wear concert clothes or should they dress to match the costumes of the production? For example, if you are performing *Carousel*, they could dress in late nineteenth-century clothes.

Whatever is decided, the rule still holds that the orchestra may integrate but it should not detract from the action onstage. To achieve this, remember that dark-colored clothes do not reflect light and perhaps should be considered over light-colored clothes.

Pit or Placement?

Besides costuming your musicians, you and the stage director may think about where you will place the orchestra. If you have a pit, you will probably want to use it. But if you are working in a space that does not have one, you may want to creatively position the musicians in relation to the action. Perhaps you could construct a decorative "box" for them at the side of the auditorium, and in certain cases you may even want to put them on the stage as directors of *Chicago* did.

In placing the orchestra, you must consider potential acoustical problems. If you put the musicians onstage, singers may complain that they cannot hear the orchestra behind them. Likewise, if there is no pit and you set up chairs for your musicians in front of the apron of the stage, singers may not hear the accompaniment because the sound is going directly out to the audience. Here, the scene designer may have to erect a baffle to reflect sound to the stage. Or the sound designer can mike the orchestra and place speakers onstage.

Working with the stage director, scene designer and sound designer, you can be creative with the placement of your orchestra, but your first goal is to obtain a unified sound with the singers onstage.

Review, Review, Review

Your orchestra should be solid—knowing its music inside and out—in time for the first rehearsals with the cast. The best way to achieve this is to constantly review the music you have already learned.

Once you add singers to the mix, there will be inevitable changes. Tempo variations are the most common problem. Perhaps your leading soprano cannot sustain her breath through a particular passage, so you might need to pick up the tempo a bit here. But if you have reviewed the music often enough with your orchestra, minor changes such as this should be no problem.

CAST AND ORCHESTRA REHEARSALS

As the conductor, you should try to put the orchestra and cast together at least a week before performances. Don't expect miracles; most likely, it will be a nightmare. For this reason, it may be wise to schedule your first rehearsal with the cast for music only, no dialogue, as suggested in chapter eight.

On hearing the orchestra play, the singers will usually be the first to complain because they have only worked with a rehearsal pianist. Now they hear the full orchestral arrangement, and many will not know how to adapt to these strange sounds coming from the pit.

Next, the dancers will complain because they have also been working with piano or a piano recording and they will lose track of their counts when they hear the full orchestra.

Finally, you will hear it from the actors, who do not expect underscoring to occur in the midst of their big scene.

The first lesson is this: *Don't panic*. This is to be expected and it happens in nearly every musical production. As the singers, dancers and actors hear the orchestra in subsequent rehearsals, they will become used to it.

During dress rehearsals, the conductor should try to balance the overall sound of the production. A usual problem is that the orchestra is too loud and is overpowering the singers and the action onstage. Besides instructing your musicians to "lighten up,"

you may also lower certain orchestral parts an octave or eliminate certain instruments from a particular passage.

Dress rehearsals also give you the chance to finalize musical cues and make sure they are made promptly. Nothing is worse than a production that lags because cues were not picked up quickly. A second here, a second there, can add minutes to the show—dead minutes where nothing happens except your spectators shift in their seats.

As conductor, you are responsible for the tempo of the entire show. If it is running away, you can pull it back—a usual occurrence on opening night—or if it is lagging, you can energize the cast. So be ready to take sight cues from the performers or—if you are wearing a headset—verbal cues from the stage manager. And always, pick them up quickly!

Orchestral Etiquette

Though stage directors often drill their actors in performance etiquette, such as "Get to the theatre an hour before curtain" and "Don't talk backstage," this type of coaching is seldom directed to the orchestra. As a result, many stage directors complain about the "amateurish" quality of the orchestra in their otherwise "professional" production. Usually this occurs because the musical director/conductor does not think to speak to the musicians about orchestral etiquette.

During run-throughs and performances, the orchestra members should arrive at "half-hour"—thirty minutes before the start of the performance—to tune their instruments and warm up. During the show, they need to sit with the orchestra at all times—even when they are not playing. This is as hard for beginners as it is for professionals who, after they have heard the joke lines in the play for the umpteenth time, find it tremendously boring to remain seated between numbers.

Moreover, they must sit *quietly*, without talking or shifting in their seats. All orchestra members should know that because they are visible to the audience any movement is distracting to the action onstage. The conductor should also sit quietly. It will help your players if you tell them that you, as conductor, must abide by the same rules.

After the Final Curtain . . .

Before you go to the cast party, make sure you gather all musical parts from your orchestra and return them to the stage manager or stage director. It is very easy to slip off with a second flute part that the saxophone player was doubling on. If the books must be returned clean to the licensor, provide some erasers so that the orchestra members can erase all marks that were made during the course of rehearsals and performances.

CHAPTER TEN

Choreographer's Rehearsals

At the first rehearsal, it is a good idea to establish a professional atmosphere right off the bat. Let your dancers know that you have ten golden rules:

1. Be present at every rehearsal.
2. Be on time.
3. No food, cigarettes or chewing gum. (Water bottles may be allowed.)
4. No jewelry or accessories that will impede movement.
5. Come dressed for dancing: If you are not using leotards and tights, sweatsuits will be fine.
6. Wear proper shoes—hopefully, the shoes you will wear in performance or similar ones.
7. No hair falling over the face. Pin it back or up.
8. Be quiet and attentive during instructions.
9. Do not leave the rehearsal without notifying the instructor.
10. Give it your all.

Before each rehearsal, you or the stage manager should use tape or chalk to mark off the floor plan for the scene. Begin by putting down a center line, then mark wing openings and set pieces. If you are using props in your dance, either get the ones that will be used in performance or find reasonable facsimiles.

At every rehearsal, your dancers *must warm up* their muscles before beginning. This may mean arriving a half hour early and running them through a quick barre or at least some slow stretches to prevent injuries. If you are working with nondancers, make sure they stretch their Achilles tendons and the muscles in their backs—these are the two most common problem areas for nondancers.

THREE STAGES OF DANCING REHEARSALS

There are three procedures in teaching a dance: blocking, reviewing and polishing.

Blocking

You will begin by blocking a dance. This means that you, as choreographer, must teach the dance you have created. And you must be a patient teacher. Always plan your rehearsal ahead of time: Know exactly what you want to accomplish and get it done in the time allotted to you. Never create your dances on the spot—rehearsal time is too valuable for that. Always work them out ahead of time and arrive prepared to teach.

Your instruction should be very specific to your dancers. Never be vague with them. Begin by demonstrating the movement in small chunks—usually two measures at a time—and counting it aloud without the music. Have the dancers "mark" the movement first, which means not dancing, just moving through it slowly. Always remember to stop and ask for questions.

Then, gradually speed up the tempo and add the music. It is a good idea to stop after sixty-four bars and give your dancers a chance to make their own notes. This way they will be able to practice at home.

Reviewing

At each rehearsal, you should review the dances already learned. Don't underestimate this stage of rehearsal. By reviewing the dances, you will cement them in the minds of your performers. If you are working with an assistant, you may ask this person to review the dances, while you work with a soloist or someone who is not involved in that particular dance.

Polishing

This comes last. After the steps have been thoroughly learned and reviewed, then you may articulate the nuances of your dance, until it looks just as you envisioned it when you created it. Dancers must also understand what emotions they are to convey within the dance. Polishing rehearsals give you the chance to integrate dance into the production as a whole.

Warning: Don't try to polish your work in the first rehearsals—that can end up being frustrating for everyone. Wait until the steps are second nature to your company before they begin to dance them emotionally.

During polishing rehearsals, it is a good idea to videotape your choreography. You may slow down the movement and study it closely to make any necessary changes. During dress rehearsals, videotape the final version of your dances for your own personal use. Except for your own notes, which may or may not be legible to anyone else, this will be the only record of your work.

TEACHING NONDANCERS TO DANCE

If you are working with people who have limited dancing experience, here is a tried-and-true method to teach them:

1. Keep the steps simple. Do not create movements that are beyond their abilities.
2. Take a light touch. Most nondancers are afraid that they will be made fools of as soon as they step on the floor. Dispel any fears by letting them know that the dance is easy and it will be fun to do.
3. Explain the situation in the production. Actors and singers think in terms of what scene they are in, so let them know that the dance they are about to learn, for example, comes in the second act after the leading lady has left the leading man.
4. Play the dance music all the way through without any movement—so that they may hear it.
5. Begin to teach the dance without music and counts. Speak in terms of right foot, left foot; for example, "Put your weight on your right foot, now cross the left foot in front and step on it, then step back on your right foot."
6. Work in very short sections, one measure at a time.
7. After they have established the overall pattern for the movement, then begin to count it for them; for example, 1-2-3-4.
8. After they have learned two measures, put the music to it.
9. While the steps may be easy, you may add excitement by snapping fingers, hand claps, toe taps or even finger lifts.
10. Always be a cheerleader, telling your nondancers that they will learn this in no time flat.

While the above method may be slow and tedious, it has proven itself in countless productions. The extra time taken to work carefully with nondancers will pay off in the end.

STAGING SONGS

Though the stage director is usually responsible for this, in certain situations, the choreographer may be asked to stage a song. In this situation, less is always more. Don't try to over-dance a song—you'll only frustrate the singers and the musical director. And remember, song lyrics need to be understood by the audience, so have your singers face front as much as possible.

In addition, ask yourself:
- What is the dramatic function of the song?
- Who has the focus onstage? (You will, of course, give instructions to the dominant singer(s), but do not neglect those who are listening to the singing.)
- Do the lyrics suggest appropriate gestures?
- Are set pieces, props and costumes usable?
- Remember, understated movement is always best for singers.

(See also "Blocking Songs" in chapter eleven.)

Stage Director's Blocking Rehearsals

This chapter deals with rehearsals held by the stage director for blocking (that is, planning the major movements) of characters. We shall start with blocking on the proscenium arch stage and then discuss stage pictures, movement, special problems in blocking, directing comedy, blocking songs, and blocking on arena, thrust and L-shaped stages.

Seven or more full rehearsals may be needed for the stage director to block the dialogue and songs (see the suggested rehearsal schedule in chapter eight); after that, the stage director may continue to alter the blocking up until dress rehearsals.

Blocking is nothing to fear if you will adopt a few commonsense suggestions:

Have a plan. As mentioned in chapter four, a way to save time in rehearsal is to think about blocking in advance. Go to a blocking rehearsal with a rough plan for the major movements, but let actors have input into deciding on their motions. Rehearsals should be a time for experimentation. Keep an open mind to performers' ideas and be flexible enough to change your way of thinking when it is for the good of the production.

Block in sequence. Block the scenes in order so that actors can better understand the progression of the plot and the reasons for certain occurrences. Each scene builds on previous happenings, and this is easier to understand if you explain the plot as you block in sequence.

Discuss each character. Before each scene you should also talk about the characters' objectives, mo-

tivations, actions and attitudes toward others. As an example, look at the character of Momma Rose in the opening scene of *Gypsy*. Uncle Jocko is trying to select child entertainers for his kiddie show. Rose's objective is to get her children's act chosen. Her motivation is her desire to make Baby June a star. Her initial action is to flatter Uncle Jocko. Her attitude toward Jocko and his assistants is that they can be manipulated.

Describe the technical elements. Next, the stage director should inform the cast about the placement of scenery, properties, furniture, steps, levels, entrances and exits. The stage manager should mark the floor with chalk or tape to indicate where scenery will stand and place rehearsal chairs and tables where furniture will be. The stage director should also tell performers about their costumes, shoes, makeup and wigs as all of these can affect movement. Encourage actors to come to rehearsals with shoes that are similar to what they will wear in performances since shoes affect how a person walks and stands. Women and men who will wear long dresses or robes in the musical should also bring to rehearsals full-length garments to help them get into character.

Block scenes of dialogue. Usually, stage directors will block scenes of dialogue first, skipping songs and dances until they have been rehearsed by the musical director and choreographer. If there is a dialogue scene in which only a few speak but many are onstage, you may find it better to call only those who have lines to the first blocking rehearsal. It may take a long time to work out the blocking for these few, and there is no reason to keep a large group waiting while you work with only several. After blocking the speakers, it should be easy at a later rehearsal to block in the nonspeakers.

Record all blocking. During a blocking rehearsal, you should be certain actors record their movements in their scripts and that all blocking is written in the stage director's and stage manager's scripts. All marks should be in pencil because blocking may be changed many times before performances. Also, if you are using rented material, all marks must be erased before returning it to the licensor. If you are working with inexperienced performers, teach them to use the symbols mentioned in chapter four: "X UL" for "cross up left" or "X to G" for "cross to Guenevere." "Cross right and look upstage" can be indicated by "X R √."

Get a good stage manager. The stage manager can be of great help to the stage director during rehearsals: marking floors, recording blocking, prompting, indicating where a technical effect will be (such as the ring of a telephone), standing in for missing performers, taking attendance, and checking on absent and late people.

PROSCENIUM ARCH STAGES

Since the proscenium arch stage is the most common American stage, we shall start by describing it and defining terms used in blocking on this type.

A "Peephole Theatre"

The *proscenium* stage (see Figures 5-1 and 11-1) has an arch that separates spectators from the acting area. This arch provides a frame for the stage picture like a frame for a painting. The proscenium arch not only focuses the audience's attention on the acting area, it also hides the machinery and technical workers that are located above and at the sides of the acting space. When a box set (a type of interior setting that depicts a room with two side walls, a back wall and a ceiling) is used onstage, the proscenium arch allows the audience to watch the show through the room's imaginary "fourth wall" that is located at the curtain line. For this reason, the proscenium arch theatre has been called a "peephole theatre."

Parts of the House

The audience faces the proscenium stage sitting in rows in the part of the building called the *house*. Those on the main floor are in *orchestra* seats while those on higher levels are in *box, loge, balcony* or *gallery* seats. The conductor and orchestra are often located in a *pit* between the audience and the stage or below the stage.

Parts of the Stage

The *acting space* (the part visible to the audience) of a proscenium stage may be divided into areas. A small- to medium-sized stage may have nine areas, while a large stage may have fifteen. Each of these areas has a name so that directors may communicate easily with performers in blocking movements and dancing. See page 79 for diagrams of these stages.

The areas are named from the performers' point of view. If an actor stands in center stage facing the audience, the left areas are to the actor's left and the right areas are to the actor's right. If the performer moves away from the audience, this person is crossing upstage, and if he or she moves toward the spectators, this actor is crossing downstage.

> *Upstage* and *downstage* are old terms that were used in the days when stage floors sloped up to the back of the stage and upstage areas were actually higher than the downstage areas. Today, most stage floors are level or almost so, but the traditional names for stage areas persist.

Some proscenium stages have an apron or forestage, which is the area from the proscenium arch to the front edge of the stage, and some may have side stages, which are acting areas in front of the proscenium arch on each side. Theatres that have an elevator forestage have the flexibility of changing the height of this floor to use it as an extension of the apron, an orchestra pit, or additional seating for the audience when it is placed at the level of the house floor and equipped with seats.

The offstage areas at the sides of the acting space are called wings, which is where performers wait to make entrances. This is another old term dating from the days when all proscenium stages used

FIGURE 11-1 **PROSCENIUM STAGE**
(DESIGNERS: MIKE MURPHY, KEVIN BANNON, MARSHALL UNIVERSITY)

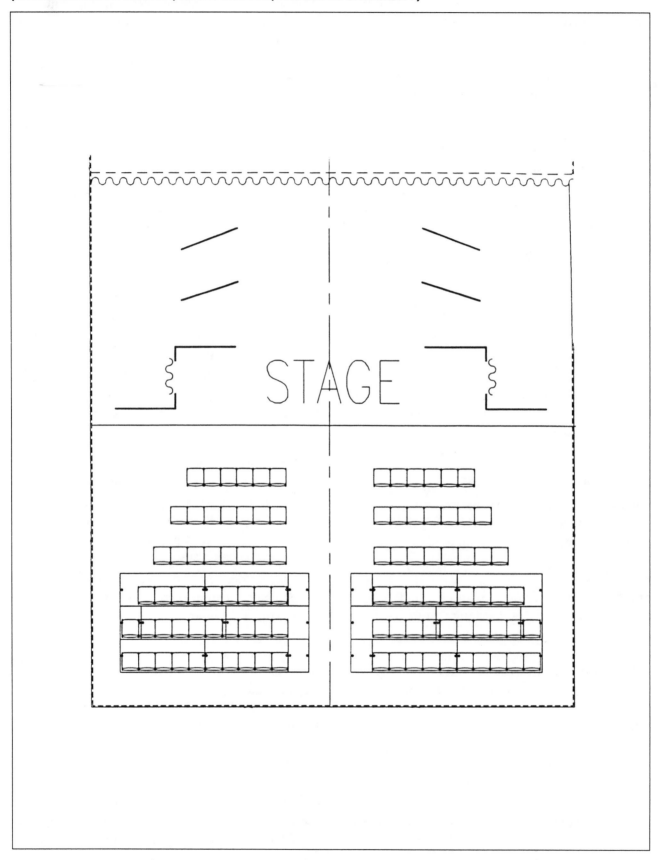

MEDIUM-SIZED PROSCENIUM STAGE

Up Right (UR)	Up Center(UC)	UP Left (UL)
Right (R)	Center (C)	Left (L)
Down Right (DR)	Down Center (DC)	Down Left (DL)

(Audience)

LARGE PROSCENIUM STAGE

Up Right (UR)	Up Right Center (URC)	Up Center (UC)	Up Left Center (ULC)	UP Left (UL)
Right (R)	Right Center (RC)	Center (C)	Left Center (LC)	Left (L)
Down Right (DR)	Down Right Center (DRC)	Down Center (DC)	Down Left Center (DLC)	Down Left (DL)

(Audience)

wing-drop-border settings that had wings as a part of the scenery at both sides of the stage, drop(s) in back, and borders hanging overhead (see Figure 11-1). This type of setting is still often used for musicals, normally with three or four wings on each side of the stage. When a script indicates that a scene, song or dance is to be done *in one*, this means that it is to be played close to the audience downstage of the first set of wings. The stage manager's desk is usually located in the left or right wings near the proscenium arch at a place where the stage manager can see the playing area. Behind the upstage areas of the acting space is backstage.

The stage floor may have *traps*, which are sections that may be removed to allow the entrance of people, props and scenery from the basement to the stage or vice versa. *Elevators* or *lifts* that can descend to the basement or rise above the stage floor may also be available. The stage floor may have a *revolve*, which is a circular turning platform that is built into the floor or is temporarily mounted on the floor. In addition, the floor may have *tracks* for the movement of wagons, scenery and properties. A *cyclorama*, which is a curved curtain or wall that is often painted to look like a sky, may be at the sides and rear of the stage.

The *fly loft* or *flies* is the space above the stage from which drops, draperies, curtains, scenery, properties and lighting equipment may hang. If needed onstage, they can be lowered through a *rigging system*. A horizontally drawn curtain is called a *traveler*, and a special curtain or set made of net or gauze that is opaque when lighted from the front but transparent when lighted from behind is a *scrim*. A *teaser* is a curtain that hangs from a batten to adjust the height of the proscenium opening, while *tormentors* are flats or drapes at the sides of the proscenium arch that may be used to alter the width of the stage opening.

Terms Used in Blocking

In blocking on a proscenium arch stage, terms are used that all directors and performers should be familiar with. The glossary explains a large number of stage and musical terms, but the following are some that you will need to know before blocking a show.

In telling actors how to stand, the stage director may use the following names for positions of the body:

↓ **FULL FRONT** The performer is facing the audience.

her left about halfway between full front and left profile. (When two are sharing a scene on a proscenium arch stage and both are equally important, they will probably be in opposite one-quarter positions.)

→ **PROFILE LEFT** The performer faces left with his or her profile (that is, the right side of the body) to the audience.

↗ **THREE-QUARTER LEFT** The performer turns to a position halfway between left profile and full back.

↑ **FULL BACK** The performer has his or her back to the audience.

↖ **THREE-QUARTER RIGHT** The performer is in a position halfway between full back and right profile.

← **PROFILE RIGHT** The performer faces right with his or her profile to the audience.

↙ **ONE-QUARTER RIGHT** The performer is in a position halfway between right profile and full front.

Other terms used in blocking are to:

CROSS To move from one place to another onstage.

CROSS IN BACK OF OR ABOVE To move on the upstage side of a person or property.

CROSS IN FRONT OF OR BELOW To move on the downstage side of a person or property.

DRESS STAGE OR COUNTER To move slightly or change position to balance the stage after another person has made a cross.

TAKE STAGE To assume a dominant position onstage, which is usually a full front or a one-quarter body position.

GIVE STAGE To take a less dominant position, which is usually a three-quarter or full back body position.

MOVE IN, ON, OR ONSTAGE To cross toward the center of the stage.

MOVE OUT, OFF, OR OFFSTAGE To cross away from the center of the stage.

MAKE AN OPEN TURN To turn toward the audience so that the spectators see the front of the actor.

MAKE A CLOSED TURN To turn away from the audience so that the spectators see the back of the actor.

OPEN UP To turn more toward the audience; for example, from a profile position to one-quarter.

TURN IN To turn away from the audience.

TURN OUT To turn toward the audience.

CHEAT To move slightly to improve the stage picture or to turn more toward the audience for better audibility.

COVER To stand in front of someone, an object, or a movement so that the audience cannot see it.

FOCUS To look at a person or object.

STEAL To move onstage without attracting the audience's attention.

STEAL A SCENE To attract attention that should be on another actor.

UPSTAGE ANOTHER PERFORMER To cross deliberately to a place upstage of another actor and assume a full front or one-quarter position, thereby forcing the other performer to turn to a three-quarter position in order to talk with the upstager. A stage director should not allow this to happen.

STAGE PICTURES

In blocking, the stage director's main concern is that the audience will be able to see, hear and understand who the characters are and what the plot is all about. To that end, the stage director must visualize how the stage will look with scenery, properties, lighting and performers in costumes and makeup; then he or she must make each stage picture communicate to the audience the situation at that moment in the plot, the intellectual and emotional content of that moment, the mood, time period and style of the musical.

The theatre's proscenium arch functions like the frame of a picture, and the stage director should be as concerned as a painter with obtaining a harmonious composition of the elements. There are differences, however, between the painter and the stage director: The visual artist works in two dimensions, the director in three; and the painter is creating one picture, while the director is creating many pictures, some of which may be very brief. The director, therefore, is concerned not only with stage pictures but also with the movement between them and the relationship of each composition to the one ahead and the one following. Knowing how to use emphasis, balance and variety can be helpful.

Emphasis

In devising stage pictures, the stage director must know how to control the spectators' attention by getting them to look at the important character(s) at that moment and ignore unimportant ones so that the audience will understand what is happening. Usually the person who should receive this emphasis is the one who is speaking, although there may be times when the reactions of others to the lines may be more important.

There are certain ways to make a character emphatic onstage—that is, the most important one at that moment. Here is how to do it:

1. A person who is facing the audience in a *full front position* is more attention-getting than those who are in other body positions. To make a character emphatic, place this individual in a position that is closer to full front than the others, so that she can "take the stage."

2. The *highest* or *tallest* character onstage will also receive attention, so to make a person emphatic, have this individual stand while all others are seated or move the performer to a level that makes him higher than the others.

3. The most attention-getting areas of the stage are the *downstage* and *center* areas, so to make someone emphatic, move this actor to one of these places.

4. *Brighly colored and light-colored costumes* are more attention-getting than clothes in subdued and dark shades; therefore, make a character emphatic by costuming this actor in a vibrant color.

5. Emphasis may be achieved through placing the person in *bright light*, such as spotlighting, while others are in darker areas.

6. Emphasis can also be achieved through *focus* because, if everyone onstage is looking at one person, the attention of the audience will be drawn to that character.

7. *Movement and gesturing* will attract the attention of the audience, so you can make a person emphatic by directing this performer to move or gesture.

8. If the emphatic person has lines, the act of *speaking* will help to attract the audience's attention.

9. A *person who is alone* will attract attention, so you can bring emphasis to an isolated individual by grouping everyone else in another location.

10. *Contrast* will bring emphasis to a character, so have the emphatic person do something different than the others. For example, (despite No. 2 above) if everyone is standing except for the emphatic person who is sitting on the floor, the contrast should force the audience to watch the one on the floor; or (despite No. 1 above) if many are full front and the emphatic person is full back, the latter will probably receive the attention.

Balance

Usually, the stage picture should appear balanced to the audience. If you have a large number of people standing for some time on one side of the stage with no people, scenery or properties on the other side, the imbalance can worry an audience.

There are two type of balance: symmetrical and asymmetrical. In *symmetrical* balance the right side of the stage up to an imaginary center line looks just like the other half from the center line to the left; that is, the scenery and lighting are approximately the same and there are about the same number of performers in the same costumes and positions on both halves of the stage. Although there may be times when you want symmetry onstage, it may seem too contrived and artificial for scenes in which you want more natural-looking arrangements.

Most of the time stage directors use many *asymmetrical* combinations to provide a balanced look without symmetry. Both halves of the stage will be different but the audience will feel that there is a visual balance—that one side of the stage is equal in emphatic weight to the other side. *Emphatic balance* is achieving equilibrium in the stage picture through the weight of the emphatic elements. One emphatic speaking and moving character at downstage right can balance many stationary, silent characters at upstage left. Consider too, how scenery may contribute to the stage picture: A house in up right center may balance a soloist at down left center.

In scenes that take place in just one area with only a few people, the audience tends to disregard the rest of the stage if there is balance within the space used. This is especially true if lighting illuminates only this area and, therefore, isolates it from the surrounding darkness.

There are times, however, when the director may

want the stage to seem unbalanced—especially in scenes that are intended to provoke tension in the audience.

Variety

Repeating compositions can be dull for spectators. They like *visual variation*, so stage directors must guard against being repetitious. In moving actors onstage, look for variety in body positions, use of stage areas, planes and levels, and spacings between people. There are many possible arrangements of characters onstage, so create fresh compositions that communicate meaning, excitement, emotions and mood.

MOVEMENT

The way to get actors from one stage picture to another is through movement, which can also help to delineate character and character relationships, contribute to the plot, reveal emotions and provide exciting actions.

All movement must be appropriate for each character, the situation, the mood, and style of the show, and it must be motivated—that is, there must be a purpose, a reason for every move. Sometimes there will be movements indicated in the script without any apparent reason for them. If the stage director or actor cannot find a justification for moving at that time, the character should not move. In moving actors to make one emphatic, the stage director must consider the motivation for the action. You cannot send someone up the stairs just because you want that person higher than the others without some reason for it. *All movement on a stage must have a purpose.* Following are some special concerns with regard to movement.

Sharing a Scene

If two standing characters are sharing a scene and both are equally important, they should usually be in opposite one-quarter or profile positions in the same plane. A *plane* is one of many imaginary lines that run parallel to the front edge of the stage. The planes are as long as the proscenium opening and as wide as a standing actor. To stand in the same plane means that the actors are an equal distance from the front edge of the stage; thus, one actor should not receive more attention from the audience than the other, provided all other elements (lighting, color of clothing, height and so forth) are equal.

Note, however, that if two actors must be in different planes, they can still share a scene if both face front.

Taking and Giving the Stage

With two standing actors, the stage director may want the character who has important dialogue or business to have more emphasis than the other. You may then direct the emphatic character to take the stage by moving slightly upstage of the other person and assuming a one-quarter or full front position while the other person gives the stage by taking a three-quarter or full back position. Another way to achieve this is to direct the nonemphatic actor to move downstage before taking a three-quarter or full back position.

Crossing Other Actors

If two actors are sharing a scene and you tell one actor to cross the other, the moving actor will normally pass in front of or below the stationary actor to the place you specify. The reason is that if the person is speaking you do not want this individual to be covered by crossing behind another character. After the cross, the stationary actor should counter or dress stage by moving slightly to be again on the same plane with the other actor. The preceding pertains to crosses made by major characters. If a minor character, perhaps a servant, is moving onstage, he or she should cross upstage of major characters unless the minor character has important lines to say.

Moving and Speaking

Normally, an actor moves when speaking and stands still when listening to others. Both speaking and moving are attention-getters, so it is better to have one character do both than to split the attention between two actors. Moving is so attention-getting that it may lessen the impact of a line. For that reason, if a line must be emphasized, the director may move the actor before the line and have the actor stand still to deliver the important line. Another possibility is to have the actor say the line and then move.

Entering and Exiting

When a performer is entering the stage, he or she must time the entrance so as to arrive onstage exactly on cue. When leaving the stage, the stage director may have the actor move to the exit on the speech before his last one, so that he can say his final lines at the door and leave quickly. If he says his last line in center stage, he may have to walk a good distance to the exit while everyone else onstage is silent waiting for him to depart. Pauses of this sort should be eliminated.

When choruses enter or exit in a realistic fashion, the best way is to move a few on or off at a time.

Triangular Arrangements

When blocking three or more performers, the stage director will sometimes use triangular arrangements with the emphatic person at the upstage apex, speaking to those who are downstage. The emphatic person may also be at a downstage apex if he or she does not have to look at the others. To get variety, triangles may be of different sizes as may the angle at the apex, and the sides may be of different lengths. Usually, equilateral and isosceles triangles should be avoided.

When deciding on the placement of a large group of people, try to get an interesting spacing between performers. In a realistic production, avoid straight lines (unless these is a good reason for them, such as people standing in line to buy something). Also, avoid semicircles, especially those where performers are standing an equal distance apart in the same body position. A triangular arrangement of performers with the emphatic person at the apex should be more interesting. Triangles should not be overworked, however, as a succession of them can seem artificial and unrealistic.

SPECIAL PROBLEMS

This section will describe some special problems that stage directors face in musicals such as handling crowds, falling, shooting, stabbing, fighting, kissing, and doing asides, soliloquies, bows and curtsies. In blocking movement in which someone could be hurt, the stage director must take all precautions. The safety of performers should be a major concern of all directors and technical workers.

Crowd Scenes

Musicals often have large choral numbers in which many people are onstage. Principals may be in the midst of the crowd or may be separated. At the beginning of Act II of *Evita*, the title character, her husband, Perón, and other dignitaries are on an elevated structure built to commemorate Perón's inauguration. On the stage floor is the chorus with backs to the audience. Standing center on this structure, Evita is in an excellent position to sing "Don't Cry for Me Argentina."

The best way to handle this crowd is to divide them into groups and give everyone a characterization: There can be family groups with a mother, father and children; a grandmother and grandchild; two old men; three teenagers; and so forth. If you have children onstage, place them with older people who can make sure that they stay in character. Explain to everyone the situation, mood, emotions and thoughts of the scene. Show them precisely where you want them to enter, to move, to stand, to focus, to exit. The focus is particularly important because the audience will look at what the crowd is watching. Demand that they listen to what is being said and react appropriately. If the people must cheer or shout words, be sure they know what to say and when to say it. For a natural appearance, have irregular spacing between small groups and use as much of the stage as possible. If you can, get them on different levels in various body positions and devise realistic business for them to do.

Falling

If an actor must fall onstage, the safest way to fall is along one side of the body. The performer should gently fall to the side of a leg, hip, torso, shoulder, and side of the head. He or she should *not* fall on the knees, put hands out to break the fall, bump the head, or let the feet bounce. Direct the actor to land, if possible, in an upstage area or behind furniture, unless the person must be visible to the audience. If the person can be seen, the head should be nearer the audience than the feet.

Usually, the fall does not have to be fast. The actor may stagger, grab a piece of furniture, and sink to the floor; however, if an actor is supposed to be shot, as in *West Side Story*, the person must appear

In some shows, the actor may pretend to shoot while recorded shots are heard or the stage manager or property master fires a prop gun offstage. If a prop gun is to be fired onstage, the property master or stage manager should be ready to fire offstage in case the onstage gun fails.

to have received a blow of great force that knocks him or her back and down.

Shooting a Gun Onstage

The gunman should aim *upstage* of the victim, who should be at least eight feet away. No one should be in the line of firing, so be sure that all performers and backstage technicians are out of the way. The reason is that a prop gun loaded with a blank cartridge can discharge a wad that may injure or kill.

Stabbing

To avoid accidents, real knives should not be used for fight scenes. For actors' safety, rubber or collapsible knives, which may be obtained from theatrical supply houses, are needed.

If a person must be stabbed, one way to conceal the action is to have the victim (with either back or front to the audience) downstage of the stabber. The attacker can hold the weapon high to show it to the audience and then bring it down with force. Just before reaching the victim the stabber turns the knife under so that it is the back of the hand that strikes the victim instead of the knife.

When stabbing an opponent with a sword, as in a duel, the attacker may pass the weapon between the upstage arm and the body of the victim.

Fighting

All stage fights must be carefully choreographed, rehearsed frequently, and strictly controlled by the stage director or a special fight director. Before beginning any fighting onstage, the combatants must establish eye contact, and they must not deviate in any way from the choreography.

To slap a person, the slapper should relax the hand, aim for the fleshy part of the cheek, avoiding the nose, eye and ear, and hit with relaxed fingers. The person hit may turn the head away from the blow.

For a blow to the midsection, the victim (with back to the audience) may conceal the action by being downstage of the hitter. The assailant can start with a clenched fist but before making contact he can open the hand so that the palm of the hand strikes the victim, who should react as though painfully hurt.

To deliver a blow to the head, a downstage hitter (with back to the audience) may cover the action with his body as he aims the punch to miss the upstage victim's chin by about an inch. The receiver can supply sound by grunting and pulling the head back and away.

To pull someone's hair, the assailant should grab the victim's hair, and the victim should grab the puller's wrist. The victim can now control the action while moving and groaning as though hurt.

To strangle someone, the strangler should place both hands on the victim's shoulders near the neck, avoiding pressure on the windpipe. The victim should place both hands over the strangler's as though trying to remove the assailant's hands. While the strangler appears to be applying pressure (but is not), the victim, who may gasp for air and moan, should control the action.

For armed combat used in various historical periods, consult a specialist in this field or books on stage fighting, several of which are listed in the bibliography of this book.

Kissing

For a standing kiss, the stage director must be certain that the couple's feet are close together because, if their feet are far apart and they lean in to kiss, their positions will look funny. The woman may put her upstage arm around the man's neck and her downstage arm on his shoulder. The man may put his upstage arm around her back and his downstage arm around her waist. His head may be downstage of hers as they tilt heads to kiss.

Because of fear of transmitting diseases, some

actors are reluctant to kiss strangers on the mouth. If so, perhaps a warm embrace with the man kissing her on the cheek or forehead will suffice. If a kiss on the mouth is necessary, the couple may open their mouths slightly as they move toward each other and then close their lips before contact. If they do not wish to touch lips, the man may kiss the woman below the lips. The man's tilted head should conceal the kiss from the audience's view.

For a seated kiss, the woman may put her head on the man's upstage shoulder as he bends to kiss her. Again, his head should cover the kiss. To kiss a woman's hand, the man should bend forward and raise her hand gently to his mouth so that he may touch the back of her hand briefly with his lips.

Asides and Soliloquies

An aside is a brief remark that a character makes to the audience that other actors onstage are not supposed to hear. Old and modern plays may contain asides, some of which are meant to be funny and some serious. To deliver an aside, the actor may turn toward the spectators or may move toward the audience while the other characters look away or freeze. After the aside is finished, all return to their prior positions.

A soliloquy is a speech given by a performer when alone onstage or when the character believes no one else is near and, therefore, he or she can reveal true thoughts and feelings to the audience. In musicals, a soliloquy may be spoken or sung, and it may be delivered as though the person is communicating to the audience or just thinking aloud. (Note Katisha's recitative and song that begin the scene from *The Mikado*.)

Bows and Curtsies

When a gentleman in a period play must bow, the stage director may want to consult a book on manners and customs (two of which are listed in the bibliography) because men's bows have changed through the years. A stage bow, though, that looks good for all periods from the Middle Ages to the early nineteenth century requires the man to step back with one foot, toes slightly turned out. He puts all of his weight on the back leg as he bends his rear knee and keeps his front leg straight. He may nod his head or bend forward as he removes his hat and places it over his heart or sweeps it back. If not wearing a hat, he may put one hand over his heart or extend the hand forward and then to the floor.

For shows that depict the middle of the nineteenth century or later, the director may ask gentlemen to put their heels together with toes slightly turned out and nod or bow from the waist with hands at the sides. A male servant may use the same bow for all periods from the Middle Ages to the present, and it is also a good bow to use at curtain calls for both men and women. For the curtain call bow, the hands may be at the sides or brought together above the knees as the actor bends forward. As the performer stands up straight, the arms return to the sides.

To make a curtsy that is good for all time periods, the woman places the ball of one foot in back of the other and keeps her weight on both feet as she bends her knees. She may also nod her head or bend forward from the waist. In another type of curtsy, the woman steps back with one foot, putting all her weight on it as she bends the rear knee and points the toe of the front foot as she bends forward. While doing either type of curtsy, she may put her hands on her dress, cross them over her heart or hold them out and back with her palms to the front.

Maids in period plays make a different type of curtsy, called the "bob" curtsy, as they enter or leave rooms. To make this quick curtsy, the maid should bend her knees slightly as she nods her head.

DIRECTING COMEDY

In directing a comedy, the stage director must analyze what is humorous about the show. Will the laughs come from funny situations in the plot, bizarre characters or witty lines? Can you, the stage director, make it funnier by adding comic movements, unusual voices, stage business, props, costuming, makeup or hairstyles?

Look at the Plot

Is it a farce or situation comedy? A satire or comedy of manners? A romantic comedy? Farce may employ a lot of slapstick and low comedic devices. Satire may rely more on wit and an intellectual approach, while romantic comedy takes a more emotional one.

Look at the Characters

Do you have characters who are obsessed with obtaining one goal? In *Guys and Dolls* Adelaide wants to marry Nathan. Nathan is just as determined to avoid marriage, and both obsessions lead to laughs. Adelaide also gets laughs through her vocal quality which, since she always has a cold, is a rather denasalized, high-pitched whine. Consider the possibilities in creating funny characters through changing the voice quality, dialect or accent of your actors.

Look at the Lines

Are there jokes that start with a "straight line" (or "feed line") that leads to a "punch line" (or "laugh line")? The actor with the straight line must set up the laugh by saying the line loudly and clearly. As for the delivery of a punch line, it often helps for the actor to play it out to the audience. Usually an actor should not cross on a laugh line as the movement may distract the audience from understanding the joke.

Are there funny words used in strange ways? Are there lines with double meanings? Puns? Malapropisms (the use of an incorrect word for one that is similar in sound)? Extreme exaggerations? Surprises? Incongruities? Mispronunciations? Look for these and direct your actors to point the key words and speak distinctly. After all, if the spectators cannot hear or understand the words, they will not laugh.

Hold for Laughs

If a big laugh results from the line, the actors should freeze, unless their humorous movements or facial expressions are feeding the laugh. When the laugh passes its peak and the next speaker thinks he or she can be heard, the actor should say the next line.

Old Comedic Devices

Can you figure out how you can get laughs from unusual props, costuming, makeup or hairstyles? Or from comic movements, stage business or facial expressions? There are old comedic devices that have been used for centuries that are still good at getting laughs, such as the *take* or *slow take*. This is done usually with the comedian looking out at the audience as he or she slowly realizes what has been said or done. A *double take* is a variation of this with the comic looking at something or someone, then looking away, then realizing what he has seen or heard, and quickly looking back. A *running gag* is comic business that is repeated throughout the musical. *Deadpanning* is getting laughs through using no facial expressions, while *mugging* is just the opposite—using excessive, exaggerated expressions. *Chasing, tripping, slipping* and *hitting* are also old farcical tricks to get laughs.

BLOCKING SONGS

After the singers have rehearsed with the musical director and have memorized the songs, the stage director should block the movement.

Determine Function, Mood, Ideas

In prerehearsal planning, the stage director should have decided on the function, mood and ideas expressed in each song and/or dance number. To repeat some of the main functions listed in chapter three:

- Will the number provide a climax to the scene?
- Set the mood?
- Give exposition?
- Advance the plot?
- Reveal characters and relationships?
- State the theme or a main idea?
- Tell a story?
- Add humor or comedy?
- Add variety and spectacle?

As an example of determining function, mood and ideas, look at a scene from *Camelot* in which King Arthur and his wife Guenevere sing "What Do the Simple Folk Do?" The functions of this number are to provide a climax to the scene, reveal what King Arthur and Queen Guenevere are thinking and feeling, set the mood and add humor. The major idea expressed in the song is that simple folk have ways to relieve their hard lives—they whistle, sing, dance, and wonder what royalty would do—but these do not help the king and queen with their burdens. So the song ends with Arthur and Guenevere looking forlornly at each other. The mood is basically melancholy.

Consider Costumes, Set and Props

The stage director may want to look for clues in the script and score as to how the number was staged originally. You do not have to follow them, but they may provide some options. Keep in mind what the set will look like and how much space will be available. If there are different levels, stairs and furniture, think about what you can use in the number to make it visually interesting. Can you use any props effectively? How will the performers be costumed? How can you use the costumes in this number?

Decide on Focus

Who should receive the primary attention of the audience? Does it change during the song? How do you make a person dominant onstage? (The answer to the last question is to use the techniques listed earlier in this chapter for making a character emphatic.) Commonly in solos the singer is given a full front center position and other people onstage are told to focus on the soloist. This is the situation in *South Pacific* when Nellie sings "Honey Bun" to an audience of sailors, marines and officers. Later when Billis enters to dance while she sings, they share the focus.

In blocking songs, never neglect the characters onstage who are watching the singers and dancers. Be sure that their eyes are focused on the performers so that the audience will do the same.

Create the Blocking

To begin, the stage director should imagine that he or she is the singer. What is your objective in singing these words? Motivation? Think the character's thoughts—feel the character's emotions. Physicalize the person's characteristics, traits, qualities, mood and attitude as you let your body move spontaneously to express the lyrics in physical motions. Then, listen to the music to determine what the melody and rhythm suggest. Let yourself go to see how you can reveal through bodily movement and facial expressions what the words and music are saying.

If your singers are nondancers, keep the movement simple. Find out what they are capable of doing. Most can walk, run, sway, turn, kick, skip, kneel, gesture with arms and hands, and do social dance steps; and some who are or have been athletes,

In repeating the song over and over to polish the movements, do not require the performers to sing at full voice. Save their singing voices by allowing them to speak or sing softly.

cheerleaders, majorettes, joggers or aerobic exercisers may surprise you.

Work on the number with a tape recording or pianist until you have a plan for the movement. Pay particular attention to places in the music where the singers are silent while the orchestra plays. In order to hold the audiences' attention, you should plan for movement there. Also, think about the ending and make it something special for the audience to remember. Then meet with the performers to discuss your plan. They may have good suggestions for movement as you work on the number together.

You can instruct them by demonstrating the motions as you recite or sing the lyrics. After they learn the movements, ask them to sing and move as they do the number with piano accompaniment.

Face the Audience

Whatever movement you decide on, have the singers face the audience as much as possible because spectators like to watch facial expressions. Also, when singers turn away from the listeners, they may not be heard (unless they are wearing microphones) and may therefore lose the audience's attention. Solos are usually sung for the most part in a full front position and duets in full front or one-quarter positions. Do not keep a singer in a profile position very long because spectators cannot see enough of the face.

In the Broadway production of *Chess*, the character of Freddie was directed to do push-ups and sit-ups while singing. Sometimes you may be tempted to have characters sing while standing on their heads or in some other weird position, but this is usually not a good idea. A stage director should not ask singers to perform actions that may hamper their singing or make it difficult to watch the conductor. Now, this does *not* mean that all singers should stand upright and face the conductor while singing. They can sing while sitting in chairs, lying on a bed, sitting or lying on the floor, moving or dancing, if they can watch the conductor through their peripheral vision. In performance, the audience should not be aware that singers are watching the conductor. The spectators should think that the performers are completely in character, thinking and feeling only the thoughts and emotions of the character as they sing.

Use Closed-Circuit TV

An aid in this matter is a closed-circuit television system with a TV camera focused on the conductor and offstage monitors that can be seen by those who must sing in the wings or with their backs to the conductor. A monitor may also be placed on a balcony rail so that performers can see the conductor on the monitor as they sing out to the audience.

Use Microphones

If singers are to hold wireless microphones, the stage director should consult with the sound designer about how close to the mouth the mike should be placed and whether the distance should be changed according to the loudness and softness of the voice. If the singer is to move while holding a mike with a cord, the stage director will have to be sure that the performer can maneuver the cord without tripping over it. Usually the singer should have the mike in one hand and loosely hold the wire in the other in order to move it as needed. Body mikes are the easiest to use because the transmitter can be taped to the body or concealed in the costume with the microphone clipped to clothing near the throat or in the wig or hair. If the sound designer plans to use floor, overhead or standing mikes, the stage director must be aware of their placements as these may affect the blocking.

BLOCKING ON NONPROSCENIUM STAGES

This section is about blocking on the most common nonproscenium stages, which are *arena* (also called theatre-in-the-round, circus, circle or central staging), *thrust* (also known as apron, open or platform),

and *L-shaped*. With arena, the audience sits on four sides of the acting area: with thrust, on three sides and with L-shaped on two (see Figures 11-2, 11-3, and 11-4).

Advantages and Disadvantages

The main advantage to these three over a proscenium theatre is that performers and audience are closer together, and the spectators, therefore, may feel more involved in the performance. Another advantage is that shows can be produced more cheaply because there is less need for elaborate scenery.

The disadvantages, as far as the audience is concerned, are that other spectators are more visible, which can distract an audience from concentrating on the performance, and these three stages cannot provide the spectacular scenic and technical marvels that a proscenium production can offer.

Actors who are accustomed to working on proscenium stages may find that playing on these alternative stages, where spectators may be only a foot away, requires greater concentration, subtler acting and more realistic costumes and makeup. On a proscenium stage, period dresses can have zippers and young people can play elderly parts; but in arena, thrust and L-shaped staging the spectators will probably spot anachronistic zippers and age lines painted on young faces.

Blocking

With all kinds of stages, the stage picture must reflect the meaning, excitement, emotions and mood of the moment. Fortunately, all of the strategies for gaining emphasis on a proscenium stage apply to nonproscenium stages with the exception of body positions and stage areas. The following are usable: *height, brightly colored and light-colored costumes, lighting, focus, movement, speaking, isolation* and *contrast.* And the need for balance and variety is as great on nonproscenium stages as on proscenium.

Since almost all modern musicals were first done on a proscenium stage, most of a script's stage directions cannot be used when blocking for nonproscenium stages. The stage director will, therefore, have to spend time adapting the musical to arena, thrust or L-shaped staging. When blocking on all three, you may direct performers in terms of the location of furniture, properties or other actors, or you may give the stage areas numbers or names. For example, you can imagine that the stage is a clock and divide it into twelve areas with the middle of the stage being a thirteenth; or you can think of the stage as a compass with areas designated as North, South, East and West.

In blocking, stage directors often try to keep the actors moving, so that they do not have their backs to one segment of the audience for too long. This is valid so long as there is motivation for the movement. While blocking, the stage director should move around to all parts of the audience to see what a scene looks like from different points of view.

Because there is usually no fly loft or curtains, lighting is extremely important because scenes begin and end through light changes. Scene changes are done in the dark unless the theatre has an elevator stage to raise or lower a set to another level for changing.

In some theatres, placement of the orchestra may be a problem. Depending on the number of musicians, they may be able to play in an aisle, a balcony, at the side of the stage, or wherever they do not interfere with the spectators' view.

Arena Stages

In arena staging, there is a playing area in the middle of a space with the audience seated around the performers. Many dinner theatres use arena staging, seating their customers at tables that surround the playing space, which may be a circle, an oval, a rectangle, or an irregular-shaped area. Usually there are four aisles leading to the playing area that can be used for performing and moving properties and scenic pieces in and out.

For audiences to see the actors, furniture, set pieces and properties must be low and movable. Tall, bulky furniture is seldom used unless it can be placed in an aisle; however, look-through scenery, such as skeleton frames of windows or walls, may be effective. A window, however, can be suggested by using only a window seat.

In blocking two performers, if one can have his back to an aisle, this will increase that actor's visibility. If the stage director will allow at least four feet between two actors, they will be more visible than if they are close together. A position called *twisting the pairs* is often used. Rather than facing each other directly, the actors make one-quarter turns in opposite directions. This provides the audience with better visibility of both performers. When one character has a long speech, the stage director must find motivation to have this person turn or move so that all parts of the audience may have a view of the actor's face.

In addition to the stage proper, the aisles may be used as acting areas; and when a performer is making an entrance through an aisle, it may help the tempo of the scene if this person starts speaking while in the aisle. Exit lines may also be given in an aisle.

In blocking three or more actors, triangular arrangements work well. With more people, such as a chorus, you can put principals on a higher level in the center with the least important characters seated around the edge of the stage or standing in the aisles.

In large arenas, performers may have difficulty projecting so that all spectators—especially those seated behind them—can hear. Being unable to hear or see the face of a performer can confuse some viewers. If this occurs, the use of microphones should be considered.

Thrust Stages

With thrust staging, the audience sits around three sides of the playing area. In back of the fourth side there may be a stagehouse or wall through which performers, scenery and props may enter and leave the stage. Some theatres combine a proscenium stage with a thrust, but usually there is no proscenium arch or a front curtain. Settings are often architectural unit sets that remain constant through a show except for changing set pieces, drapes or properties to indicate different locales. In some theatres, tunnels that run from offstage to the thrust have been built underneath the house seats in order to get performers on and off stage quickly.

Like arena staging, furniture and properties on the thrust must be low, but there is a difference: In the back there can be tall scenery, windows, doors, or a stairway to an upstairs room. Generally, though, the scenery tends to be rather simple.

L-Shaped Stages

With L-shaped staging, the audience sits on two sides of a rectangular playing area. On the other two sides can be scenery, doors, windows, drapes, a stairway and other scenic elements, but there is no proscenium arch or front curtain. The stage itself can accommodate low furniture and properties.

The L-shaped stage offers the stage director greater use of scenery than arena, yet gives the close contact between audience and performers that is desirable for some musicals, especially small-cast, easily staged ones, such as *The Fantasticks* or *You're a Good Man, Charlie Brown*.

FIGURE 11-2 **ARENA STAGE**
(DESIGNERS: MIKE MURPHY, KEVIN BANNON, MARSHALL UNIVERSITY)

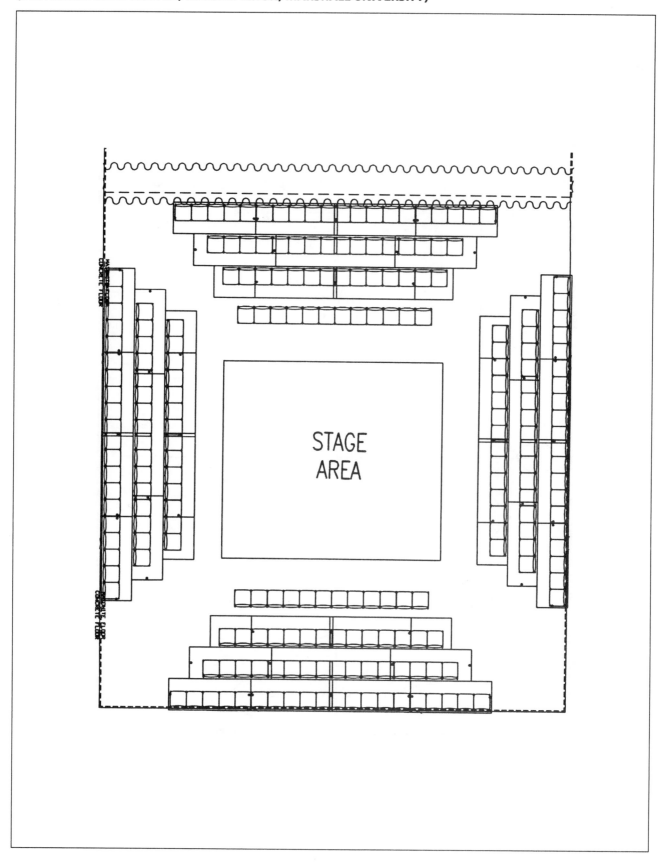

FIGURE 11-3 **THRUST STAGE WITH TABLES SET FOR DINNER THEATER**
(DESIGNERS: MIKE MURPHY, KEVIN BANNON, MARSHALL UNIVERSITY)

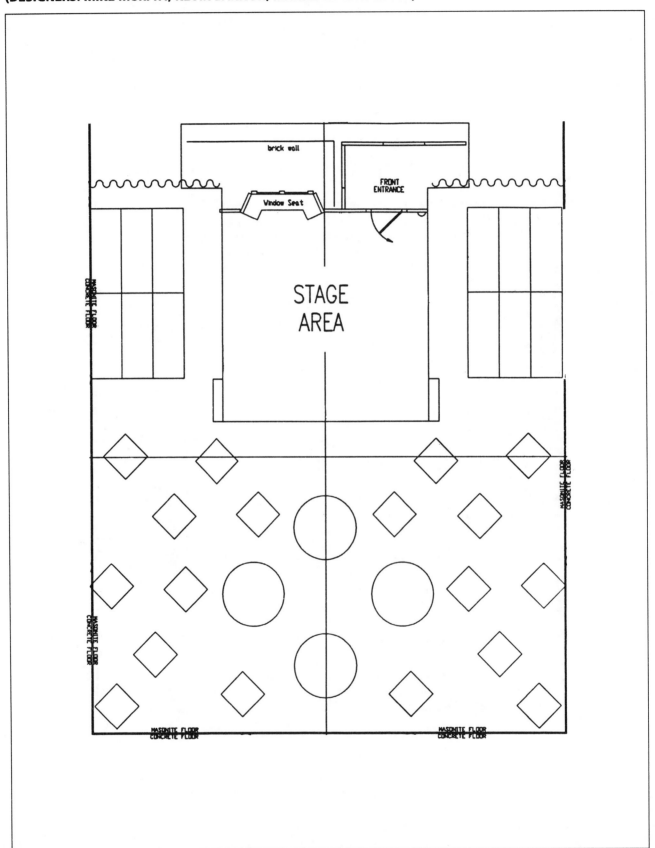

FIGURE 11-4 **L-SHAPED STAGE**
(DESIGNERS: MIKE MURPHY, KEVIN BANNON, MARSHALL UNIVERSITY)

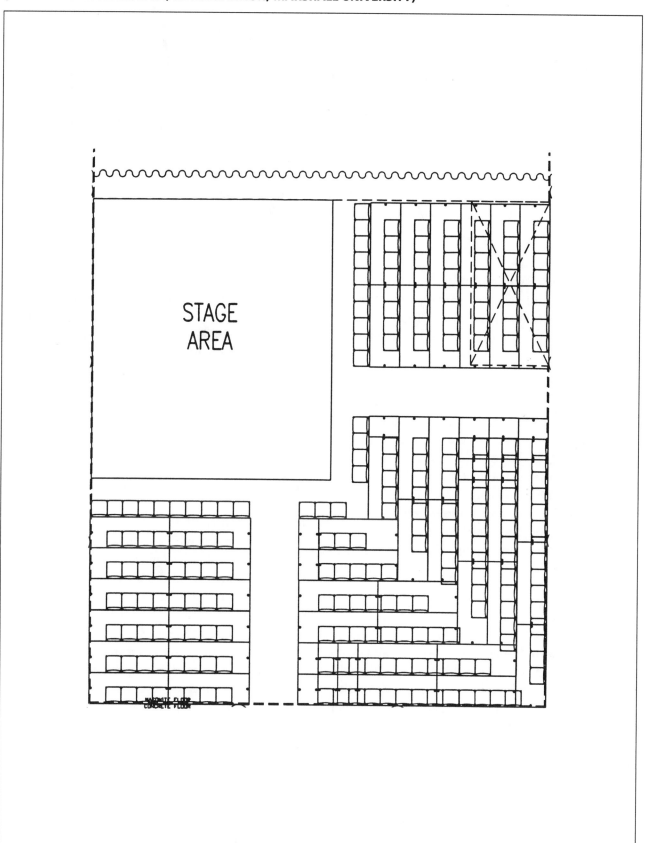

CHAPTER TWELVE

Developing, Polishing, Final Rehearsals and Performances

The stage director will probably continue to adjust the blocking until dress rehearsals, but attention must also be paid to other matters. These concerns and performances are discussed in this chapter.

DEVELOPING REHEARSALS

From the first to the last rehearsal, the stage director should talk to the cast about characterizations, vocal characterizations, line interpretations, projection, articulation, stage business and listening. While blocking the show, the stage director should be aware of how each actor is developing a characterization and help the performer to proceed in the right direction; but after the musical is blocked, the stage director must give priority to developing well-rounded characters and integrating the singing, dancing and acting.

Characterizations

Everyone who walks onstage, including extras with no lines to say or sing, should have a characterization. In working with performers who have studied acting, the stage director may find that they prefer to develop a characterization in a particular way, and this preference will influence how you work with them. An actor can prepare emotionally, technically, or use a combination of the two, and the stage director should adapt to the actor's system. Talk to each actor in terms that he or she understands and finds helpful.

Emotional Actors

Some performers, who may be called *emotional*, *intuitive* or *Method* (this is the American version of the Stanislavski System) actors, prefer to work from the inside to the outside. After a thorough analysis of the play and role, they concentrate on thinking the thoughts and feeling the emotions of the character. While their emphasis may be on the inner experience, they are also concerned with valid external expressions. Popularized by Konstantin Stanislavski, whose books on acting are listed in the bibliography, the Stanislavski System is widely used.

Technical Actors

Other performers, who are categorized as technical actors, prefer to work from the outside to the inside. They think carefully about the outer manifestations of the thoughts and emotions rather than trying to experience them internally. After a careful analysis of the play and role, they adopt an appropriate posture, movements, gestures, facial expressions, voice and dialect or accent for the part, and they rely on their technical skills to present a well-rounded character. While they may not consciously work on the inner feelings, these may occur when the external details are done well.

Internal-External Actors

A third group of actors prefers to combine these two approaches and focus both on the internal and the external. In working with beginning actors, you should encourage them to explore all three methods and then make up their minds as to how they want to develop characterizations.

Analyzing a Role

With beginning actors, you must also teach them how to analyze a role by determining the following:

- *Objectives*: What is your character's major goal for the entire musical? What does your character want in each scene that he or she is in?
- *Motivations*: What motivates your character to take action?
- *Actions*: What does your character do to achieve his or her objectives?
- *Obstacles*: What obstacles keep your character from achieving the objectives?
- *Attitudes*: What attitudes does your character exhibit toward others in the musical?
- *Thoughts*: What are you thinking in each scene?
- *Feelings*: What are you feeling in each scene?

In chapter three we noted that the stage director should analyze each character by examining the following. The same pertains to actors who can get ideas for their parts by determining:

- What the stage directions reveal about your character. (Be sure to look at the character's first entrance as well as throughout the script.)
- What your character says about himself or herself in the script.
- What other characters say about your character (if they are speaking the truth).
- What your character has done prior to the opening of the musical and what she or he does during the musical.
- How the character changes throughout the musical.

Observations

The following exercises may give actors ideas they can incorporate in their characterizations:

- Ask them to observe people who are similar in age, occupation, temperament or some significant way to their characters. If, for example, an actor is playing a character who is forty years older than he is, he may get ideas for posture, movements, stage business and voice by observing someone of that age.
- Have them explore their own memories for experiences they have had that are close to their characters'. If they can remember how they reacted to a similar incident, this may help them obtain a realistic reaction onstage.

Research

Many times, though, there are no people available to observe and the actors have no past experiences that will help them; then they should try research. Perhaps they can read the source of the musical. Certainly anyone cast in *Mame* will get help from reading the preceding play, *Auntie Mame*, and the novel by Patrick Dennis that inspired both. If they are playing historical people, such as John Adams, Thomas Jefferson and Benjamin Franklin in *1776*, they may profit from reading a biography and looking at pictures of the person. Also they may get ideas from seeing a film or videotape of the musical or listening to a CD or audio tape of the music.

Imagination

If all else fails, there are still the actors' imaginations. Stanislavski wrote about the "magic if." He said that an actor should ask, "What would I do IF I were this person in this situation?" Tell your actors to let their imaginations go to see what they can create. If you are directing *My Fair Lady*, you might have the actress playing Eliza Doolittle ask herself, "If I were a poor young cockney girl in 1912 in London, what would I do to sell flowers to wealthy operagoers?" Let her imagine the situation and then improvise a monologue.

It may also stimulate the actors' imaginations if you give them a chance to ask questions about the plot, subtext, characters' attitudes, motivations, symbolism or any other problem that is bothering them.

Build Actors' Confidence

Beginning actors are sometimes consumed by fears, insecurities and doubts. The stage director should encourage them and build their confidence in being able to perform. Praise them on what they do well and *never* ridicule the bad. Instead, offer ideas on how to improve what is wrong. Do not allow anyone to say, "I can't do it." Tell them they *can* do it if they will try. It may be, of course, that they cannot accomplish what you want because they are trying too hard. Then, urge them to relax. Stanislavski believed that if there was no relaxation, there could be no creativity.

Give Criticism Gently

No one likes to receive criticism, but you can soften it somewhat if you criticize the character, not the actor. Say: "King Arthur crept onstage when he should have entered boldly and taken the stage." The next time through the scene, comment on the entrance again. Praise the actor if he did it right or tell him again how to improve it.

Actors like to receive positive comments, so be generous in telling them what they do well.

Exercises for Trouble Spots

If actors are having difficulty with certain scenes, you may want to try the following exercises:

• Have the actors improvise what the characters were doing for approximately five minutes before the hard scene begins.

• Ask the actors to speak out loud what the character is thinking and feeling before saying each line of the dialogue of the difficult scene. Stanislavski called this "vocalizing the inner monologue," and it is a good way for the director to determine if the actors really understand what the character is thinking and feeling at that time.

• Have two actors who share a troublesome scene reverse roles. This may help the performers understand the scene better by looking at the situation from the other character's point of view.

• Ask them to play opposite values. If a performer is supposed to be excited in a scene, ask him to play it calmly. If she is supposed to be sad, ask her to play it happily. In life we vacillate emotionally, and this exercise may help actors realize that they have options and that, perhaps, they should display more than one emotion in a scene.

As mentioned earlier, rehearsals are the times for experimentation. Be daring and bold! Try unconventional, unusual, even bizarre renditions. Something usable may come out of these experiments.

If an actor needs help with a dialect or accent, consult the dialect/accent books with accompanying tapes listed in the bibliography. Or, if it is a common dialect or accent, there may be people in your community who can aid the performer. In some cities, too, there are dialect coaches. The theatre department of almost any college or university should be able to put you in touch with someone who can help you with this problem.

Vocal Characterizations

After an actor has ideas about a characterization, ask how this can be expressed through the voice and speech of the character. Point out that the voice can reflect the character's age, home environment, intellect, education and emotional state. Discuss with the actor how the character's voice may be different from the actor's usual way of speaking.

• Should the *quality* of the character's voice be different from the actor's voice? Is it more harsh, gentle, throaty, strident, thin, full, nasal or denasal?

• How about the *pitch* of the character's voice? Is it usually higher or lower than the actor's voice? Does the character use a monotone? Does the character use excessive pitch variations?

• Does the character speak at a faster or slower *rate* than the actor normally uses?

• Does the character speak *louder or softer* than the actor?

• What about the character's *articulation*? Is the character overly precise in speaking? Inarticulate? Does the character have a dialect or accent that is different from the actor's?

Line Interpretations

If an actor does not understand a line, the stage director must discuss the desired interpretation of the words. Perhaps the performer does not know what the character's objective, motivation and action are for the scene; what the character's attitude is toward others in the scene; and what the character is thinking and feeling. It is possible that the character is saying one thing but thinking something else; therefore, the actor must examine the subtext of the scene. If the actor understands these factors, she should be able to speak the line in an acceptable way. Only as a last resort should you say the line and ask the actor to mimic you.

Memorization

Check also to see that the actors have memorized their lines accurately. Do no permit them to paraphrase the lines. They must say the words exactly as written by the authors.

If an actor is having difficulty memorizing lines, demonstrate several ways to learn them:

• Read all of the roles in a scene. Think about what the characters are thinking and feeling. Pay particular attention to what your character is thinking before each line. Now, as you read your cue, place your hand over your first speech and try to say your lines. Look to see if you got it right. If you didn't, repeat this procedure until you do. Then move on to your next speech.

• Record all of the lines in a scene and listen to the playback. Speak your lines with the recording.

• Ask someone to read the other parts and prompt you when necessary.

• Relate your lines to the blocking and learn both at the same time.

Variety

The stage director must be sure that the actors have enough variety in their delivery to capture and hold the audience's attention. They can do this by varying the pitch, rate, loudness and quality of their voices to communicate their interpretation of the lines. If a performer does not have appropriate variety for the role, try taping the voice and playing it back so that the person can hear the faults.

Projection and Articulation

All performers in your musical must be heard and understood, so check frequently on projection and articulation. Sit in the back of the theatre and stop anyone whom you cannot hear or understand. Tell the speaker to sharpen his articulation and to imagine that he is aiming his voice to those seated in the back row of the theatre. Have her repeat the line until it is satisfactory, because there is nothing more irritating to an audience than not being able to understand a performer.

After the orchestra joins the cast, you must check to determine if everyone can be heard during musical underscoring and songs. If not, the actors and singers must use better articulation and/or more energetic projection, the orchestra must play softer, or the stage director must order microphones for the performers.

Stage Business

Stage business is the name for the small, detailed activities that actors do to help get across to an audience their characterizations. Typical stage business includes small motions like drinking, eating, smoking, sewing, arranging flowers, filing nails, writing and reading—not major movements as in blocking. Some business may be suggested by the author, but it is often devised by the stage director or the actor to give the latter something to do onstage that will make the scene appear more believable. The stage director must keep in mind, though, that any movement can be attention-getting, and if using a prop like a fan or handkerchief is attracting too much attention to a person who should not have it, then the activity must be curtailed.

Listening to Other Characters

Look out for performers who are merely waiting onstage to hear their cue line so that they can say or sing their lines. Actors should be listening to the others onstage, thinking about what they hear, and responding as though they just had the idea that causes them to speak, sing or do what the script stipulates.

Listening to a song onstage demands special attention. The listener must think of the feelings expressed in the lyrics and the singer's interpretation. The listener may react, if it is in a way that will not take the audience's attention away from the person who should receive it; but the stage director should be on guard against those egotistical performers who try to steal attention away from a soloist.

Integration of Singing, Dancing and Acting

After dialogue and songs have been blocked by the stage director (see chapter eleven) and dances have been choreographed by the choreographer (see chapter ten), the stage director should supervise combining them. The purpose is to unify the production. From this point on, the entire cast, stage and musical directors and choreographers should be present at all integrated rehearsals.

The first rehearsal of this type is likely to be rough as performers struggle to remember dialogue, songs and dances for the first act, but the stage director should be patient, helpful and understanding. If a scene is particularly bad, ask that it be repeated. Analyze where the problems lie and turn to your fellow directors for help. Perhaps a song or a dance or an acting scene needs more work; then additional separate rehearsals will have to be scheduled until the unit is running smoothly. The integrated rehearsals should continue, however, as planned with the extra rehearsals scheduled at other times.

Now performers must be urged to memorize their lines, blocking, songs and dances as quickly as possible. Set a date and put it on the rehearsal schedule as to when everything must be memorized. Write on the schedule: "No books onstage from here on." (With a rehearsal period of seven weeks, this should be about three weeks before opening. See the suggested rehearsal schedule in chapter eight.)

As soon as actors have memorized their lines, hand props should be introduced; if the ones to be used in performances are not yet available, substitute props should be devised. It is important that the actor have a cane or sword or eyeglasses to rehearse with as soon as the script is out of the person's hands. And if the performer wears glasses but the character does not, he or she should now begin to rehearse without them. Also, encourage your actors to wear shoes and clothes to rehearsal that are similar to those that will be worn in performances; for example, women in *Hello, Dolly!*, which is set in the 1890s, should rehearse in long skirts and low-heeled shoes.

At this time, the stage director or the stage manager should check on the progress of the technical elements. As soon as props and scenic pieces become available, they should be used in rehearsals.

POLISHING REHEARSALS

In run-throughs, the show is not stopped unless absolutely necessary. The stage and musical directors, choreographer, conductor and stage manager take notes that are given to the cast at the end of an act or the show. Now, the directors are involved with putting the finishing touches on the show, tightening it, unifying it, and checking on tempos, climaxes, concentration, spontaneity, energy and ensemble playing. Above all, the stage director must be certain that the audience will understand the story, theme and major ideas.

Normally, after a run-through the cast and directors assemble and written notes are handed to the performers or the notes are given orally. The notes concern everything that the directors want changed before the next rehearsal and may range in importance from correcting one kick in a dance to criticizing an actor's entire performance. Be careful, though, about chastising a performer in front of the entire cast. If you must speak sharply to someone, do it in a private conversation.

Tempos

The tempos of songs, dances and scenes are a concern of the stage and musical directors, choreographer and conductor. The conductor will control musical tempos during performances, but until then the directors have input into this matter: the musical director for songs; the choreographer for dances; and the stage director for dialogue, each scene, scene changes, and the musical as a whole.

Musical underscoring of dialogue may present problems. This can occur anywhere in the script, but it is often found at the beginning, in the middle, or at the end of songs. These places involve careful timing so that the spoken words and movements fit with the music exactly. If the conductor is late starting the accompaniment or it is too slow, the performers may have an awkward pause as they finish the dialogue and have to wait for their musical cue to sing. If the conductor starts the music too early or it is played too fast, the actors will have to speak very quickly to get through the dialogue by the time they must sing. Rehearse until the best word cue is determined for starting the accompaniment and the best rate of playing the music and speaking is decided upon. To repeat: *Musical underscoring of dialogue may present problems that must be resolved through careful rehearsals with performers, stage director and conductor.*

The stage director is concerned with a proper pace and flow throughout the musical. Some scenes will have an overall rate of fast, some will be medium, and a few slow, but in all scenes there will be many variations of speed. If the stage director believes that the dialogue of a scene is going too slowly, he or she should demand that cues be picked up promptly or overlapped (this means that an actor starts talking before the previous actor has stopped) and that pauses be shortened or eliminated. Check especially to see if pauses can be eliminated when characters are entering or exiting. Also, there should be no waiting for scene or costume changes. As soon as the applause is dying out on one scene, the next scene should start. If technical changes are holding up the show, the changes must be rehearsed until they can be done quickly.

To keep the musical going forward at a good tempo, the stage director should not permit encores unless they are in the score. If they are there, do not let them be used unless the audience demands an encore by tremendous applause. The stage manager is the one who must decide at each performance whether there is sufficient demand for an encore. If so, the stage manager then quickly notifies the conductor and performers to do it.

Building to Climaxes

Most songs, dances and scenes build to a climactic moment, and the entire musical builds to a major climax, which was defined in chapter three as the point of greatest emotional involvement on the part of the audience. The major climax is usually found shortly before the denouement or ending. (Note the analysis of the plot of *1776* in chapter three.)

The stage director's responsibility is to see that actors build to these exciting moments in the musical. The word *building* implies increasing the intensity, tempo, volume and movement and raising the pitch; however, some climactic moments may be reached by increasing the tension but slowing down the tempo and movement and lowering the volume and pitch. Both ways may, of course, be accompanied by changes in lighting, sound and music.

These climactic moments are the high points of the performance—the ones audiences remember—so be sure they will enthrall your viewers.

Concentration

During run-throughs, the stage director must insist that performers concentrate on staying in character and in the scene. If actors are truly concentrating, they should not be distracted by anything. If a performer is not concentrating, find out what she is thinking and feeling by asking her to vocalize the inner monologue. (See the exercise on vocalizing the inner monologue mentioned earlier in this chapter.) The goal is for performers to listen to other actors and think the thoughts and feel the emotions of the character.

If anything unusual happens, such as someone being late for an entrance, the other actors must adapt to the changed circumstances and ad lib in character until such time as they can return to the script. If the actors understand the situation and their characters' thoughts and emotions at that point, they should be able to do this.

Spontaneity

Even though performers have rehearsed for weeks, they are required to show onstage a spontaneous quality that is often called the *illusion of the first time*. To achieve it, actors must listen to the others, think about what they hear, and respond as though this were the first time this situation had occurred. Watch especially to make sure that actors are not anticipating a cue by reacting before the cue is given. If they are really listening and thinking before responding, this cannot happen.

Energy

Audiences respond well to performers who are dynamic and energetic and who know how to sell their songs and dances. Actors should have a great desire to get onstage and communicate this musical to an audience, but sometimes they are tired or ill or unhappy and not in the right frame of mind to perform well. Then, it is up to the stage director to stimulate them to give a good performance. Like the coach of the football team, the director may have to give pep talks before run-throughs and performances to make them forget their problems. Exercises may also be needed to warm up the performers' voices and bodies and to get their energy level up. Use some of the exercises described in chapter eight.

Remind the performers that it takes a lot of energy and stamina to work in a musical and that they must get enough rest and take care of their health because they will not perform well if they are sick or exhausted.

Ensemble Playing

By the time of the run-throughs the performers should be working well together for the good of the show. They should have learned that they can trust and depend on each other, which can only happen if there is good communication among performers both onstage and offstage. Group creativity or ensemble playing should be the goal as all work harmoniously to achieve a great performance.

FINAL REHEARSALS

Final rehearsals are concerned with integrating the orchestra and the technical elements into the production and taking care of all last-minute problems.

Dress Parade

Several days before dress rehearsals, the dress parade may take place as performers try on their costumes for the costume designer, stage director, choreographer (for dance costumes) and others to approve. Of course, any needed adjustments must be made before dress rehearsals begin. This may be an appropriate time too for the stage director and/or costume designer to talk with the performers about stage makeup and hairstyles so that they understand how to achieve the desired appearance.

First Orchestra-Cast Rehearsal

Around this time, the first rehearsal of cast and orchestra is often held. As described in chapter eight, this is usually a special rehearsal at which all of the music is rehearsed, but scenes of dialogue are not unless there is underscoring to the scene. This rehearsal is desirable because until now performers have worked only with piano, and they will find that the music sounds different when played by an orchestra. Often singers will have difficulty finding

Lights for the musicians may be a problem. You must provide adequate lighting so that the musicians can read the notation comfortably, but this light must not detract from the stage picture or produce a glare in the audience. The best solution is directional music lights, which sit atop lowered music stands.

their first note in a number, and it may take several repetitions before they get it right.

Sometimes this rehearsal is the first one that the orchestra has in the theatre's pit. If this is the case, the conductor must allow sufficient time before rehearsal to supervise the placement of music stands, chairs and lights so that the musicians can see the conductor.

Adding the Technical Elements

Scenery, curtains, properties, lighting and sound may be added gradually to the musical over several rehearsals or all at once. In any event, there is usually one rehearsal for just technical cues. The orchestra is not called to this rehearsal, and performers may or may not be called. If they are, they and the rehearsal pianist usually do not perform all of the musical but just the parts that have cues for technical changes. If performers are not called, the stage manager and rehearsal pianist may give these cues so that the designers and technical crews can perfect scene, curtain, property, lighting and sound changes plus special effects.

Curtains may close or drop at different speeds: slow, medium or fast. The stage director should decide what speed will be used for each curtain and so inform the stage manager.

Instructions to the Cast

Before dress rehearsals, the stage director should give the performers instructions to help them through final rehearsals and performances. These may be given orally or in writing. You can select from the following list those instructions that apply to your situation:

• Keep the stage director's and stage manager's telephone numbers handy so you can notify one of them in case of accident or illness. Be sure the stage manager has your phone number and address.

• Warm up vocally and physically before dress rehearsals and performances. (If there will be group warm-ups for dancers, singers and actors, tell them when and where they will occur.)

• Don't eat a big meal before dress rehearsals or performances, and be careful of what you eat during a performance. Avoid carbonated beverages that may make you belch onstage and food, such as nuts, that may stick in your throat. Drink only water.

• Don't take any alcohol or drugs before or during a rehearsal or performance.

• Notify the stage manager if you have a medical condition that may require emergency attention.

• Since performers and crews work closely together, be aware of your breath and body odors and be sure that they are not offensive. Don't wear strong perfumes, colognes or scented hairsprays, as some people are allergic to these odors.

• Sign in (at the place specified) as soon as you arrive at the theatre. This should be at least one hour before curtain. Do not leave the theatre without notifying the stage manager.

• Obey the theatre's smoking regulations. (Tell them exactly what they are.)

• Don't leave valuables (watches, money, jewelry, etc.) in unlocked dressing rooms. Give them to the stage manager to keep during a rehearsal or performance.

• Remember that the stage manager is in charge backstage, and you must cooperate fully with him or her.

• You are responsible for providing your own makeup and doing your makeup and hairstyle according to the stage director's instructions. Don't change them without getting the stage director's or stage manager's approval. (If you have beginners, it may be wise to appoint a couple of experienced people to supervise makeup, hairstyles and wigs.)

• Be sure your hands are clean before handling costumes and accessories. Take care of them and hang costumes up after taking them off. If any become soiled or damaged, notify the wardrobe supervisor. Never go outside the theatre in costume.

• Check on your props *before* you need them onstage and be sure you know where to find them. Handle all props carefully and return them to the prop table when you are finished with them. Offstage, don't play with the props or eat prop food. If you have a problem with a property, see the property master.

• Stay away from all areas where the audience might be before the show or at intermission.

• Never peek through the curtain, and, when waiting for an entrance in the wings, be certain that the audience cannot see you.

• Stay aware of the progress of the show and never miss an entrance.

• Be quiet in the wings and other areas near the stage while the show is on.

• During scene changes, be consistent in your usual way of exiting or entering the stage. The technical crews have planned to move scenery and properties around your movements, so don't change them. And look out for flying drops and moving set pieces.

• If anything unusual happens onstage, such as a telephone not ringing at the right time, stay in character. Adapt to the different circumstances, which may require ad libbing until you can return to the script.

• If a prop or part of a costume accidentally falls to the floor, pick it up if you are close by because an audience will watch it until someone removes it.

• Hold for laughs. If you have the line that follows a big laugh, wait until the laugh is almost out and you believe that you can be heard; then say the line loudly and clearly.

• If you forget your lines, ad lib until you can get back to the correct lyrics or dialogue. Don't wait to be prompted.

• At curtain call, there will be no presentation of flowers or curtain speeches. After the last curtain call, clear the stage quickly. (Inform them where they may meet their friends backstage after the show.)

• When finished with rented scripts and vocal parts, return *clean* books to the stage manager.

• (If performers are expected to assist with striking the set, tell them when to report.)

FIGURE 12-1 *HELLO, DOLLY!* CHORUS NUMBERS

| ACT 1 | | | | |
Scene	Place	People	Costumes	Songs/Dances
1	N.Y. Street	Women Men	Dress #1, hat, gloves Town suit, hat	"Opening"
2	Feed Store	Men	Trousers, vest, shirt (no coat, hat)	"It Takes a Woman"
	Railroad Station	Women Men	Dress #2, hat, gloves, parasol Town suit, hat, vest, gloves, spats	"Put on Your Sunday Clothes"
3	N.Y. Street	Women Men	Same dress (no hat) Suit (no hat, gloves, spats)	"Dancing"
		Women Men	Same Suit, hat, gloves, spats	"Before the Parade Passes By"

Dress Rehearsals

The last few rehearsals are dress rehearsals at which costumes, makeup, hairstyles and wigs are worn and the show is performed with full accompaniment and all technical elements. These rehearsals should be as much like performances as possible. Now the stage director must be certain that the appearance of each character is correct. During the first dress rehearsal you will find out where costume or makeup changes are taking too long. You may have to ask the stage manager to arrange for dressers and quick-change places close to the stage so that performers can make entrances on time in the right costume and makeup.

Dress rehearsals are the directors' and designers' last opportunity to work for the desired interpretation of the work. They should sit in the house and take notes on everything they do not like about the production and then try to get it corrected before the next rehearsal or performance. The conductor and the stage manager will also have notes for performers and technical crews.

If chorus members have not been adequately rehearsed and seem to be in doubt as to the order of their numbers and what costume to wear when, have the stage manager post a reminder. Write in large letters on big posterboard the scene number, the place, the people involved, the costumes to be worn and the songs and dances in that scene. See figure 12-1 for an example for the first act of *Hello, Dolly!*

The poster should be positioned so performers can see it when leaving the stage to refresh their memories as to what costume and number are next.

Curtain Call and Exit Music

The end of the first dress rehearsal is a good time to block and rehearse the curtain call. For some, but not all, musicals there is music in the score for curtain calls and the exit of the audience. If there is none, the conductor may repeat several numbers from the show or the stage director may decide to use no music.

Usually for curtain calls the performers wear their last costume or their most striking costume. The custom is to bring the cast on in order from the least important to the most important to take a bow. Be sure they smile and move quickly. If they don't, the applause may die out before the leads arrive. After the stars bow, the entire company may join hands for another bow. Then the performers may point with one hand to the conductor and orchestra

A suitable bow for everyone can be made by putting your heels together with toes slightly turned out and bending from the waist. Hands may stay at the sides or be brought together above the knees. On rising to an erect posture, return your hands to the sides. If women are wearing long skirts, they may prefer to curtsy.

To get everyone to bow or curtsy at the same time for a company bow, appoint someone who is downstage center as the leader, and when this person bows, everyone else does too.

who if they are not playing, may bow from their location. After this, the lights may black out or the curtain may descend. All onstage should hold their positions because, if there is great applause from the audience, the stage manager may call for another company bow. The stage manager is the one who must determine whether the demand is sufficient for additional bows. At the end of curtain calls, houselights are brought up as the orchestra plays the exit music.

The curtain call should be rehearsed until it is executed quickly and proficiently; then it should be used at dress rehearsals and performances.

At performances, some may wish to give flowers onstage at curtain calls to the leading actors, directors and others. The producer and other leaders should decide whether this will be permitted. Most school/community organizations do not allow the presentation onstage of flowers, gifts or curtain speeches. If you adopt this policy, performers and the house manager should be informed of it. If flowers or gifts are sent to the theatre, they may be placed in the recipient's dressing room.

Photographs

The organization's production photographs are usually taken during or after a dress rehearsal. Some photographers prefer to take them while the rehearsal is in progress, but others like to have a pic-

ture call at which preselected poses are shot. If this is after a dress rehearsal, the best way to shoot the pictures is from the curtain call back to the beginning of the musical, so that performers have one less costume change.

Some directors like to invite a small number of friends of the company to the final dress rehearsal so that the cast can become accustomed to the reactions of an audience. Since picture-taking should never be permitted during performances, you may want to allow photographs to be taken by these friends at this rehearsal.

PERFORMANCES

The first to arrive for performances may be the stage manager, who is often charged with opening and closing the theatre. Others, such as the technical director and assistant stage managers, may also be assigned to this duty to see that doors are unlocked, lights are turned on, and check-in lists are in place for technicians and cast.

Usually at ninety minutes to curtain time, the technicians arrive to make sure that all of the technical elements are ready before the house is opened to the audience. Upon entering the theatre, they check in with the stage manager, who is in charge backstage during performances. Then the stage floor may be mopped; scenery, curtains, and props examined; lighting and sound equipment checked; and the stage set for the first scene. Meanwhile, in the dressing rooms, the wardrobe supervisor and costume crew are preparing the costumes.

Ticket sellers should be in the box office at least ninety minutes before curtain. The house manager should also get to the theatre about this time to make sure that the house is clean, the heating or cooling system is operating, enough programs are on hand, and everything is ready to receive the audience.

Performers should appear before the time specified by the stage director in instructions to the cast. This is usually one hour before curtain, but perform-

> The publicized starting time for a performance is usually referred to as the *curtain time*. Today, for some productions, a front curtain may not be used, but the term is still customary.

ers who have difficult makeups to put on may be asked to come in earlier. On arrival, they should check in with the stage manager. If a performer or technician is not present at the time deadline, the stage manager must telephone to try to find this person. If the absentee cannot be found, the stage manager must plan quickly to cover for this individual during the performance. If this person comes late, the stage manager should reprimand her or him. If the person is absent and has no excuse, he or she should be dismissed from the company.

Some companies like to do warm-ups of about fifteen minutes. The choreographer can work with the dancers while the musical director warms up all singers. If, however, the dancers sing and the singers dance, the choreographer and musical director may have to split the time. These warm-ups may be at one hour to curtain and may be followed by brief announcements and pep talks by directors, producer, conductor or stage manager that total no more than five minutes. Then the performers will have about forty minutes to dress, make up, and get into character before "Places, please."

At forty-five minutes to curtain, ticket-takers, sellers of refreshments and souvenirs, and ushers with small flashlights should be appropriately attired and at their posts. The house manager should then instruct new ushers about the seating plan, location of rest rooms, telephones and water fountains, and procedures for seating the disabled. The house manager should also remind them to hand to each customer a program, smile and be gracious.

The conductor will notify the orchestra of what to wear, when to arrive at the theatre (allowing enough time for them to warm up their instruments and themselves before the overture), and where to leave coats and instrument cases. If possible, tuning instruments should be done backstage. If not possible, the orchestra should enter the pit early enough to tune instruments so that there can be, at least, a few minutes of silence from the pit before the conductor enters.

If all technical elements are ready at thirty minutes to curtain, the stage manager will inform the house manager that the house may be opened. Until that time, the audience should be kept in the lobby.

Before the performance, the stage and musical

directors, choreographer and conductor may be backstage with the performers, encouraging them, checking their costumes, makeup and hair, and answering last-minute questions, but now is *not* the time to make any significant alterations in blocking, lines, songs or dances because the actors are probably too nervous to remember them. If, however, any changes are made, the stage manager must be notified because, for example, a line change may affect a technical cue.

The stage manager keeps track of the time and warns everyone backstage with traditional calls of "Half hour, please," "Fifteen minutes, please," and "Five minutes, please." The proper response to these calls is "Thank you." At about five minutes to curtain, the stage manager should check to see that all orchestra members are in the pit and technical crews are in place. At two minutes to curtain, the stage manager calls backstage "Places, please," and all performers in the first scene go immediately to the stage.

At curtain time, the stage manager must confer with the house manager about whether the musical can begin. If a large number of spectators is waiting to be seated, the house manager may request that curtain be delayed five minutes, but as soon as possible, the stage manager should call for the houselights to fade out. If the conductor is visible as he or she enters the pit, a spotlight may call attention to this entrance. If there is applause, the conductor should acknowledge it by bowing. Then the performance begins.

As soon as the overture starts, the house manager or ushers should close the doors to the house. Latecomers should be kept outside until there is a break in the action onstage (such as at the end of a musical number or scene); then they can be ushered to vacant seats near the door without disturbing the rest of the audience too much.

During performances, the stage manager prompts, gives cues for technical elements, maintains order backstage, and keeps a record of the running time of acts and intermission. If there is no stage-monitoring system in the dressing rooms and greenroom, the stage manager will also have to notify performers before their entrances. The stage manager is very busy before and during performances and, for this reason, may have one or two assistants.

At the end of Act I, when the houselights come up for intermission, the house manager or ushers should open the doors. Ushers should remain at the doors to answer questions, lead latecomers to their correct seats, or direct patrons to the rest rooms, refreshments, telephones and water fountains. Near the end of the intermission, which is usually ten to fifteen minutes long, a warning (such as a bell or flashing lights or an announcement on a public address system) should notify the spectators that the second act is about to start.

Backstage at intermission, the stage manager calls "Five minutes, please" and (a few minutes later) "Places, please" as he or she makes sure that performers, crews, conductor and orchestra are ready to start Act II. The houselights fade out, the conductor enters the pit, and the second act begins, as the house manager or ushers close the doors. At the end of curtain calls, the stage manager brings up the houselights and the house manager or ushers open the doors as the exit music is played.

During performances, the place for the stage and musical directors, choreographer, designers and producer is in the audience, watching to see how the spectators react to the performance. They should also be taking notes on everything they dislike so they can fix the faults before the next performance.

Before leaving the theatre, the performers should hang up their costumes and clean up the makeup and dressing rooms so that everything is ready for the next performance. The crews should put away props and scenery, clean up any messes, and lock up their equipment so that they will not have too much to do before the next performance; and ushers may be asked to pick up used programs and trash on the floor of the house.

After everyone has left the theatre, the stage manager and assistants lock up. (See Figure 12-2 for a "Suggested Time Guide for Performances.")

FIGURE 12-2 **SUGGESTED TIME GUIDE FOR PERFORMANCES**

100 Minutes to Curtain	Stage manager and assistants open the theatre, unlock doors, turn on lights, and prepare check-in lists.
90 Minutes	Technical workers check in and prepare technical elements for performance.
	Ticket sellers open the box office.
	House manager arrives.
60 Minutes	All performers check in and go to a fifteen-minute warm-up.
45 Minutes	Ticket-takers, ushers, sellers of refreshments/souvenirs arrive.
	Announcements and pep talks given to performers.
40 Minutes	Performers go to dressing and makeup rooms.
30 Minutes	If all technical elements are ready for the performance, the house manager opens the house to the audience.
	Orchestra members warm up.
	Backstage the stage manager gives the first call of "Half hour, please."
15 Minutes	Backstage the stage manager calls "Fifteen minutes, please."
5 Minutes	Stage manager checks to be sure orchestra members are in the pit.
	Backstage the stage manager calls "Five minutes, please."
	Technical workers go to their positions.
2 Minutes	Backstage the stage manager calls "Places, please."
	Performers in the first scene go to the stage.
Curtain Time for Act I	House manager and stage manager confer about starting the performance. If customers are waiting to be seated, they may decide to wait five minutes.
	After people are seated, fade out houselights.
	Conductor enters the pit and the performance begins.
	House manager and ushers close the doors to the house.
Intermission	Houselights are up.
	House manager and ushers open the doors to the house.
5 Minutes to Curtain for Act II	Backstage the stage manager calls "Five minutes, please."
2 Minutes to Curtain for Act II	Warning (bell, flashing lights or announcement) is given to the audience that the next act is about to start.
	Backstage the stage manager calls "Places, please."
	Performers needed to start Act II go to the stage.
	Orchestra returns to the pit.
	Technicians go to their positions.
Curtain for Act II	Houselights fade out.
	Conductor enters the pit and the act begins.
	House manager and ushers close the doors to the house.
After Curtain Calls	Houselights are up.
	House manager and ushers open the doors so the audience may leave as exit music is played.
	Performers, crews and ushers clean up.
After Everyone Has Left	Stage manager and assistants lock the theatre.

CHAPTER THIRTEEN

Staging Revues

Since the nineteenth century, the revue has been one of the chief forms of theatrical entertainment in this country. The word *revue* comes from the French word for "review"; and early French, English and American revues did review contemporary events, customs and celebrities, making satirical comments about them. In the United States, the revue has been known by various other names: vaudeville, variety show, burlesque, minstrel show, showboat olio, music hall entertainment, cabaret or nightclub show.

Revue can cover a wide range of theatrical productions from a large, spectacular musical revue, like a *Ziegfeld Follies*, to a small, satirical revue, such as *Beyond the Fringe*. It may offer a variety of different kinds of acts (songs and dances that range from solos to large production numbers, comedy monologues and duologues, blackout sketches, parodies, running gags, instrumental solos and ensembles, and specialty acts like magicians, acrobats and jugglers), or it may consist entirely of one type of act (for example, all singing or all dancing). There may be a large number of people onstage or just a few. There may be a lot of theatrical production (scenery, properties, lighting, sound, costumes and special effects) or there may be practically none. There is, however, one characteristic common to all revues. There is no overall plot or storyline to unite the whole show, although there may be a theme.

This chapter will examine two types of revues produced by amateur groups today, the production teams needed and the directors' and designers' responsibilities.

PRODUCING TWO TYPES OF REVUES

A school/community group that wants to present a revue may decide to select one that was popular professionally or to create its own revue. The following is a description of what is involved with producing these two types.

Producing a Broadway Revue

There are Broadway and off-Broadway revues that can be produced by amateurs like *Jacques Brel Is Alive and Well and Living in Paris*, which consists of songs by Brel; *Tintypes*, a nostalgic look at the songs of 1890 to 1917; *Ain't Misbehavin'*, which features music written or popularized by Fats Waller; *Sugar Babies*, a "memory of burlesque" that recreates some of the great acts of the past; and *A Day in Hollywood/A Night in the Ukraine*, which pokes fun at movies of the 1930s and presents a Russian play as it might have been filmed by the Marx Brothers.

To produce a Broadway revue, the procedure and the production team are the same as for a musical (see chapter two). You can rent (and in some cases you can buy) the scripts, scores, vocal parts and orchestrations and pay royalty to the licensor for the right to present it. Most well-known revues are licensed for amateur production by Music Theatre International, Rodgers and Hammerstein Theatre Library, and Samuel French, Inc., whose addresses and telephone/fax numbers are listed in chapter two.

Producing Your Own Revue

A revue may also be put together by an amateur group who can then tailor it to fit the number and talents of available performers, the tastes of local audiences, and the amount of money in the budget. Some amateurs, who have never seen a professional stage revue, have for years watched television variety revues, such as those starring Bob Hope or Carol Burnett, and sketch-comedy shows like *Saturday Night Live*. They, therefore, have a good idea of what a revue should be like. Also, school/community organizations often like the idea of being able to display the talents of many of their members, unlike a musical that may "star" only a couple of people. In addition, amateur performers may find a revue easier to rehearse than a musical. Rather than having to practice every weekday evening for six or seven weeks for a musical, some people who are just in one or two revue numbers may rehearse for only about two or three hours a week until the final week. This appeals to a lot of amateurs who are going to school or have full-time jobs.

Acquiring a Production Team

To create a revue, the team for its production should be similar to the one suggested in Figure 2-2 of chapter two for an amateur musical with two exceptions. The first difference is that the producer and/or stage director should supervise several writers who decide on the theme for the show, create a format, and write or obtain the music, sketches, monologues and other material that is needed. By getting permission to use copyrighted material and paying all required royalties, old and new music, sketches and monologues written by top professionals may be used. But if you should have local writers, composers and lyricists, the musical revue is the ideal form to allow them to exhibit their work. After all, Richard Rodgers, Lorenz Hart, Oscar Hammerstein II and others started their brilliant careers by writing original college musicals.

The second difference is that there must be a musical arranger and orchestrator, working under the supervision of the musical director, to prepare arrangements, orchestrations and vocal parts.

Deciding on the Theme

One of the first decisions to be made is the theme or point of view for the revue. The units in *Call Me Mister* were concerned with various aspects of postwar adjustment; the numbers of *As Thousands Cheer* were inspired by different sections of a newspaper; *At Home Abroad* used an around-the-world format; the songs of *Working* looked at the life of ordinary workers in the United States; and *Dancin'* displayed the powerful choreography of Bob Fosse. Other themes that could be used are these: particular time periods or years; holidays; the works of certain composers or authors; special locales (New York City, the South, Paris); historical events (the Civil War, the World Wars); months of the year; or any subject that can hold units together (a showboat, circus, magazine or amusement park).

Determining the Units

The range of possible units for a musical revue is extensive. All types of songs should be considered: popular, standard, folk, country, jazz, rock and roll, spiritual, operatic, humorous and others. All kinds of dancing and song-and-dance numbers can be used. Comedy can be in the form of blackout sketches, comedy teams or monologues, and impressions. Consider also using instrumentalists and specialty acts like gymnasts, mimes and trained animals. Each unit should be short: Most should be under five minutes, except in the case of sketches that may run a little longer.

Planning the Scenery

The units are short, but this does not mean that the scenery has to be changed every few minutes since several units may use the same setting or there may be a simultaneous set or architectural set in place for the entire show with just a change of props, drapes or scenic pieces to indicate different locales. The writers, in consultation with the scene designer and stage director, should decide on the types of scenery needed as they plan the units.

Formatting the Show

Getting the numbers into the best order is probably the most important part of putting together a good revue. Here is where an astute stage director is needed. If the director is a person of taste who understands the potential audience, he or she may be of great assistance to the writers in routing the revue.

The format for a large revue that offers a balanced variety of different kinds of acts may be like the following: The overture, which should be lively and cheerful, may be separate or it may lead into the opening unit. This is usually a large production number that is fast, impressive, often funny, and designed to get the show off to a good start by capturing the audience's interest. From there on, contrast and variety are necessary. For that reason, big production numbers are often followed by a solo or small group, a beautiful act by a comedic one, and a nonmusical unit by a musical one. Generally, you do not schedule two dance numbers or two singing choruses together, but you try to get a good mix of songs, dances, comedy and specialty acts.

The staging of the numbers must be considered. If you are using wing-drop-border sets, large choruses needing the full stage may be followed by a soloist or a few people who can work "in one" in front of a downstage drop while the stage behind this drop is readied for the next big number.

To bring down the curtain to great applause at the end of Act I, the last unit should be climactic. After the intermission, brief entr'acte music may lead into the opening of Act II. To provide a major climax, the best number in the show should be placed immediately before the closing unit of Act II. Then a spectacular finale that includes all of the performers may conclude the revue. Before the production format is finalized, however, the producer, stage director, choreographer, musical director and designers should have an opportunity to offer suggestions for possible changes.

Writing the Script

After the format meets with everyone's approval, the writers should prepare a script for the show. At a minimum, they may write monologues or dialogues for introductions to acts or continuity between units. If the writers can provide comic material, they may want to write blackout sketches. Unless you have a serious theme (which most revues do not), the tone of the writing should be light and happy, and, if it is funny, so much the better.

As to the length of the show, two hours or less, including an intermission, should please most audiences. Usually the first act is longer than the second, so a one-hour first act, a fifteen-minute intermission, and a forty-five-minute second act may be the goal.

After the script is ready, it should be approved by the producer and stage director before work on the production is started. Then complete scripts must be prepared for the producer, stage director, musical director/conductor, choreographer and designers and dialogue parts for the actors, comedians and narrators. The writers' work is not finished, though. They should attend rehearsals and make changes as needed.

DIRECTORS

Prerehearsal planning for a revue is the same as for a musical. The stage director must be sure that scripts and music are available for rehearsals and that the choreographer and musical director know which numbers they are responsible for. As with a musical, the stage director is in charge of the acting, staging of songs, scheduling the cast's rehearsals, and unifying the entire production. The choreographer handles all of the dancing and may assist with the movement for songs. The musical director coaches all of the singers and obtains rehearsal pianists and orchestra. The conductor schedules the orchestra's rehearsals and conducts at performances.

DESIGNERS

The stage director must also discuss the revue with the designers to be sure that they understand what is needed for scenery, props, lighting, sound, costumes and special effects and then supervise their work with the help of the stage manager. To assist the designers, the stage director may prepare a production analysis and a list of needed costumes and wigs, such as the ones recommended in chapter three (see Figures 3-3 and 3-4).

Scenery and Properties

Realistic scenery is usually not desired for the amateur musical revue, but theatricality is; therefore, most of the time the sets and properties may be frankly make-believe, artificial and decorative—something that would be found nowhere but in a theatre. But the sets and properties should add color, gaiety, glamour and spectacle to the production, harmonize with the style and color of the costumes, suggest the period and locale of the scene, enhance the mood, and provide sufficient entrances and enough space for the desired staging. When a large number of people are to be onstage, the designer should consider using levels, ramps or steps so that more people can be easily seen.

Lighting and Sound

Lighting and sound will depend on the requirements of the script and acoustics of the theatre. Follow spotlighting is used for many revues in addition to the usual stage lighting. Sound amplification is often needed to assure the audibility of performers.

Costumes

The costumes should be appropriate for the characters, the time period, place and mood of each unit and add to the excitement and spectacle of the show. They should allow the dancers to move freely and attract attention to the principal performers. Colors used must be compatible with the scenery and the lighting.

All three directors should plan their numbers before designers finalize their plans. The directors may discover a need for an entrance in a particular place, a certain type of costume, a special prop, or a desired lighting, sound or special effect that may affect the designing of the technical elements.

AUDITIONS AND REHEARSALS

Auditions for the revue may be either general or specific, open or closed, depending on the wishes of the directors. Generally, the rehearsal schedule for a revue will look much like that for a musical. Usually, separate rehearsals are held at the beginning: The musical director rehearses with the singers; the choreographer with the dancers; and the stage director with actors, comedians and narrators.

In directing blackout sketches, the stage director should work to establish a comic mood quickly. Because the sketch is brief, the audience should learn as soon as the scene begins that laughs are expected and wanted. The pace of the sketch should be fast yet have variety, and it should gather momentum as the climax is reached. Above all, the actors should strive for spontaneity in performing. (See "Directing Comedy" in chapter eleven.)

If you are directing burlesque material, such as found in *Sugar Babies*, remember that comedians usually relied heavily on a percussionist to punctuate every punch line, blow or comedic movement with drums, cymbals, slide whistle, woodblock, whipcrack or taxi horns.

After the singers know the words and music, the stage director or choreographer should block the movement for the songs. In planning the movement, be guided by the music, the meaning of the lyrics, the mood of the scene, the abilities of the performers, the costumes to be worn, the amount of space available, and the scenery, steps, levels and furniture onstage. (See "Staging Songs" in chapter ten and "Blocking Songs" in chapter eleven.)

As soon as singers know the songs and movements, dancers know the dances, and actors know their lines and blocking, integration rehearsals should be held to combine the elements. All three directors should attend these rehearsals in case there is trouble with any portion of a number. After all units have been rehearsed individually until they are running smoothly, run-throughs should be held to put Act I together, then Act II, and eventually the entire show. After one or two technical rehearsals and three or four full-dress rehearsals with orchestra, the show is on.

During the last run-throughs and dress rehearsals, the stage manager should work for speed, vitality and perfection. Numbers may have to be shortened or even cut out of the show; stage waits for the changing of scenery or costumes must be eliminated or covered by additional material; and all units must be played with enthusiasm, energy, and an eagerness to please. At a dress rehearsal, the stage director should also block the curtain call, which may be like the musical's curtain call described in chapter twelve.

CHAPTER FOURTEEN

Staging Operas

In the early days of opera in Europe, the choirmaster, who was often also the composer, directed the singers, and the concertmaster directed the orchestra. In the nineteenth century, some composers took over both jobs in conducting their works. Later, some conductors came to prominence who were not composers but were nevertheless in charge of the orchestra and singers. Stage directors came along a little later. Some of the first were composers, such as Richard Wagner, who was the stage director for the first complete production of his *Der Ring des Nibelungen* in 1876. Known as the régisseur or metteur en scène in Europe, the stage director was in charge of the mise-en-scène, the staging and designing of the production, which included the arrangements and movements of performers and the scenery, properties, lighting, costumes, makeup and special effects. One of the first great important directors of opera was Max Reinhardt, who presented the premiere of *Der Rosenkavalier* in Dresden in 1911.

In professional opera at the present, the power of the stage director seems to be increasing as management turns to stage directors and designers to make productions more visually spectacular and exciting. Famous professional directors like Franco Zeffirelli, Peter Brook, Jonathan Miller, Harold Prince and Peter Sellars are conceiving new ways of bringing life to old favorites, and they are receiving the critical reviews, not the singers. As might be expected, some critics are now complaining that in a *director's opera* too much attention is being paid to the staging, scenery and lighting and not enough to the singing; the director, they charge, is intruding on the spectators' enjoyment of the music by telling them what to think about the opera's events.

In school/community productions of opera, the musical director/conductor and the stage director will probably be joint heads of the artistic aspects of the production, each person with important responsibilities.

Next is a description of the work of today's producer, musical director/conductor, stage director, choreographer and designers. This is followed by information about auditions and rehearsals for amateur operatic productions.

PRODUCER

If there is someone in the producing group who functions as a producer (although the title may be general director, general manager, executive director, artistic director, impresario or something else), this person works much like the producer of musicals and revues, as described in chapter two. He or she may be responsible for these tasks:

- Seeking grants and donations
- Getting the money for initial expenditures
- Acquiring the production team
- Organizing the administrative and financial aspects of the production
- Preparing a budget
- Hiring personnel

- Providing rooms and theatre for auditions, rehearsals, technical preparations and finally, performances
- Supervising the publicity, selling of tickets, preparing the program, and management of the house during performances

The producer may or may not be involved in the artistic aspects of the production, depending on his or her preference, but in all probability, the producer, musical director/conductor and stage director will decide together on the opera to be presented. The producer should then rent or buy scores, choral parts and orchestrations.

DIRECTORS

If there is no producer, the musical director/conductor or the stage director will probably assume the producer's duties with the help of a business manager to oversee the financial aspects.

Because the music is so important in determining the interpretation to be given the work, the stage director should have a knowledge of music. The noted designer Adolphe Appia stated that the music must be expressed in corresponding visual images as the music determines the character and timing not only of performers' movements but also of the scenery, costumes and lighting.

Both the musical and stage directors must study the score and libretto and, probably, the source of the opera, deciding together on the style, plot, characterizations, character relationships, theme, symbolism, moods, staging, movements, scenery, properties, lighting, costumes and special effects. Some operas have explicit stage directions, but others do not. If available, these should be considered carefully and either accepted or rejected. Older operas have traditional ways of being staged, which should also be accepted or rejected. If there is dancing in the opera, a choreographer should be brought into these conferences as well as the designers, so that all may exchange their thoughts. The result of these conferences should be an imaginative concept for the production and a clear idea of the style, mood and colors to be used.

DESIGNERS

The stage director must work closely with the scene designer as they plan the stage environments and the decor. Research should reveal descriptions and pictures of scenery used by previous designers that may stimulate ideas for the settings. They must, however, consider the size and facilities of the stage and the capabilities of their construction crews. They must also keep in mind the open spaces, the entrances and different levels needed for the chorus and dancers. As suggested in chapter three, the stage director may prepare a production guide that describes the scenery, properties, lighting, special effects and their cues (see Figure 3-3).

The stage director should also provide the costume designer with a costume list indicating preferences for types of clothes and colors (see Figure 3-4). With the lighting designer, the stage director should discuss the relationship of the lighting to the music because the changes of light must be coordinated with the changes in the music.

The scene designer should prepare ground plans and models or renderings; the costume designer, sketches; and the lighting designer, a light plot and an instrument schedule. All are submitted to the stage director for approval. When this has been obtained, the crews can go to work so that all technical elements will be ready for technical rehearsals.

AUDITIONS AND REHEARSALS

Opera auditions and rehearsals may be somewhat different from those for musicals and revues, but there are many similarities. Let's see what they are.

Auditions

The musical and stage directors should organize auditions and see that they are publicized. Open or closed auditions may be held in which the candidates sing an aria of their choice or a selection from the opera to be presented. To test for acting ability, they may be asked to read sections of the libretto, but the most important qualification in selecting principals should be their singing ability. If time permits, the directors may wish to talk with each one about his stage experiences and concept of the opera and different roles. If voices must blend in duets and groups, the candidates for these roles may be asked to sing portions of these passages together.

The dancing audition should be handled by the choreographer, who will cast all dancers. The principals and all other singers should be cast by the musical and stage directors and the producer, if he or she wishes to be consulted.

Rehearsal Schedule

Because of the complexities of the score, the total number of rehearsals needed will probably be more than for a musical or revue. The total amount will depend on the difficulty of the opera and the experience and dedication of the cast, orchestra, directors, designers and crews. The directors will have to make an educated guess as to the number of rehearsals needed based on their past experiences and knowledge of the people. Although the total number may be more than the rehearsal schedule for a musical, the types of rehearsals are similar:

- Listening to the opera and discussing it
- Separate rehearsals for soloists, chorus and orchestra with musical director/conductor and dancers with choreographer
- Blocking rehearsals with stage director (after music is learned)
- Developing: work on characterizations and integration of singing, dancing, acting
- Polishing: have run-throughs with piano accompaniment
- Technical: addition of scenery, properties, lighting, curtains
- Orchestra, cast and technical rehearsals
- Dress rehearsals: addition of costumes and makeup

First Rehearsals

At the first meeting, the cast and directors may listen to a pianist play the score or a recording, or they may watch a film or videotape of the complete opera to give everyone an idea of what the work is like. Then, the directors should explain their concept for the opera and the theme and meaning of the plot. They must be sure that the performers understand the style, time period, locale, the customs and clothes associated with that era and place, the historical facts behind the creation of this opera and the writers' purpose. The singers must try to understand each character by studying the ideas that the character expresses in the opera, the actions this person takes, and information about the character found in stage directions and in the words of other characters. The changes that occur in characters during the course of the opera should be discussed as well as character relationships. In addition, each character has a major goal for the entire opera as well as an objective for each scene that should be identified. Performers should also figure out for each scene their characters' motivations, actions taken to achieve their objectives and attitudes toward others.

Musical Director/Conductor's Rehearsals

Rehearsals for singers will begin with learning the music. The musical director should coach the singers, setting tempos and instilling the desired interpretation. Assistants should be present so that they can take over many subsequent rehearsals because this coaching must continue until performances. The musical director must also give complete instructions to the choreographer concerning the tempos of the dance music and to the choral director, if there is one, for the choral music. The conductor, who may also be the musical director, schedules and rehearses the orchestra.

Choreographer's Rehearsals

The choreographer will rehearse the dancers separately until the dances are learned; then the dances will be integrated into the show. Polishing of the dances will continue, however, until performances.

Stage Director's Rehearsals

The stage director will normally not work with the singers until the music has been memorized; then, the stage director will begin to stage the opera. When *Tannhäuser* was first rehearsed, Wagner insisted that the cast read the libretto out loud under the direction of the stage director and in the presence of the conductor. Other stage directors have followed this procedure, stopping frequently to talk about characterizations, meaning of the plot and words, and performers' objectives, motivations, actions and attitudes. Wagner also encouraged his performers to articulate their words distinctly.

In blocking singers, the composer Gian-Carlo Menotti, who is also a stage director, advises the stage director to work closely with the singer. At first, the stage director should stand near the artist in order to understand how it feels to sing these lines. Feeling the emotions should help the director and performers create the proper movements.

During rehearsals the stage director should strive for a sense of communication between characters. To believe that the singers are listening to each other and communicating their thoughts and emotions is the goal. Because many repetitions are needed in staging rehearsals, the director may allow the performers to speak their lines or sing softly in these rehearsals in order to save their voices.

The singing chorus may be rehearsed separately by the stage director, who should make sure that the chorus members have characterizations and know their objectives, motivations, actions and attitudes toward others. As they work in small groups or as individuals, they should have natural-looking business to do. The stage director should strive for irregular spacings and various body positions in different stage areas, but in addition to a visual balance the director must consider the musical balance of voices.

Use of Closed-Circuit TV

If the blocking requires singers to turn their backs to the conductor, they should then be able to see an assistant conductor in the wings, unless the theatre has a closed-circuit TV system. As mentioned in chapter eleven, a television camera focused on the conductor and monitors placed offstage may guide those who must sing in the wings or prepare for an entrance. Also, a TV monitor on the front of the balcony may allow singers to play to the audience, rather than focusing on the conductor in the pit.

Integration of Singing, Dancing, and Acting

As soon as the singing, dancing and blocking have been learned, there should be several rehearsals to integrate the soloists, chorus and dancers. The musical director/conductor, stage director, choreographer and choral director should be present for these rehearsals, which will have a piano accompaniment.

Run-Throughs and Final Rehearsals

At run-throughs the opera is rehearsed from beginning to end with piano accompaniment—hopefully without stopping. At theatres that have a prompt-

er's box, a prompter may help forgetful singers. If there is no prompter's box, the conductor may assume this responsibility.

When the opera is running smoothly, the technical elements—scenery, properties, lighting and curtains—may be introduced with the stage manager calling the cues. If necessary, an assistant conductor may be stationed with the stage manager to be sure that technical cues are given at the correct place in the music.

Now the stage director should move farther back in the house so that he or she can be sure that singers can be heard, seen and understood throughout the theatre. The stage director must also make sure that the dramatic timing is right and that the action of the opera is building appropriately to minor and major climaxes.

Next the orchestra is added, and last of all, performers put on costumes and makeup for full dress rehearsals. At one of these, the stage director should block a curtain call in which the cast, conductor and orchestra are recognized for their work.

Locating Information About an Opera

If you have seen an opera that you would like to produce (for example, suppose you saw *Amahl and the Night Visitors* on television), how do you find out about the costs to present it and the place to get scores, choral parts and orchestrations? You might look at a list of operas in the appendix of this book to discover that *Amahl* is handled by G. Schirmer, Inc., and contact them at the address given below.

Another way is to inquire at your local music store. They may be able to order the material or provide the publisher's name and address so that you can write or call/fax the publisher about materials and performance fees.

If you do not have a "local music store," go to the music section of your library to see if a score is available. If the opera you want is not there, ask the librarian if it can be obtained through interlibrary loan. Once you have the score, look to see who published it. For a current address of that publisher, inquire again at the library.

Another source of information is:
Opera America
1156 Fifteenth Street, N.W., Suite 810

Washington, DC 20005
(202) 293-4466
Fax (202) 293-0735

The Information Services Department of Opera America is a clearinghouse for information on all aspects of operas. They are primarily a membership organization, but nonmembers may call with simple reference questions.

If you do not have a particular opera in mind, consult publishers' catalogs. The opera catalog of G. Schirmer, Inc., contains information about many operas and includes lists of operas, operettas and comic operas for the following:

- In several acts or in one act
- With chamber orchestra, ensemble or solo accompaniment
- In English or in other languages
- For college or community groups
- For young performers or young audiences
- About Christmas and other religious subjects

Two of the best opera catalogs are published by:

Boosey & Hawkes, Inc.
For information:
24 E. Twenty-first St.
New York, NY 10010-7200
(212) 228-3300
Fax (212) 473-5730

For rentals and performance rights:
52 Cooper Square, Tenth Floor
New York, NY 10003-7102
(212) 979-1090
Fax (212) 979-7057

G. Schirmer, Inc.
Promotion and Copyright Departments:
257 Park Ave. S.
New York, NY 10010
(212) 254-2100
Fax (212) 254-2013

Rental and Performance Department:
P.O. Box 572
5 Bellvale Road
Chester, NY 10918
(914) 469-2271
Fax (914) 469-7544

If you are interested in presenting opera for young audiences with juvenile and/or adult performers, you may be interested in joining the following organization:

Opera for Youth, Inc.
318 N. Main St.
Bowling Green, OH 43402

They can provide information about operas for young people, including new works.

CHAPTER FIFTEEN

Scenes for Practice

To give you the opportunity to practice stage and musical directing, choreographing and performing, we are including in this chapter excerpts for two or three performers from two comic operas by W.S. Gilbert and Arthur Sullivan: *The Pirates of Penzance* and *The Mikado*. While these were written over a hundred years ago, they are still popular today. In recent years *The Pirates of Penzance* was presented on Broadway with two rock stars, Linda Rondstadt and Rex Smith, and George Rose and Kevin Kline. Directors Peter Sellars and Jonathan Miller tried nontraditional productions of *The Mikado* with Sellars locating it in a modern Japanese corporation and Miller placing it in a 1920s English resort with Dudley Moore in a starring role. The Australian Opera's interpretation set the show in a London department store in about 1900.

Perhaps these productions may inspire you to break away from tradition. Let your imagination roam to see how you can make these comic operas appealing to modern audiences.

You learn by doing; so if you are in a class or workshop situation, analyze, cast, rehearse and present these selections for your classmates. Aspiring stage directors, musical directors, choreographers and performers can gain valuable experience this way.

Following are suggestions for preparing these scenes:

1. All directors should study the entire work.

2. All directors should analyze it. This involves doing research and analyzing the plot, characters, thoughts, words of the dialogue and lyrics, music, movement, dances, spectacle, sound and special effects.

3. The stage director should decide on the interpretation to be given the comic opera.

4. The stage director should prepare a description of the characters in the excerpt.

5. The stage director should devise a simple ground plan for the scene, indicating where scenery and furniture should be placed, even though you will not have them. For a class presentation, you do not need a theatre, stage, scenery, stage lighting, sound effects, costumes or stage makeup. Perform at one end of a room; or if the place has movable chairs or desks, arrange them in an arena, thrust or L-shaped configuration. You will need a piano and an accompanist or a recording. Also, you may want to use some hand props if they are easy to find. If they are not obtainable, the actors can pantomime handling them or use substitute props.

6. All directors may be involved in casting.

7. The stage director should discuss with the performers the desired interpretation of the work and the characters' objectives, motivations, actions, thoughts, feelings and attitudes toward others in the scene.

8. The musical director may help the singers with tempos, dynamics, phrasing and other musical matters.

9. The choreographer may block the movements for songs.

10. The stage director may do the following:

☐ Block the movements for dialogue.

☐ Make sure that performers understand and give the desired interpretation of the characters, dialogue and lyrics.

☐ Check up on their articulation and projection.

☐ Insist that they communicate with each other.

☐ Demand that they concentrate on staying in character.

☐ Urge them to show energy and vitality while playing.

☐ For a class performance, request them to wear clothing and shoes from their own wardrobe that suggest what their characters might wear. An appropriate hairstyle may also help them get into character.

Enjoy this challenge to your creativity—have fun!

Scene for one woman and two men from Act II of *The Pirates of Penzance* (1879) by W.S. Gilbert and Arthur Sullivan

CHARACTERS Frederic, an apprentice to the pirates

The Pirate King

Ruth, an older woman who is a maid of all work

SETTING A moonlit, ruined chapel (with Gothic windows at the back) on the coast of Cornwall

TIME Night

SITUATION When Frederic was very young, his nurse-maid, Ruth, apprenticed him to a pirate until his twenty-first birthday. (She had been told to take him to a *pilot*, but she misunderstood the word.) Having reached the age of twenty-one, Frederic, who has met a beautiful young lady, Mabel, is eager to leave the pirates, and he has sought the aid of the police to eliminate them.

COMMENTS Frederic is a tenor, the Pirate King is a bass, and Ruth is an alto.

(Mabel, her sisters, the General, and others have exited. Frederic remains.)

RECITATIVE—FREDERIC, PIRATE KING, AND RUTH

FRED Now for the pirates' lair! Oh, joy unbounded!

Oh, sweet relief! Oh, rapture unexampled!

At last I may atone, in some slight measure,

For the repeated acts of theft and pillage

Of which, at a sense of duty's stern dictation,

I, circumstance's victim, have been guilty.

(KING and RUTH appear at the window, armed.)

KING Young Frederic! *(Covering him with pistol.)*

FRED Who calls?

KING Your late commander!

RUTH And I, your little Ruth! *(Covering him with pistol.)*

FRED Oh, mad intruders,

How dare ye face me? Know ye not, oh rash ones,

That I have doomed you to extermination?

(KING and RUTH hold a pistol to each ear.)

KING Have mercy on us, hear us, ere you slaughter.

FRED I do not think I ought to listen to you.

Yet, mercy should alloy our stern resentment,

And so I will be merciful—say on!

SOLOS, TRIO, AND CHANT—RUTH, FREDERIC, AND PIRATE KING

RUTH When you had left our pirate fold

We tried to raise our spirits faint,

According to our customs old,

With quips and quibbles quaint.

But all in vain the quips we heard,

We lay and sobbed upon the rocks,

Until to somebody occurred

A startling paradox.

FRED A paradox?

RUTH *(laughing).* A paradox!

A most ingenious paradox!

We've quips and quibbles heard in flocks,

But none to beat this paradox!

ALL A paradox, a paradox, a most ingenious paradox.

Ha! ha! ha! ha! ha! ha! ha! ha! this paradox!

KING We knew your taste for curious quips,

For cranks and contradictions queer,

And with the laughter on our lips,

We wished you there to hear.

We said, "If we could tell it him,

How Frederic would the joke enjoy!"

And so we've risked both life and limb

To tell it to our boy.

FRED *(interested).* That paradox?

KING (*laughing*). That paradox? That most ingenious paradox!
We've quips and quibbles heard in flocks,
But none to beat that paradox!

ALL A paradox, a paradox, a most ingenious paradox.
Ha! ha! ha! ha! ha! ha! ha! ha! that paradox!

KING (*chant*). For some ridiculous reason, to which, however, I've no desire to be disloyal,
Some person in authority, I don't know who, very likely the Astronomer Royal,
Has decided that, although for such a beastly month as February, twenty-eight days as a rule are plenty.
One year in every four his days shall be reckoned as nine-and-twenty.
Through some singular coincidence—I shouldn't be surprised if it were owing to the agency of an ill-natured fairy—
You are the victim of this clumsy arrangement, having been born in leap-year, on the twenty-ninth of February,
And so, by a simple arithmetical process, you'll easily discover,
That though you've lived twenty-one years, yet, if we go by birthdays, you're only five and a little bit over!

KING and RUTH Ha! ha! ha! ha! ha! ha! Ho! ho! ho! ho!

FRED Dear me! Let's see! (*counting on fingers*)
Yes, yes; with yours my figures do agree!

ALL Ha! ha! ha! ha! ha! ha! ha! ha!

(*FREDERIC more amused than any.*)

FRED How quaint the ways of Paradox!
At common sense she gaily mocks!
Though counting in the usual way,
Years twenty-one I've been alive,
Yet, reckoning by my natal day,
Yet, reckoning by my natal day,
I am a little boy of five!

RUTH and KING He is a little boy of five!

ALL Ha! ha! ha! ha! ha! ha! ha! ha!
A paradox, a paradox,
A most ingenious paradox!
Ha! ha! ha! ha! ha! ha! ha! ha!
A paradox, Ha! ha! ha! ha! ha! ha! ha! ha!

A curious paradox, ha! ha! ha! ha! ha! ha! ha! ha!
A most ingenious paradox!

(*RUTH and KING throw themselves back on seats, exhausted with laughter.*)

FRED Upon my word, this is most curious—most absurdly whimsical. Five-and-a-quarter! No one would think it to look at me!

RUTH You are glad now, I'll be bound, that you spared us. You would never have forgiven yourself when you discovered that you had killed *two of your comrades*.

FRED My comrades?

KING (*rises*). I'm afraid you don't appreciate the delicacy of your position. You were apprenticed to us—

FRED Until I reached my twenty-first year.

KING No, until you reached your twenty-first birthday (*producing document*), and, going by birthdays, you are as yet only five-and-a-quarter.

FRED You don't mean to say you are going to hold me to that?

KING No, we merely remind you of the fact, and leave the rest to your sense of duty.

RUTH (*rises*). Your sense of duty!

FRED (*wildly*). Don't put it on that footing! As I was merciful to you just now, be merciful to me! I implore you not to insist on the letter of your bond just as the cup of happiness is at my lips!

RUTH We insist on nothing; we content ourselves with pointing out to you *your duty*.

KING Your duty!

FRED (*after a pause*). Well, you have appealed to my sense of duty, and my duty is only too clear. I abhor your infamous calling; I shudder at the thought that I have ever been mixed up with it; but duty is before all—at any price I will do my duty.

KING Bravely spoken! Come, you are one of us once more.

FRED Lead on, I follow. (*Suddenly.*) Oh, horror!

KING and RUTH What is the matter?

FRED Ought I to tell you? No, no, I cannot do it; and yet, as one of your band—

KING Speak out, I charge you by that sense of conscientiousness to which we have never yet appealed in vain.

FRED General Stanley, the father of my Mabel—

KING and RUTH Yes, yes!

FRED He escaped from you on the plea that he was an orphan!

KING He did!

FRED It breaks my heart to betray the honoured father of the girl I adore, but as your apprentice I have no alternative. It is my duty to tell you that General Stanley is no orphan!

KING and RUTH What!

FRED More than that, he never was one!

KING Am I to understand that, to save his contemptible life, he dared to practise on our credulous simplicity? *(FREDERIC nods as he weeps.)* Our revenge shall be swift and terrible. We will go and collect our band and attack Tremorden Castle this very night.

FRED But—stay—

KING Not a word! He is doomed!

TRIO—RUTH, PIRATE KING, AND FREDERIC

RUTH and KING Away, away! my heart's on fire,
  I burn this base deception to repay,
  This very night my vengeance dire
  Shall glut itself in gore. Away, Away!

FRED Away, away! ere I expire—
  I find my duty hard to do today!
  My heart is filled with anguish dire,
  It strikes me to the core. Away, away!

KING With falsehood foul
  He tricked us of our brides.
  Let vengeance howl;

The Pirate so decides!
Our nature stern
He softened with his lies,
And, in return,
Tonight the traitor dies.

RUTH and FRED Yes, yes! tonight the traitor dies.

ALL Yes, yes! tonight the traitor dies.

RUTH Tonight he dies!

KING Yes, or early tomorrow.

FRED His girls likewise?

RUTH They will welter in sorrow.

KING The one soft spot

RUTH In their natures they cherish—

FRED And all who plot

KING To abuse it shall perish!

ALL Tonight he dies!
  Yes, or early tomorrow.
  His girls likewise,
  They will welter in sorrow.
  The one soft spot
  In their natures they cherish—
  And all who plot
  To abuse it shall perish!
  Away, away, away!
  Tonight the traitor dies!
  Away, away, tonight, tonight,
  Tonight the traitor dies!
  Tonight! away!

(Exeunt KING and RUTH. FRED throws himself on a stone in despair.)

NOW FOR THE PIRATES' LAIR! Recitative—Frederic, Pirate King, and Ruth
(From *The Pirates of Penzance*), Words by W.S. Gilbert, Music by Arthur Sullivan

NOW FOR THE PIRATES' LAIR! (continued)

NOW FOR THE PIRATES' LAIR! (continued)

WHEN YOU HAD LEFT OUR PIRATE FOLD Solos, Trio, Chant—Ruth, Frederic, Pirate King
(From *The Pirates of Penzance*), Words by W.S. Gilbert, Music by Arthur Sullivan

WHEN YOU HAD LEFT OUR PIRATE FOLD (continued)

WHEN YOU HAD LEFT OUR PIRATE FOLD (continued)

WHEN YOU HAD LEFT OUR PIRATE FOLD (continued)

WHEN YOU HAD LEFT OUR PIRATE FOLD (continued)

WHEN YOU HAD LEFT OUR PIRATE FOLD (continued)

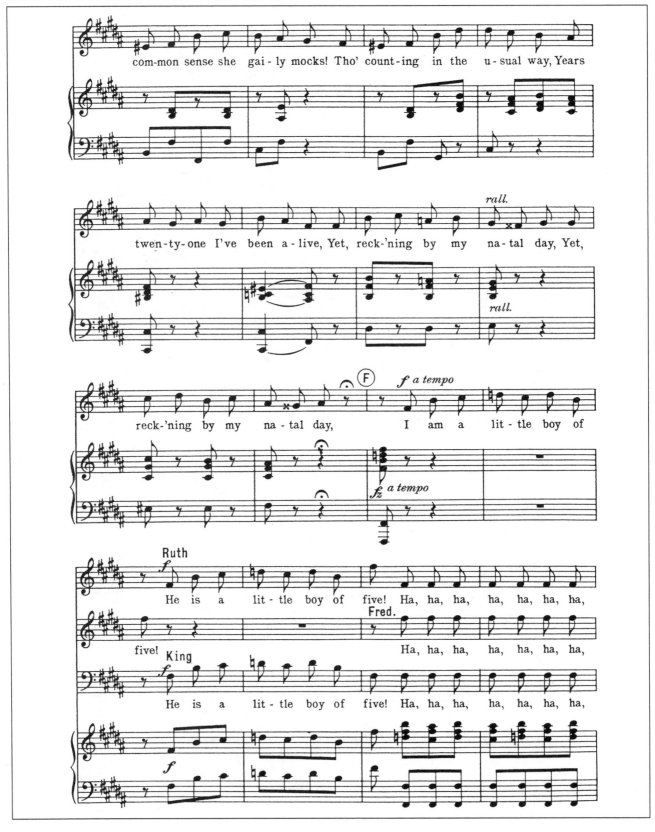

WHEN YOU HAD LEFT OUR PIRATE FOLD (continued)

WHEN YOU HAD LEFT OUR PIRATE FOLD (continued)

AWAY! AWAY! MY HEART'S ON FIRE Trio—Ruth, Pirate King, Frederic
(From *The Pirates of Penzance*), Words by W.S. Gilbert, Music by Arthur Sullivan

AWAY! AWAY! MY HEART'S ON FIRE (continued)

AWAY! AWAY! MY HEART'S ON FIRE (continued)

AWAY! AWAY! MY HEART'S ON FIRE (continued)

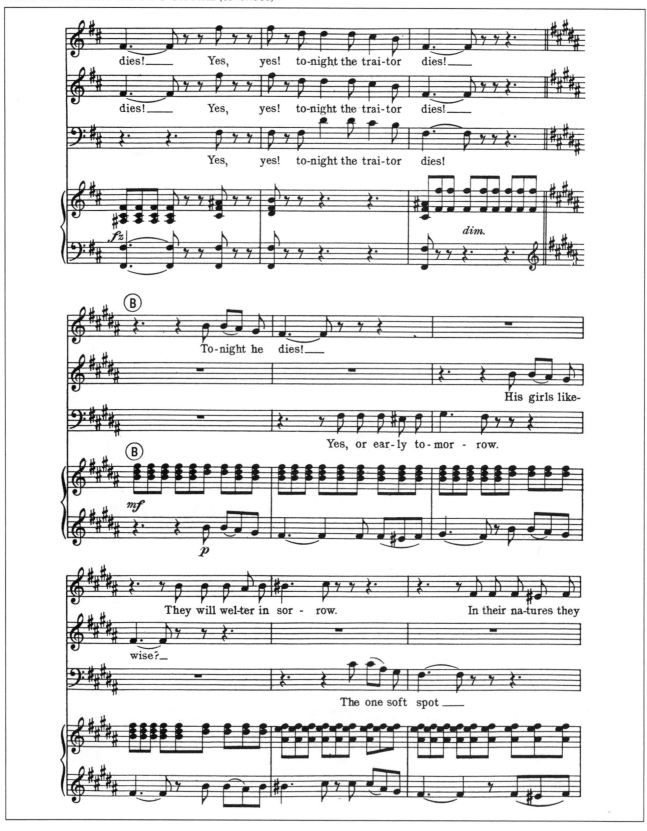

AWAY! AWAY! MY HEART'S ON FIRE (continued)

AWAY! AWAY! MY HEART'S ON FIRE (continued)

AWAY! AWAY! MY HEART'S ON FIRE (continued)

Scene for one woman and one man from Act II of *The Mikado* (1885) by W.S. Gilbert and Arthur Sullivan

CHARACTERS Katisha, an older lady who is in love with Nanki-Poo

Ko-Ko, the Lord High Executioner of Titipu

SETTING Ko-Ko's garden in Titipu, Japan

TIME Shortly after Katisha has arrived in Titipu with the Mikado, who is searching for his son, Nanki-Poo

SITUATION The Mikado and Katisha have been told that Nanki-Poo, her intended husband, has been executed. In punishment, the Mikado has said that Ko-Ko and two others will be executed. Actually, Nanki-Poo is alive and married to Yum-Yum, but he does not wish to reveal this because Katisha will insist on his execution if she finds out that he is married; and if Nanki-Poo is executed, Yum-Yum will be buried alive. As a way out of their difficulties, Nanki-Poo and Yum-Yum have persuaded Ko-Ko to ask Katisha to marry him.

COMMENTS Katisha is a mezzo-soprano and Ko-Ko is a baritone. While Gilbert and Sullivan set this comic opera in Japan, some modern directors have changed the location.

(Enter KATISHA.)

RECITATIVE and SONG—KATISHA Alone, and yet alive! Oh, sepulchre!
My soul is still my body's prisoner!
Remote the peace that Death alone can give—
My doom, to wait! my punishment, to live!

SONG Hearts do not break!
They sting and ache
For old love's sake
But do not die,
Though with each breath
They long for death
As witnesseth
The living I, the living I.
Oh, living I!
Come, tell me why,
When hope is gone,
Dost thou stay on?
Why linger here,
Where all is drear?
Oh, living I!
Come, tell me why,
When hope is gone,
Dost thou stay on?

May not a cheated maiden die?

KO *(Entering and approaching her timidly.)* Katisha!

KAT The miscreant who robbed me of my love! But vengeance pursues—they are heating the cauldron!

KO Katisha—behold a suppliant at your feet! Katisha—mercy!

KAT Mercy? Had you mercy on him? See here, you! You have slain my love. He did not love *me*, but he would have loved me in time. I am an acquired taste—only the educated palate can appreciate *me*. I was educating *his* palate when he left me. Well, he is dead, and where shall I find another? It takes years to train a man to love me. Am I to go through the weary round again, and, at the same time, implore mercy for you who robbed me of my prey—I mean my pupil—just as his education was on the point of completion? Oh, where shall I find another?

KO *(Suddenly, and with great vehemence.)* Here!—Here!

KAT What!!!

KO *(With intense passion.)* Katisha, for years I have loved you with a white-hot passion that is slowly but surely consuming my very vitals! Ah, shrink not from me! If there is aught of woman's mercy in your heart, turn not away from a lovesick suppliant whose every fibre thrills at your tiniest touch! True it is that, under a poor mask of disgust, I have endeavoured to conceal a passion whose inner fires are broiling the soul within me! But the fire will not be smothered—it defies all attempts at extinction, and, breaking forth, all the more eagerly for its long restraint, it declares itself in words that will not be weighed—that cannot be schooled—that should not be too severely criticised. Katisha, I dare not hope for your love—but I will not live without it! Darling!

KAT You, whose hands still reek with the blood of my betrothed, dare to address words of passion to the woman you have so foully wronged!

KO I do—accept my love, or I perish on the spot!

KAT Go to! Who knows so well as I that no one ever yet died of a broken heart!

KO You know not what you say. Listen!

SONG—KO-KO On a tree by a river a little tom-tit
Sang "Willow, titwillow, titwillow!"
And I said to him, "Dicky-bird, why do you sit
Singing 'Willow, titwillow, titwillow'?"
"Is it weakness of intellect, birdie?" I cried,

"Or a rather tough worm in your little inside?"
With a shake of his poor little head, he replied,
"Oh, willow, titwillow, titwillow!"
He slapped at his chest, as he sat on that bough,
Singing "Willow, titwillow, titwillow!"
And a cold perspiration bespangled his brow,
Oh, willow titwillow, titwillow!
He sobbed and he sighed, and a gurgle he gave,
Then he plunged himself into the billowy wave,
And an echo arose from the suicide's grave—
"Oh, willow, titwillow, titwillow!"
Now I feel just as sure as I'm sure that my name
Isn't Willow, titwillow, titwillow,
That 'twas blighted affection that made him
exclaim,
"Oh, willow, titwillow, titwillow!"
And if you remain callous and obdurate, I
Shall perish as he did, and you will know why,
Though I probably shall not exclaim as I die,
"Oh, willow, titwillow, titwillow!"

(During this song KATISHA has been greatly affected, and at the end is almost in tears.)

KAT *(Whimpering.)* Did he really die of love?

KO He really did.

KAT All on account of a cruel little hen?

KO Yes.

KAT Poor little chap!

KO It's an affecting tale, and quite true. I knew the bird intimately.

KAT Did you? He must have been very fond of her.

KO His devotion was something extraordinary.

KAT *(Still whimpering.)* Poor little chap! And—if I refuse you, will you go and do the same?

KO At once.

KAT No, no—you mustn't! Anything but that! *(Falls on his breast.)* Oh, I'm a silly little goose!

KO *(Making a wry face.)* You are!

KAT And you won't hate me because I'm just a little teeny weeny wee bit bloodthirsty, will you?

KO Hate you? Oh, Katisha! is there not beauty even in bloodthirstiness?

KAT My idea exactly.

DUET—KATISHA and KO-KO

KAT There is beauty in the bellow of the blast,
There is grandeur in the growling of the gale,
There is eloquent outpouring
When the lion is a-roaring,

And the tiger is a-lashing of his tail!

KO Yes, I like to see a tiger
From the Congo or the Niger,
And especially when lashing of his tail!

KAT Volcanoes have a splendour that is grim,
And earthquakes only terrify the dolts,
But to him who's scientific
There is nothing that's terrific
In the falling of a flight of thunderbolts!

KO Yes, in spite of all my meekness,
If I have a little weakness,
It's a passion for a flight of thunderbolts!

BOTH If that is so,
Sing derry down derry!
It's evident, very,
Our tastes are one.
Away we'll go,
And merrily marry,
Nor tardily tarry
Till day is done!

KO There is beauty in extreme old age—
Do you fancy you are elderly enough?
Information I'm requesting
On a subject interesting:
Is a maiden all the better when she's tough?

KAT Throughout this wide dominion
It's the general opinion
That she'll last a good deal longer when she's tough.

KO Are you old enough to marry, do you think?
Won't you wait until you're eighty in the shade?
There's a fascination frantic
In a ruin that's romantic;
Do you think you are sufficiently decayed?

KAT To the matter that you mention
I have given some attention,
And I think I am sufficiently decayed.

BOTH If that is so,
Sing derry down derry!
It's evident, very,
Our tastes are one!
Away we'll go,
And merrily marry,
Nor tardily tarry
Till day is done!

(Exeunt together.)

ALONE, AND YET ALIVE! Recitative and Song—Katisha
(From *The Mikado*), Words by W.S. Gilbert, Music by Arthur Sullivan

ALONE, AND YET ALIVE! (continued)

ALONE, AND YET ALIVE! (continued)

ALONE, AND YET ALIVE! (continued)

WII.LOW, TIT-WILLOW Song—Ko-Ko
(From *The Mikado*), Words by W.S. Gilbert, Music by Arthur Sullivan

WILLOW, TIT-WILLOW (continued)

WILLOW, TIT-WILLOW (continued)

cold per-spi - ra-tion be-span-gled his brow, Oh, wil-low, tit-wil-low, tit-

wil-low!   He sobbed and he sighed, and a gur-gle he gave, Then he

plunged him-self in - to the bil-low-y wave, And an ech-o a-rose from the

su - i-cide's grave—"Oh, wil-low, tit-wil-low, tit-wil-low!"

WILLOW, TIT-WILLOW (continued)

WILLOW, TIT-WILLOW (continued)

THERE IS BEAUTY IN THE BELLOW OF THE BLAST Duet—Katisha and Ko-Ko
(From *The Mikado*), Words by W.S. Gilbert, Music by Arthur Sullivan

THERE IS BEAUTY IN THE BELLOW OF THE BLAST (continued)

THERE IS BEAUTY IN THE BELLOW OF THE BLAST (continued)

THERE IS BEAUTY IN THE BELLOW OF THE BLAST (continued)

THERE IS BEAUTY IN THE BELLOW OF THE BLAST (continued)

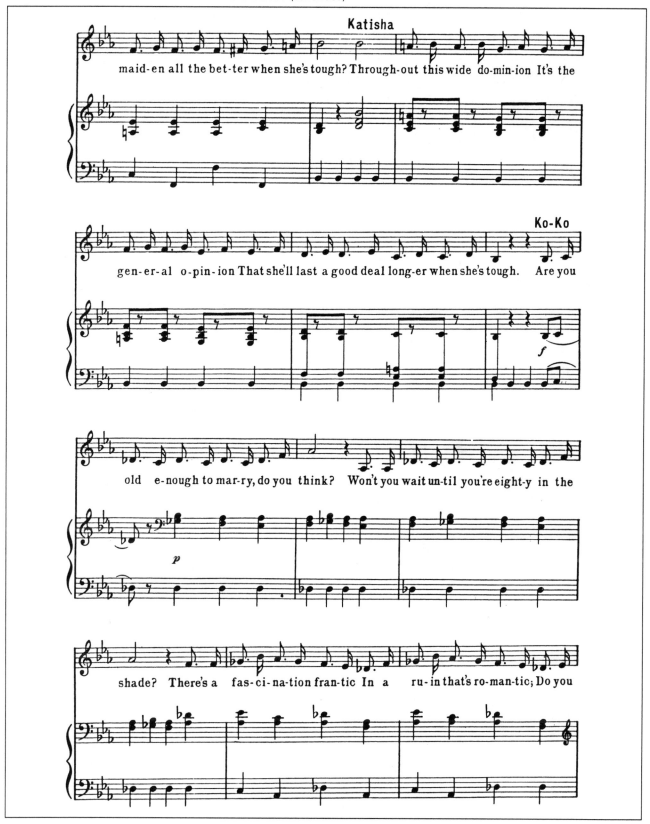

THERE IS BEAUTY IN THE BELLOW OF THE BLAST (continued)

THERE IS BEAUTY IN THE BELLOW OF THE BLAST (continued)

THERE IS BEAUTY IN THE BELLOW OF THE BLAST (continued)

We purposely chose shows that are copyright-free. This gives you the opportunity to photocopy and distribute the lyrics and music to your cast members, directors, choreographers or classes for use in rehearsals. The scenes require a variety of skills that will exercise the abilities of all involved.

These comic operas attest to the fact that even the oldest productions can still be enjoyed by modern audiences in their original formats.

On the other hand, remember that you can be creative when adapting these musicals to your cast or class. Even the recent Broadway productions of these shows were quite different than what the authors originally intended.

Appendix

NOTABLE MUSICALS, REVUES, OPERAS, COMIC OPERAS AND OPERETTAS

In this section you'll find information about some musicals, revues, operas, comic operas and operettas that are popular with school/community organizations. The musicals and revues are licensed by the following:

> Music Theatre International (abbreviation used in the lists: MTI)
>
> Rodgers and Hammerstein Theatre Library (abbreviation: RH)
>
> Samuel French, Inc. (abbreviation: SF)
>
> Tams-Witmark Music Library, Inc. (abbreviation: TW)

For their addresses and telephone and fax numbers, see chapter two.

In the list of operas, comic operas and operettas, some of the above companies are noted, but most are handled by these two:

> Boosey & Hawkes, Inc. (abbreviation: BH)
>
> G. Schirmer, Inc. (abbreviation: GS)

For their addresses and telephone and fax numbers, see chapter fourteen.

Following this introduction are descriptions of thirty-nine large musicals in alphabetical order.

After these descriptions are four lists of titles and licensors.

- Ninety-two more large musicals
- Ten small musicals (By "small" we mean that only ten or fewer performers are needed.)
- Twenty-five revues
- Forty-eight operas, comic operas and operettas

If you would like more information about one of these works, contact the company indicated by the abbreviation.

ANNIE

Book by Thomas Meehan—Music by Charles Strouse
Lyrics by Martin Charnin

With regard to the sets indicated in these descriptions, you may find that some of them are not needed or you may be able to think of a simpler way to suggest the location of a scene. Sometimes a slide projection, a fragmentary set, a screen, a few pieces of furniture, or creative lighting can be used instead of large, elaborate scenery. At times, too, one set can be repeated with slight changes to indicate different places.

Based on the Comic Strip *Little Orphan Annie*
Licensor: Music Theatre International
First opened in New York in 1977.

SYNOPSIS During the Depression of 1933, Annie is in an orphanage in New York City. She escapes but is returned; then Oliver Warbucks's secretary selects her to spend Christmas at the Warbucks mansion. Oliver tries to find Annie's parents; but when it is learned that they are deceased, Oliver adopts Annie.

BEST MUSICAL NUMBERS "Tomorrow," "It's the Hard Knock Life," "Easy Street," "I Don't Need Anything but You"

CAST 3 men, 3 women, 7 girls, 1 dog, chorus

SETS Orphanage, St. Mark's Place, homeless community, various rooms in the Warbucks mansion, New York City, radio studio, White House in Washington, DC

COSTUMES Early 1930s clothes

INSTRUMENTATION 5 reeds, 2 trumpets, 2 trombones, 1 tuba, 1 violin, 1 cello, 1 bass, 1 guitar-banjo, 2 percussion, 1 piano-conductor

ANNIE GET YOUR GUN

Music and Lyrics by Irving Berlin—Book by Herbert and Dorothy Fields

Licensor: Rodgers and Hammerstein Theatre Library

First opened in New York in 1946.

SYNOPSIS In the latter part of the nineteenth century in the Midwest, Annie Oakley, a great sharpshooter, is discovered by Buffalo Bill and she joins his Wild West Show. She falls in love with the star Frank Butler, but when she becomes well-known, Frank cannot take the competition and leaves to join a rival show. Later, in a shooting contest between the two, Annie lets Frank win with the result that they are going to be partners as the two shows are combined.

BEST MUSICAL NUMBERS "There's No Business Like Show Business," "The Girl That I Marry," "You Can't Get a Man With a Gun," "I Got the Sun in the Morning," "Doin' What Comes Natur'lly," "They Say It's Wonderful," "Anything You Can Do"

CAST 8 men, 3 women, 1 boy, 3 girls, large number of small roles and chorus

SETS Outside a summer hotel, a train's Pullman parlor, fairgrounds, arena of tent, dressing room tent, deck of cattleboat, hotel ballroom, ferryboat, outside a fort

COSTUMES Late nineteenth-century clothes

INSTRUMENTATION (Orchestrations by Robert Russell Bennett for 1966 production) 1 flute I-II (doubling piccolo), 1 oboe (optional doubling English horn), 1 clarinet I-II, 1 bassoon, 1 horn, 1 trumpet I-II, 1 trumpet III, 1 trombone I, 1 trombone II, 1 trombone III, 2 percussion I-II, 2 violin A-B-C-D, 1 viola, 1 cello, 1 bass, 1 harp, 1 guitar, 1 piano-conductor vocal score

THE BOY FRIEND

Book, Music and Lyrics by Sandy Wilson

Licensor: Music Theatre International

First opened in New York in 1954.

SYNOPSIS The year is 1926; the place is a fashionable finishing school on the French Riviera. A wealthy young lady, Polly, falls in love with a delivery boy, Tony, who eventually turns out to be wealthy also. To hold his interest, Polly pretends to be a working girl. At the end, everything turns out favorably for Polly and Tony and other couples.

BEST MUSICAL NUMBERS "Perfect Young Ladies," "The Boy Friend," "Won't You Charleston With Me?," "I Could Be Happy with You," "It's Never Too Late to Fall in Love"

CAST 8 men, 8 women (may be expanded)

SETS Drawing room of a finishing school, the beach, the terrace of a cafe

COSTUMES 1920s clothes (short skirts and cloche hats for the women)

INSTRUMENTATION 3 reeds, 2 trumpets, 1 trombone, 1 percussion, 2 violins, 1 bass, 1 banjo (or guitar), 1 piano-conductor

BRIGADOON

Music by Frederick Loewe—Book and Lyrics by Alan Jay Lerner

Original Dances Created by Agnes de Mille

Licensor: Tams-Witmark Music Library, Inc.

First opened in New York in 1947.

SYNOPSIS Tommy Albright and Jeff Douglas, two New Yorkers who are lost in the Scottish highlands, discover the village of Brigadoon, which comes to life for only one day in each century. Tommy falls in love with a Scottish lass, Fiona, and Jeff has a comic involvement with Meg Brockie. Tommy and Fiona part, but at the end Tommy is drawn back to Brigadoon to be with his love.

BEST MUSICAL NUMBERS "Almost Like Being in Love," "The Heather on the Hill," "There but for You Go I," "Come to Me, Bend to Me," "My Mother's Wedding Day"

CAST 12 men, 5 women plus townsfolk, including Scottish dancers and bagpipers

SETS Forest, road, town square, open shed, living room, outside of a house and church, New York City bar

COSTUMES Scottish dress that is based on clothes of the eighteenth-century for the townspeople and contemporary wear for the Americans

INSTRUMENTATION 3 violins, 1 viola, 1 cello, 1 bass, 1 flute-piccolo, 1 oboe, 2 clarinets, 1 bassoon, 1 horn, 3 trumpets, 1 trombone, 1 percussion, 1 piano-celeste, 1 piano-conductor

BYE BYE BIRDIE

Book by Michael Stewart—Music by Charles Strouse

Lyrics by Lee Adams

Licensor: Tams-Witmark Music Library, Inc.

First opened in New York in 1960.

SYNOPSIS Conrad Birdie, an Elvis Presley-type rock-and-roll singer, is about to be inducted into the army. Rose Grant, secretary to Conrad's agent, Albert Peterson, devises a plan for a contest in which a typical teenage girl will get to kiss Conrad goodbye on national television. The winner is Kim MacAfee of Sweet Apple, Ohio, who has just been pinned to Hugo. When Conrad arrives in Sweet Apple, a great commotion ensues. At the end, however, Kim is with Hugo and Rose is with Albert.

BEST MUSICAL NUMBERS "Kids," "A Lot of Livin' to Do," "Put on a Happy Face," "Rosie," "We Love You, Conrad"

CAST 6 men, 6 women, 1 boy, teenagers

SETS Office, home, 2 railroad stations, courthouse, stage, roadside retreat, nightspot, a structure used by teenagers for "The Telephone Hour"

COSTUMES 1960s clothes plus a dazzling costume for Conrad

INSTRUMENTATION 3 violins, 1 cello, 1 bass, 4 reeds, 1 horn, 3 trumpets, 2 trombones, 2 percussion, 1 guitar-banjo, 1 piano-conductor

CABARET

Book by Joe Masteroff—Music by John Kander—Lyrics by Fred Ebb

Based on the Play by John Van Druten and Stories by Christopher Isherwood

Licensor: Tams-Witmark Music Library, Inc.

First opened in New York in 1966.

SYNOPSIS A young American named Clifford Bradshaw arrives in Berlin in 1929 to get material for a new novel. Among others, he meets Fraulein Schneider, who rents him a room, and an English girl, Sally Bowles, who moves in with him. Months later, she has an abortion, and Cliff leaves alone for America. A bizarre emcee opens and closes the show and appears frequently within it.

BEST MUSICAL NUMBERS "Wilkommen," "Cabaret," "Don't Tell Mama," "Perfectly Marvelous," "Two Ladies," "It Couldn't Please Me More," "If You Could See Her"

CAST 13 men, 9 women plus a 4-piece female on-stage band, 6 Kit Kat Girls, and German sailors

SETS Nightclub with a large illuminated sign that reads "Cabaret" and a spiral staircase, train compartment, Cliff's room, Schneider's living room and bedroom, fruit shop

COSTUMES 1929-1930 clothes, including some chorus girl costumes and Nazi uniforms

INSTRUMENTATION 2 violins, 1 viola, 1 cello, 1 bass, 4 reeds, 1 horn, 2 trumpets, 2 trombones, 1 percussion, 1 accordion-celeste, 1 drum, 1 piano-conductor

Stage band: 1 saxophone, 1 trombone, 1 piano, 1 drum

Note: Orchestra parts have been cross-cued so that the horn, violins I-II, viola and cello parts can be eliminated from the instrumentation.

CAMELOT

Book and Lyrics by Alan Jay Lerner—Music by Frederick Loewe

Based on *The Once and Future King* by T.H. White

Licensor: Tams-Witmark Music Library, Inc.

First opened in New York in 1960.

SYNOPSIS In the twelfth century, a young King Arthur nervously awaits the arrival of his betrothed, Guenevere. The couple marries and the years pass. Arthur forms the Round Table at which knights meet with no one sitting at the head. Lancelot arrives from France and falls in love with Guenevere. Mordred, Arthur's illegitimate son, fosters Guenevere's love for Lancelot, then has her arrested for treason. She escapes to France with Lancelot, and Arthur forgives them.

BEST MUSICAL NUMBERS "Camelot," "If Ever I Would Leave You," "What Do the Simple Folk Do," "Lusty Month of May," "How to Handle a Woman," "I Wonder What the King Is Doing Tonight"

CAST 14 men, 5 women, knights, ladies, nymphs, 1 sheepdog

SETS Hilltop, near Camelot, Arthur's study, countryside, garden, terrace, tents, grandstand of jousting field, corridor, grand hall, forest, queen's bedchamber, battlefield

COSTUMES Twelfth-century clothes, including half-animal, half-human nymphs who are followers of Morgan Le Fey

INSTRUMENTATION 3 violins, 1 viola, 1 cello, 1 bass,

1 flute-piccolo, 1 oboe-English horn, 2 clarinets, 1 bassoon, 3 horns, 3 trumpets, 2 trombones, 1 percussion, 1 guitar-lute-mandolin, 1 harp, 1 piano-conductor

Also available is an orchestration for an 11-or 12-piece combo.

CAROUSEL

Music by Richard Rodgers—Book and Lyrics by Oscar Hammerstein II

Based on Ferenc Molnár's Play *Liliom* as Adapted by Benjamin F. Glazer

Licensor: Rodgers and Hammerstein Theatre Library

First opened in New York in 1945.

SYNOPSIS In 1873 at an amusement park in New England, a young naive millworker, Julie, meets Billy, a carnival barker. After marrying, Billy loses his job, learns that Julie is pregnant, and is caught in the act of robbery. Rather than go to prison, Billy commits suicide. "Up there" Billy is permitted to return to earth for one day. He does so to help his fifteen-year-old daughter, Louise, and to tell Julie that he loved her.

BEST MUSICAL NUMBERS "If I Loved You," "Mister Snow," "June is Bustin' Out All Over," "You'll Never Walk Alone"

CAST 5 men, 5 women, small roles, children, singing-dancing ensemble

SETS Amusement park, path along a shore, Nettie's spa, island, waterfront, "up there," beach, outside Julie's cottage, outside a schoolhouse

COSTUMES 1873 and 1888 clothes

INSTRUMENTATION (Orchestrations by Don Walker) 1 flute I-II (doubling piccolo), 1 oboe (doubling English horn), 1 clarinet I-II, 1 bassoon, 1 horn I-II, 1 horn III, 1 trumpet I-II, 1 trombone I, 1 trombone II, 1 tuba, 1 percussion, 1 violin A-B, 1 violin C, 1 viola, 1 cello, 1 bass, 1 harp, 1 piano-conductor score

Also available is a two-piano arrangement.

CHICAGO

Book by Fred Ebb and Bob Fosse—Music by John Kander

Based on the Play *Chicago* by Maurine Dallas Watkins

Licensor: Samuel French, Inc.

First opened in New York in 1975.

SYNOPSIS In Chicago in the roaring 1920s, Roxie shoots her lover. She and Velma, another murderer, try to get publicity in order to be acquitted and to have stage careers. A smart lawyer gets them off and they proceed to play vaudeville.

BEST MUSICAL NUMBER "All That Jazz"

CAST 9 men, 10 women

SETS Unit set with scenic pieces for a bedroom, jail, office, and courtroom (Note: The original production had the orchestra onstage on top of a platform.)

COSTUMES Late 1920s clothes

INSTRUMENTATION 3 reeds, 2 trumpets, 2 trombones, 1 tuba-bass, 1 percussion, 1 violin, 1 banjo, 2 keyboards (piano-harmonium and piano-accordion), 1 piano-conductor score

A CHORUS LINE

Music by Marvin Hamlisch—Book by James Kirkwood and Nicholas Dante

Lyrics by Edward Kleban

Conceived and Originally Directed and Choreographed by Michael Bennett

Licensor: Tams-Witmark Music Library, Inc.

First opened in New York in 1975.

SYNOPSIS A director of a Broadway musical is holding auditions for dancers. In the process, the dancers tell personal stories about how they got into show business or why they became performers or what their dreams are. At the end the director makes his selection, and the cast reappears in brilliant costumes to dance the finale.

BEST MUSICAL NUMBERS "What I Did for Love," "One," "Dance: Ten; Looks: Three," "At the Ballet," "Hello, Twelve, Hello, Thirteen, Hello Love," "The Music and the Mirror," "Nothing," "The Tap Combination"

CAST 14 men, 12 women (The choreography and dancing must be excellent.)

SET A bare stage with a mirrored rear wall

COSTUMES Dance and street clothes until the end when the dancers wear spectacular costumes

INSTRUMENTATION 4 reeds, 3 trumpets, 3 trombones, 2 percussion, 1 harp, 1 bass, 1 guitar, 1 keyboard, 1 keyboard-conductor

EVITA

Lyrics by Tim Rice—Music by Andrew Lloyd Webber

Licensor: Music Theatre International

First opened in New York in 1979.

SYNOPSIS This operatic musical (there are only a few spoken lines) tells the story of the rise to fame and power in Argentina of Eva Perón. It begins in 1952 in Buenos Aires on the day of Eva's death. Another political figure, Che Guevara, relates the story of her life from the time she was 15 in 1934 to her death.

BEST MUSICAL NUMBERS "Don't Cry for Me Argentina," "Another Suitcase"

CAST 3 men, 2 women, chorus of adults and children (Excellent singing voices are needed.)

SETS Unit set with projections of slides, scenic pieces, and props to portray a cinema, nightclub, Buenos Aires, bedroom door, radio station, charity concert, bedroom, the balcony of Casa Rosada

COSTUMES 1934 to 1952 clothes and military uniforms

INSTRUMENTATION 4 reeds, 2 horns, 2 trumpets, 1 trombone/bass trombone, 2 violins, 1 cello, 1 bass, 2 guitars (acoustic and electric), 2 percussion, 1 drum, 1 harp, 2 keyboards, 1 piano-conductor

FIDDLER ON THE ROOF

Book by Joseph Stein— Music by Jerry Bock—Lyrics by Sheldon Harnick

Based on Sholem Aleichem Stories

Licensor: Music Theatre International

First opened in New York in 1964.

SYNOPSIS The time is 1905; the place is Anatevka, a village in Czarist Russia. The plot concerns one of the hard-working families in this Jewish community: a dairyman, Tevye, his wife, and five daughters. Three of his daughters marry—two with Tevye's blessing and one without. A pogrom interrupts one of the wedding celebrations, and later the constable informs the villagers that they must leave their homeland. The final scene depicts the Jews departing for other lands with their meager possessions.

BEST MUSICAL NUMBERS "Tradition," "Matchmaker," "If I Were a Rich Man," "Sunrise, Sunset," "Now I Have Everything," "Do You Love Me?"

CAST 12 men, 10 women, a fiddler, chorus

SETS Exterior and interior of Tevye's house, kitchen, inn, street, bedroom, Motel's tailor shop, railroad station, barn

COSTUMES Early twentieth-century Russian peasant clothes

INSTRUMENTATION 5 reeds, 3 trumpets, 1 trombone, 1 horn, 3 violins, 1 viola, 1 cello, 1 bass, 1 accordion, 1 guitar, 1 percussion, 1 piano-conductor

42ND STREET

Music by Harry Warren—Lyrics by Al Dubin

Book by Michael Stewart and Mark Bramble

Based on the Novel by Bradford Ropes

Licensor: Tams-Witmark Music Library, Inc.

First opened in New York in 1980.

SYNOPSIS In 1933, stage auditions are being held for the chorus of a new Broadway musical, *Pretty Lady.* Young, naive Peggy Sawyer auditions, and eventually the director hires her. Later, however, in rehearsal she accidentally causes the leading lady to break an ankle, and the director is persuaded that Peggy should substitute. She learns the part, and the show and Peggy are big hits.

BEST MUSICAL NUMBERS "You're Getting to Be a Habit with Me," "We're in the Money," "Lullabye of Broadway," "Shuffle Off to Buffalo," "42nd Street"

CAST 11 men, 6 women, small roles, chorus (Needed are excellent dancers.)

SETS Stage, cafe, dressing rooms, hotel suite, sets for *Pretty Lady,* railroad station

COSTUMES Early 1930s clothes; dazzling costumes for production numbers

INSTRUMENTATION 5 reeds, 1 horn, 3 trumpets, 2 trombones, 1 bass, 1 percussion, 1 piano-celeste, 1 piano-conductor
Optional parts: 1 guitar-banjo, 1 harp
Also available is a part for a keyboard synthesizer that can substitute for five reed parts.

A FUNNY THING HAPPENED ON THE WAY TO THE FORUM

Book by Burt Shevelove and Larry Gelbart
Music and Lyrics by Stephen Sondheim
Based on *Pseudolus* and Other Plays by Plautus
Licensor: Music Theatre International
First opened in New York in 1962.

SYNOPSIS The time is about 200 B.C.; the place, a street in Rome. A slave, Pseudolus, yearns to be free. Hero, his young master, promises this if Pseudolus can acquire for him the beautiful Philia, whom Hero has admired from afar. Unfortunately, Philia has been sold to the great captain, Miles Gloriosus. After much farcical trickery, Hero and Philia are together and Pseudolus is free.

BEST MUSICAL NUMBERS "Comedy Tonight," "Everybody Ought to Have a Maid"

CAST 11 men, 7 women

SETS A unit set consisting of the exterior of three houses on a street in ancient Rome

COSTUMES Roman togas and gowns

INSTRUMENTATION 5 reeds, 3 trumpets, 3 trombones, 1 percussion, 3 violins, 1 viola, 1 cello, 1 bass, 1 harp, 2 drums, 1 piano-conductor
Note: Following instruments may be eliminated: reed V, trumpet III, trombones II and III, all violins, viola, cello and harp.

GREASE

Book, Music and Lyrics by Jim Jacobs and Warren Casey
Licensor: Samuel French, Inc.
First opened in New York in 1972.

SYNOPSIS In a great satire of the rock-and-roll era, Rydell High's class of '59 shows the fads of the 1950s, such as the pajama party, the drive-in movie, the prom and others. Danny Zuko, Sandy Dumbrowski and Betty Rizzo are memorable characters in this fun show.

BEST MUSICAL NUMBERS "Look at Me, I'm Sandra Dee," "Beauty School Dropout," "It's Raining on Prom Night," "Alone at a Drive-In Movie," "All Choked Up," "Greased Lightnin' "

CAST 9 men, 8 women

SETS Platform stage with drops or projections for 12 different locations; 1950s car needed for two scenes

COSTUMES 1950s poodle skirts, leather jackets, and other fashions of the time

INSTRUMENTATION 1 piano-conductor score (and optional electric piano), 2 saxophones, 2 guitars, 1 bass, 1 drum

GUYS AND DOLLS

Music and Lyrics by Frank Loesser—Book by Jo Swerling and Abe Burrows
Based on a Story and Characters by Damon Runyon
Licensor: Music Theatre International
First opened in New York in 1950.

SYNOPSIS In New York City in 1950, a chorus girl, Adelaide, has been trying to get Nathan Detroit, a gambler, to marry her for fourteen years. Nathan bets another gambler, Sky Masterson, that Sky cannot persuade Sarah Brown of the local mission to go with him to Havana. She makes the trip, but when she discovers that gamblers used the mission while they were away, she breaks up with Sky. To get her back, Sky plays a crap game with gamblers in which the losers have to attend a mission meeting. At the end, Sky and Sarah are together, as are Adelaide and Nathan.

BEST MUSICAL NUMBERS "The Oldest Established," "A Bushel and a Peck," "Guys and Dolls," "If I Were a Bell," "I've Never Been in Love Before," "Luck Be a Lady," "Sit Down, You're Rockin' the Boat"

CAST 15 men, 4 women, chorus

SETS Broadway, interior and exterior of mission, phone booth, nightclub, street off Broadway, dining room in hotel in Havana, cheap street cafe, Havana exterior, sewer, street near Times Square

COSTUMES Mid-twentieth century clothes

INSTRUMENTATION 5 reeds, 3 trumpets, 1 trombone, 1 horn, 4 violins, 1 cello, 1 bass, 1 percussion, 1 piano-conductor

GYPSY

Book by Arthur Laurents—Music by Jule Styne
Lyrics by Stephen Sondheim
Suggested by the Memoirs of Gypsy Rose Lee

Licensor: Tams-Witmark Music Library, Inc.

First opened in New York in 1959.

SYNOPSIS The plot reveals the early lives of Louise, her sister, June, and her mother, Rose, as they struggle to make a living in vaudeville in the early 1920s. Eventually, June leaves them and Louise rises to fame in the early 1930s as the burlesque stripper, Gypsy Rose Lee.

BEST MUSICAL NUMBERS "Let Me Entertain You," "Some People," "Small World," "You'll Never Get Away From Me," "Everything's Coming Up Roses," "Together Wherever We Go"

CAST 13 men, 9 women plus Newsboys, Farmboys, Hollywood Blondes, showgirls, 1 dog, 1 lamb

SETS Stages of 7 theatres, kitchen, road with cutout of fancy touring car, backstage, hotel rooms, Chinese restaurant, office, theatre, alley, railroad platform, Texas desert country, 2 dressing rooms, corridor

COSTUMES Clothes of 1920s to early 1930s, costumes for various vaudeville and burlesque acts, including a cow costume, and coats for Rose, June, Louise, and the dog that are made from hotel blankets like those used in preceding scene

INSTRUMENTATION 3 violins A-B, 1 viola, 1 cello, 1 bass, 5 reeds, 1 horn, 3 trumpets, 3 trombones, 2 percussion, 1 piano-conductor

HELLO, DOLLY!

Book by Michael Stewart—Music and Lyrics by Jerry Herman

Based on the Play *The Matchmaker* by Thornton Wilder

Licensor: Tams-Witmark Music Library, Inc.

First opened in New York in 1964.

SYNOPSIS The story, which is set in New York City and Yonkers in the 1890s, involves Mrs. Dolly Gallagher Levi's efforts to marry a prosperous merchant, Horace Vandergelder, and to match up Irene with Cornelius, Barnaby with Minnie, and Ambrose with Ermengarde. A complex farcical plot ensues that culminates in a happy ending for all.

BEST MUSICAL NUMBERS "Hello, Dolly!," "Before the Parade Passes By," "It Takes a Woman," "Put on Your Sunday Clothes," "It Only Takes a Moment"

CAST 7 men, 6 women, small roles, chorus

SETS 1890s street, feed store, railroad station, hat shop, restaurant with private dining rooms, courtroom

COSTUMES 1890s clothes plus 1 horse costume

INSTRUMENTATION 3 violins, 1 viola, 1 cello, 1 bass and optional tuba, 4 reeds, 3 trumpets, 2 trombones, 2 percussion, 1 guitar-banjo, 1 piano-celeste, 1 piano-conductor

Note: Orchestra parts are cued so score may be played with the following: 3 reeds, 2 trumpets, 1 trombone, 1 percussion, 1 bass, 1 piano

JESUS CHRIST SUPERSTAR

Music by Andrew Lloyd Webber—Lyrics by Tim Rice

Licensor: Music Theatre International

First opened in New York in 1971.

SYNOPSIS This rock opera (all lines are sung) tells the story of the last week in the life of Jesus Christ, including his betrayal by Judas, arrest, trial and crucifixion.

BEST MUSICAL NUMBERS "Everything's Alright," "I Don't Know How to Love Him," "Superstar"

CAST 21 men, 2 women, chorus (Leads must have excellent singing voices.)

SETS Bethany, Jerusalem, Pontius Pilate's house, the Last Supper, garden of Gethsemane, Calvary

COSTUMES Togas and other clothes appropriate for this biblical period

INSTRUMENTATION Rock combo: 1 electric/acoustic guitar, 1 electric bass guitar, 1 piano/organ, 1 drum/percussion

Bandstration (add): 1 flute/piccolo, 1 flute/clarinet, 1 oboe, 1 bassoon, 2 trumpets, 1 trombone, 1 horn

Orchestration (add): 2 violins, 1 viola, 1 cello, 1 piano-conductor

THE KING AND I

Music by Richard Rodgers—Book and Lyrics by Oscar Hammerstein II

Based on *Anna and the King of Siam* by Margaret Landon

Licensor: Rodgers and Hammerstein Theatre Library

First opened in New York in 1951.

SYNOPSIS In 1862 an English widow, Anna, arrives in Bangkok with her young son to tutor the royal children and wives. The king wishes to change his image of being a barbarian and seeks Anna's help. Eventually they come to understand one another. In a contest of wills over the whipping of one of his wives, the king gives in, becomes ill and dies. His son, the new king, indicates that he will be a better ruler than his father.

BEST MUSICAL NUMBERS "I Whistle a Happy Tune," "Hello, Young Lovers," "Getting to Know You," "Shall We Dance?"

CAST 7 men, 4 women, 2 boys, large singing-dancing ensemble

SETS Deck of ship, palace corridor, king's study, palace grounds, schoolroom, Anna's bedroom, theatre, room in Anna's house

COSTUMES 1860s clothes for the English and Siamese garments for the others

INSTRUMENTATION (Orchestrations by Robert Russell Bennett) 1 flute I, 1 flute II (doubling piccolo), 1 oboe (optional doubling English horn), 1 clarinet I-II, 1 clarinet III (doubling bass clarinet), 1 bassoon, 1 horn I-II, 1 horn III, 1 trumpet I-II, 1 trumpet III, 1 trombone I, 1 trombone II, 1 tuba, 2 percussion, 1 violin A, 1 violin B, 1 violin C, 1 viola, 1 cello, 1 bass, 1 harp, 1 piano-conductor score
Also available is a two-piano arrangement.

LES MISÉRABLES

A Musical by Alain Boublil and Claude-Michel Schönberg
Lyrics by Herbert Kretzmer
Based on the Novel by Victor Hugo
Licensor: Music Theatre International
First opened in New York in 1987.

SYNOPSIS In 1815 in France Jean Valjean is released on parole after nineteen years on a chain gang. Embittered by years of hardship, he steals silver from the Bishop of Digne. Valjean is caught but the Bishop lies to save him. Eight years pass and Valjean, having broken his parole and changed his name, has become a factory owner and mayor of a town. Inspector Javert, who has been pursuing Valjean, recognizes him, but Valjean escapes. Javert's pursuit continues until 1832

when he commits suicide. Later, Valjean dies.

BEST MUSICAL NUMBERS "Bring Him Home," "I Dreamed a Dream," "Who Am I?," "Master of the House," "One Day More"

CAST 4 men, 5 women, 1 boy, 2 girls, chorus

SETS Various scenes set in Digne, Montreuil-sur-Mer, Montfermeil and Paris

COSTUMES Early nineteenth-century French clothes

INSTRUMENTATION 1 flute-piccolo, 1 oboe-English horn, 1 clarinet-alto saxophone, 2 horns, 3 trumpets, 1 trombone, 1 drum, 1 percussion, 1 guitar, 2 keyboards, 4 violins, 1 viola (optional), 1 cello, 1 bass, 1 piano-conductor

LI'L ABNER

Book by Norman Panama and Melvin Frank
Lyrics and Music by Johnny Mercer and Gene de Paul
Based on Characters Created by Al Capp
Licensor: Tams-Witmark Music Library, Inc.
First opened in New York in 1956.

SYNOPSIS The time is the 1950s and Daisy Mae has her eyes set on Li'l Abner for her husband. Unfortunately, the government has declared that Dogpatch is the most unnecessary place in the country and that the town should be evacuated so that atomic testing can take place there. The townsfolk are determined to prove that their town is necessary, and after several complications, the town is spared when a letter from Abraham Lincoln is found under the statue of Jubilation T. Cornpone. The letter declared Dogpatch to be a national shrine because of its help in the Civil War. Abner and Daisy Mae can now be married.

BEST MUSICAL NUMBERS "Jubilation T. Cornpone," "Namely You"

CAST 7 men, 3 women, small roles, chorus

SETS Dogpatch's cabins, fishing hole, town square, and roads; Washington, DC, settings of a laboratory, Oval Office, and general's office and mansion

COSTUMES Look at Al Capp's comic strip for ideas on hillbilly wear

INSTRUMENTATION 3 violins, 1 viola, 1 cello, 1 bass, 5 reeds, 3 trumpets, 3 trombones, 1 percussion, 1 guitar-banjo, 1 piano-conductor

Also available is a part for a keyboard synthesizer that can substitute for violin, viola and cello parts.

A LITTLE NIGHT MUSIC

Book by Hugh Wheeler—Music and Lyrics by Stephen Sondheim

Suggested by the Film *Smiles of a Summer Night* by Ingmar Bergman

Licensor: Music Theatre International

First opened in New York in 1973.

SYNOPSIS About 1900 in Sweden, lawyer Fredrik has a beautiful 18-year-old bride, Anne, and a grown son, Henrik. Because Anne remains a virgin, Fredrik turns to Desirée, who already has a jealous lover in Carl-Magnus. The latter then has his wife tell Anne about Fredrik and Desirée. All of the principals are together at the Armfeldt residence for a weekend in the country. At the end, Anne is with Henrik, Carl-Magnus is with his wife, and Fredrik is with Desirée.

BEST MUSICAL NUMBERS "Send in the Clowns," "A Weekend in the Country"

CAST 7 men, 10 women

SETS Two rooms: parlor and master bedroom, stage and two stage boxes of theatre, Desirée's apartment, breakfast room, Armfeldt terrace, lawn with two period cars (if not available, they can be cut), garden, dining room, Desirée's bedroom, trees

COSTUMES Elegant 1900 period clothes for the wealthy and uniforms for servants

INSTRUMENTATION 5 reeds, 3 horns, 2 trumpets, 1 trombone, 2 violins, 1 viola, 1 cello, 1 bass, 1 harp, 1 celeste (piano), 1 percussion, 1 piano-conductor

MAN OF LA MANCHA

Book by Dale Wasserman—Music by Mitch Leigh—Lyrics by Joe Darion

Licensor: Tams-Witmark Music Library, Inc.

First opened in New York in 1965.

SYNOPSIS At the end of the sixteenth century, the poet Miguel de Cervantes, a man in his late 40s, is in a prison in Seville awaiting trial by the Spanish Inquisition. A kangaroo court of fellow prisoners decides to confiscate his possessions, including an incomplete manuscript of a novel he has written entitled *Don Quixote*. To save his work, Cervantes proposes to defend it by acting out the story of the idealistic Quixote. At the end, the manuscript is returned to Cervantes who then leaves for his trial confident that he will survive.

BEST MUSICAL NUMBERS "The Impossible Dream," "Dulcinea," "I Really Like Him," "Aldonza"

CAST 16 men, 5 women, guards

SETS A unit set represents the common room of a prison; a flight of stairs centerstage is used by guards to enter from above; various places are shown by additional scenic pieces

COSTUMES Late sixteenth-century clothes

INSTRUMENTATION 5 reeds, 2 horns, 2 trumpets, 2 trombones, 1 bass, 2 Spanish guitars, 1 timpani, 2 percussion, 1 piano-conductor

MISS SAIGON

A Musical by Alain Boublil and Claude-Michel Schönberg

Music by Claude-Michel Schönberg

Lyrics by Richard Maltby, Jr. and Alain Boublil

Licensor: Music Theatre International

First opened in New York in 1991.

SYNOPSIS Inspired by a novel, *Madame Chrysantheme* by Pierre Loti, a story, "Madame Butterfly" by John Luther Long, a play by David Belasco and an opera by Giacomo Puccini, Boublil and Schönberg decided to write their own version, *Miss Saigon*. They set their story in Vietnam, and the lovers are an American soldier, Chris, and a Vietnamese girl, Kim.

BEST MUSICAL NUMBERS "I'd Give My Life for You," "The American Dream"

CAST 4 men, 2 women, 1 boy, chorus

SETS Various scenes in Saigon, Ho Chi Minh City, Atlanta, Bangkok, including an onstage helicopter

COSTUMES 1970s clothes and uniforms

INSTRUMENTATION 1 flute-piccolo, 1 flute-piccolo-Asian flutes, 1 oboe-cornet, 1 clarinet, 1 bass clarinet-clarinet-saxophone, 1 bassoon, 2 horns, 2 trumpets, 1 trombone, 1 bass trombone-tuba, 1 synthesized percussion, 1 electric guitar-acoustic guitar, 2 synthesizers, 4 violins, 1 viola, 2 cellos, 1 bass-electric bass, 1 piano-conductor

THE MUSIC MAN

Book, Music and Lyrics by Meredith Willson
Based on a Story by Meredith Willson and Franklin Lacey
Licensor: Music Theatre International
First opened in New York in 1957.

SYNOPSIS The year is 1912 when a con man, Harold Hill, comes to River City, Iowa, to start a children's band. The librarian, Marian, is not taken in by his glib persuasiveness but the rest of the town is. Eventually, though, Marian succumbs to his charms. Despite the fact that Harold is not a musician, the youngsters do perform.

BEST MUSICAL NUMBERS "Seventy-Six Trombones," "Goodnight, My Someone," "Marian the Librarian," "Lida Rose," "Till There Was You"

CAST 13 men, 10 women, 1 boy, 1 girl, chorus

SETS Railway coach, center of town, gymnasium, exterior and interior of library and a modest home, street, hotel porch, footbridge, park, high school assembly room

COSTUMES Early twentieth-century clothes including many band uniforms

INSTRUMENTATION 5 reeds, 3 trumpets, 3 trombones, 3 violins, 2 cellos, 1 bass, 1 percussion, 1 piano-conductor
Also available is a more difficult, modified orchestration.

MY FAIR LADY

Book and Lyrics by Alan Jay Lerner—Music by Frederick Loewe
Adapted from George Bernard Shaw's Play and Gabriel Pascal's Film Entitled *Pygmalion*
Licensor: Tams-Witmark Music Library, Inc.
First opened in New York in 1956.

SYNOPSIS In 1912, a poor flower girl, Eliza Doolittle, meets a famous phonetician, Professor Henry Higgins. Later she asks him to teach her how to talk like a lady, and he makes a bet with Colonel Pickering that after six months of work he will pass her off as a duchess. Months later, Eliza is successful in doing this; however, conflict erupts between Henry and Eliza, and she leaves. She later informs him that she will marry Freddy. Henry now begins to realize that he has grown accustomed to Eliza and, at the end, she returns.

BEST MUSICAL NUMBERS "I Could Have Danced All Night," "Wouldn't It Be Loverly," "With a Little Bit of Luck," "On the Street Where You Live," "Get Me to the Church on Time," "I've Grown Accustomed to Her Face"

CAST 15 men, 10 women, buskers, cockney men and women, servants

SETS Outside the Royal Opera House, tenement section, Higgins's study, near the race at Ascot, inside a club tent at Ascot, outside Higgins's house, ballroom, upstairs hall, Mrs. Higgins's conservatory

COSTUMES Early twentieth-century clothes

INSTRUMENTATION 3 violins, 1 viola, 1 cello, 1 bass, 1 flute-piccolo, 1 oboe-English horn, 2 clarinets, 1 bassoon, 2 horns, 3 trumpets, 2 trombones, 1 tuba, 1 percussion, 1 harp, 1 piano-conductor
Also available are band and combo instrumentations and a special arrangement for two pianos.

OKLAHOMA!

Music by Richard Rodgers—Book and Lyrics by Oscar Hammerstein II
Based on the Play *Green Grow the Lilacs* by Lynn Riggs
Licensor: Rodgers and Hammerstein Theatre Library
First opened in New York in 1943.

SYNOPSIS In the early 1900s in a Western Indian territory, Curly, a handsome cowboy, and Laurey, a pretty farm girl, are attracted to each other. When a villainous hired hand, Jud, attempts to cut in, Curly and Laurey marry. In an attempt to slay Curly, Jud is accidentally killed; but in a quick trial Curly is acquitted and the newlyweds leave for their honeymoon.

BEST MUSICAL NUMBERS "Oh, What a Beautiful Mornin'," "The Surrey With the Fringe on Top," "Kansas City," "People Will Say We're in Love," "I Cain't Say No," "Oklahoma"

CAST 6 men, 4 women, small roles, large singing-dancing ensemble

SETS Front of Laurey's farmhouse, smokehouse, grove, Skidmore ranch, kitchen porch, back of

Laurey's house

COSTUMES Early twentieth-century western farm and cowboy clothes

INSTRUMENTATION (Orchestrations by Robert Russell Bennett) 1 flute (doubling piccolo), 1 oboe (optional English horn), 1 clarinet I-II (clarinet I doubling bass clarinet), 1 bassoon, 1 horn I-II, 1 trumpet I-II, 1 trombone, 1 percussion, 2 violin A-B, 1 viola, 1 cello, 1 bass, 1 guitar (doubling banjo), 1 harp, 1 piano-conductor score

Also available are a bandstration and a two-piano arrangement.

OLIVER!

Music, Lyrics and Book by Lionel Bart
Based on *Oliver Twist* by Charles Dickens
Licensor: Tams-Witmark Music Library, Inc.
First opened in New York in 1963.

SYNOPSIS Oliver Twist, an orphan in Victorian London, is in an orphanage run by Mr. Bumble. He sells Oliver to an undertaker, but Oliver runs away and becomes involved with Fagin, his group of thieves, the Artful Dodger, and Nancy, girlfriend of Bill Sikes. Oliver is apprehended by the police and placed in the home of a rich old gentleman, but Nancy finds him and takes him back to Fagin. Then, Bumble discovers that Oliver belongs to a wealthy family. Nancy tries to return Oliver to the rich man but is killed by Sikes, who is then shot dead. Oliver is reunited with his wealthy grandfather, and Fagin considers going straight.

BEST MUSICAL NUMBERS "As Long as He Needs Me," "Consider Yourself," "Where Is Love?," "I'd Do Anything," "It's a Fine Life," "Who Will Buy?"

CAST 6 men, 6 women, other adults, 2 excellent boys, and more boys to play orphans and thieves

SETS Inside and outside the workhouse, undertaker's establishment, Fagin's kitchen, city streets, tavern, Oliver's bedroom, London Bridge

COSTUMES Mid-nineteenth-century clothes

INSTRUMENTATION 3 violins, 1 viola, 1 cello, 1 bass, 4 reeds, 2 horns, 2 trumpets, 2 trombones, 2 percussion, 1 piano-conductor

Also available is a reduced orchestration.

THE PAJAMA GAME

Book by George Abbott and Richard Bissell
Music and Lyrics by Richard Adler and Jerry Ross
Based on the Novel *7½ Cents* by Richard Bissell
Licensor: Music Theatre International
First opened in New York in 1954.

SYNOPSIS In the 1950s in the Sleep Tite Pajama Factory in Cedar Rapids, Iowa, the employees want a raise of seven and one-half cents per hour, but management is opposed. Babe Williams heads the Grievance Committee and Sid Sorokin is the superintendent. Eventually, the employees get their raise and Babe and Sid acknowledge their love for each other.

BEST MUSICAL NUMBERS "Hey, There," "Steam Heat," "Hernando's Hideaway"

CAST 10 men, 6 women, chorus

SETS Factory shop with sewing machines, hallway, office, wooded path, picnic area with knife-throwing trick board, kitchen, meeting hall, Hernando's Hideaway

COSTUMES Mid-twentieth-century clothes

INSTRUMENTATION 5 reeds, 3 trumpets, 3 trombones, 4 violins, 1 viola, 1 cello, 1 bass, 1 guitar, 1 percussion, 1 piano-conductor

PETER PAN

Music by Mark Charlap and Jule Styne
Lyrics by Carolyn Leigh, Betty Comden and Adolph Green
Additional Incidental Music by Trude Rittman and Elmer Bernstein
Licensor: Samuel French, Inc.
First opened in New York in 1954.

SYNOPSIS Around 1900 in London, Peter Pan takes Wendy, Michael and John to Never-Never Land where they meet Captain Hook, pirates and others before returning home to grow up.

BEST MUSICAL NUMBERS "I'm Flying," "I've Got to Crow"

CAST Peter can be played by a young man or woman; 3 men, 4 women, 2 boys, 2 girls, pirates, Indians, orphan boys, actors to play animals

SETS Nursery of Darling house, Never-Never Land, pirate ship (Peter, Wendy, Michael and John must be rigged to fly.)

COSTUMES 1900 clothes, Indian costumes, animal suits. Captain Hook needs hook in place of one hand.

INSTRUMENTATION 2 flutes-piccolos, 1 oboe, 1 bassoon, 2 clarinets, 3 trumpets, 1 horn, 1 trombone, 1 drum, 4 violins, 1 viola, 1 cello, 1 bass, 1 harp, 1 piano-conductor score

1776

Music and Lyrics by Sherman Edwards—Book by Peter Stone
Based on a Concept by Sherman Edwards
Licensor: Music Theatre International
First opened in New York in 1969.

SYNOPSIS In Philadelphia, the hot summer of 1776 disturbs the deliberations of the Second Continental Congress where historical figures such as John Adams, Benjamin Franklin and Thomas Jefferson are engaged in lively debates. The climax is reached in July when the Declaration of Independence is passed and signed.

BEST MUSICAL NUMBERS "The Lees of Old Virginia," "He Plays the Violin," "Momma Look Sharp," "Is Anybody There?"

CAST 25 men, 2 women

SETS Chamber, mall, Thomas Jefferson's room, High Street, anteroom

COSTUMES Late eighteenth-century clothes and wigs

INSTRUMENTATION 4 reeds, 2 trumpets, 2 horns, 3 trombones, 1 violin, 1 viola, 1 cello, 1 bass, 1 harp, 1 harpsichord, 1 percussion, 1 piano-conductor

SHE LOVES ME

Book by Joe Masteroff—Music by Jerry Bock—Lyrics by Sheldon Harnick
Based on a Play by Miklos Laszlo
Licensor: Music Theatre International
First opened in New York in 1963.

SYNOPSIS In a perfume shop in Budapest in the early 1930s, two clerks, Georg and Amalia, are feuding, unaware that they are pen pals who have fallen in love with each other without meeting. Other clerks have their problems too, but by the end all is resolved satisfactorily.

BEST MUSICAL NUMBER "She Loves Me"

CAST 7 men, 2 women, chorus

SETS In and around Maraczek's Parfumerie, Café Imperiale, hospital, apartment

COSTUMES Early 1930s clothes

INSTRUMENTATION 2 reeds, 1 trumpet-flugelhorn, 1 violin, 1 cello, 1 bass, 1 percussion, 2 keyboards, 1 piano-conductor

SHOW BOAT

Music by Jerome Kern—Book and Lyrics by Oscar Hammerstein II
Based on the Novel by Edna Ferber
Licensor: Rodgers and Hammerstein Theatre Library
First opened in New York in 1927.

SYNOPSIS The plot covers the years from 1880 to 1927 in the life of Magnolia, the daughter of a captain of a show boat. She marries a gambler, moves to Chicago, has a daughter, and is deserted by her husband. Eventually they are reunited.

BEST MUSICAL NUMBERS "Ol' Man River," "Make Believe," "Why Do I Love You?," "You Are Love," "Can't Help Lovin' Dat Man," "Life Upon the Wicked Stage," "Bill"

CAST 9 men, 8 women, 1 girl, small roles, large singing-dancing chorus (Outstanding bass is needed to sing "Ol' Man River.")

SETS Show boat, kitchen, auditorium, outside of a saloon and newspaper office, 1893 Chicago World's Fair, boardinghouse, convent

COSTUMES Clothes span a 47-year period from 1880 to 1927

INSTRUMENTATION (Orchestrations of 1946 production by Robert Russell Bennett) 1 flute (doubling piccolo), 1 oboe (optional English horn doubling), 1 clarinet I-II, 1 bassoon, 1 horn I-II, 1 trumpet I-II, 1 trombone, 2 percussion, 3 violin A-B-C-D, 1 viola, 1 cello, 1 bass, 1 banjo-guitar, 1 piano-conductor vocal score

THE SOUND OF MUSIC

Music by Richard Rodgers—Lyrics by Oscar Hammerstein II
Book by Howard Lindsay and Russel Crouse
Suggested by *The Trapp Family Singers* by Maria Augusta Trapp

Licensor: Rodgers and Hammerstein Theatre Library

First opened in New York in 1959.

SYNOPSIS In the 1930s in Austria, a postulant, Maria, is sent by the Mother Abbess to be a governess for the seven children of the widowed Captain Georg von Trapp. Eventually Maria wins the love of the children and father, whom she marries. After the family sings at a festival concert, they escape to the abbey. Although the Nazis are searching for them, the family eludes them and sets out on foot to walk over the mountains to Switzerland.

BEST MUSICAL NUMBERS "The Sound of Music," "My Favorite Things," "Do-Re-Mi," "Climb Ev'ry Mountain," "Edelweiss," "Sixteen Going on Seventeen"

CAST 6 men, 9 women, 3 boys, 5 girls, neighbors, nuns, novices

SETS Interior of abbey, mountainside, office, corridor, living room, outside of Trapp villa, bedroom, hallway, terrace, cloister, concert hall, garden

COSTUMES 1930s Austrian clothes, uniforms, nuns' habits

INSTRUMENTATION (Orchestrations by Robert Russell Bennett) 2 flutes (II doubles piccolo), 1 oboe (doubling English horn), 2 clarinets, 1 bassoon, 3 horns, 3 trumpets, 2 trombones, 1 tuba, 1 percussion, 2 violins, 1 viola, 1 cello, 1 bass, 1 harp, 1 guitar (doubling mandolin), 1 piano, 1 piano-conductor

Also available is a two-piano arrangement.

SOUTH PACIFIC

Music by Richard Rodgers—Lyrics by Oscar Hammerstein II

Book by Oscar Hammerstein II and Joshua Logan

Adapted from *Tales of the South Pacific* by James A. Michener

Licensor: Rodgers and Hammerstein Theatre Library

First opened in New York in 1949.

SYNOPSIS Ensign Nellie Forbush, a nurse from Little Rock, is stationed on an island in the South Pacific during World War II. She becomes romantically involved with Emile de Becque, an older French plantation owner; but when she finds out about his two children by a Polynesian, she is upset. Later, after Emile does heroic work for U.S. forces, Nellie and the children welcome him home.

BEST MUSICAL NUMBERS "Some Enchanted Evening," "A Cockeyed Optimist," "There is Nothin' Like a Dame," "Bali Ha'i," "I'm Gonna Wash That Man Right Outa My Hair," "A Wonderful Guy," "Younger Than Springtime," "Honey Bun," "This Nearly Was Mine"

CAST 20 men, 13 women, 1 young boy, 1 young girl, islanders

SETS Terrace of Emile's home, company street, beach, commander's office, exterior of Bali Ha'i, native hut, stage, backstage, radio shack

COSTUMES World War II uniforms and island native garb

INSTRUMENTATION (Orchestrations by Robert Russell Bennett) 1 flute (doubling piccolo), 1 oboe (doubling English horn), 1 clarinet I-II, 1 bassoon, 1 horn I-II, 1 horn III, 1 trumpet I-II, 1 trumpet III, 1 trombone I, 1 trombone II, 1 tuba, 1 percussion, 1 violin A, 1 violin B, 1 violin C, 1 violin D, 1 viola, 1 cello, 1 bass, 1 harp, 1 piano-conductor score

Also available is a two-piano arrangement.

THE THREEPENNY OPERA

Music by Kurt Weill—Book and Lyrics by Bertolt Brecht

Based on John Gay's Ballad Opera *The Beggar's Opera*

English Adaptation by Marc Blitzstein

Licensor: Rodgers and Hammerstein Theatre Library

The Blitzstein adaptation first opened in New York in 1954.

SYNOPSIS The place is London at the time of Queen Victoria's coronation. A scoundrel, Mack the Knife, secretly marries the daughter of an underworld boss but is betrayed by his in-laws and sent to prison. After the police chief's daughter frees him, he is turned in by a prostitute and sentenced to death. Because it is the day of the queen's coronation, she sets Macheath free, raises him to the peerage, and gives him a castle and a pension.

BEST MUSICAL NUMBER "The Ballad of Mack the Knife"

CAST 7 men, 4 women, several small roles, singing-dancing ensemble

SETS Peacham's shop, stable, heaths of Highgate, whorehouse, prison

COSTUMES 1830s clothes

INSTRUMENTATION (Orchestrations by Kurt Weill for 1954 production) 2 reeds, 2 trumpets, 1 trombone, 1 guitar, 1 percussion, 1 keyboard, 1 conductor

WEST SIDE STORY

Book by Arthur Laurents—Music by Leonard Bernstein
Lyrics by Stephen Sondheim
Based on a Conception of Jerome Robbins
Licensor: Music Theatre International
First opened in New York in 1957.

SYNOPSIS On the west side of New York City, the tragic love story of Tony and Maria is told. Two rival gangs, the Jets and the Sharks, are fighting, but at the end the death of Tony brings the gangs together.

BEST MUSICAL NUMBERS "Maria," "Tonight," "I Feel Pretty," "Somewhere"

CAST 25 men, 14 women (Can be done with a smaller cast.)

SETS Street, backyard, bridal shop, gym, back alley with fire escape to apartment window, drugstore, neighborhood, under the highway, bedroom, another alley, cellar

COSTUMES 1950s street wear with jackets for gang members

INSTRUMENTATION 5 reeds, 3 trumpets, 1 horn, 2 violins, 1 cello, 1 bass, 1 electric guitar-Spanish guitar-mandolin, 1 piano-celeste, 1 percussion, 1 piano-conductor
Also available is a more difficult orchestration.

WHERE'S CHARLEY?

Music and Lyrics by Frank Loesser—Book by George Abbott
Based on Brandon Thomas's *Charley's Aunt*
Licensor: Music Theatre International
First opened in New York in 1948.

SYNOPSIS In the 1890s, two Oxford University students, Jack and Charley, invite two young ladies to lunch in their rooms. When the chaperone, Charley's aunt from Brazil, fails to arrive, Charley dresses as the chaperone and himself as he tries to avoid a suitor to the aunt.

BEST MUSICAL NUMBERS "Once in Love With Amy," "Better Get Out of Here," "Make a Miracle," "The Woman in His Room"

CAST 9 men, 4 women (An excellent male dancer is needed for Charley.)

SETS Room at Oxford University in England, street, garden, powder room, ballroom

COSTUMES 1890s clothes

INSTRUMENTATION 5 reeds, 3 trumpets, 1 horn, 1 trombone, 3 violins, 1 viola, 1 cello, 1 bass, 1 percussion

MORE LARGE MUSICALS

Abbreviations after titles are for the licensors:
MTI for Music Theatre International
RH for Rodgers and Hammerstein Theatre Library
SF for Samuel French, Inc.
TW for Tams-Witmark Music Library, Inc.

Anything Goes—TW
Applause—TW
Barnum—TW
Bells Are Ringing—TW
The Best Little Whorehouse in Texas—SF
Big River—RH
Blood Brothers—SF
The Boys From Syracuse—RH
Bring Back Birdie—TW
Calamity Jane—TW
Call Me Madam—RH
Candide—MTI
Carmen Jones—RH
Carnival—TW
A Christmas Carol—RH
Cinderella—RH
City of Angels—TW
Company—MTI
Damn Yankees—MTI
Do Black Patent Leather Shoes Really Reflect Up?—SF
Dreamgirls—TW
Drood: The Mystery of Edwin Drood—TW
Fame—MTI

Finian's Rainbow—TW
Fiorello!—TW
Flower Drum Song—RH
Follies—MTI
Funny Girl—TW
Gentlemen Prefer Blondes—TW
George M!—TW
Gigi—TW
Girl Crazy—TW
Golden Boy—SF
Good News—TW
Grand Hotel—SF
Hair—TW
High Button Shoes—TW
How to Succeed in Business Without Really Trying—MTI
Into the Woods—MTI
I Remember Mama—RH
Irene—TW
Joseph and the Amazing Technicolor Dreamcoat—MTI
Kismet—MTI
Kiss Me Kate—TW
Kiss of the Spider Woman—SF
La Cage aux Folles—SF
Lady in the Dark—RH
Little Mary Sunshine—SF
Lost in the Stars—RH
Mack and Mabel—SF
Mame—TW
Me and My Girl—SF
Meet Me in St. Louis—TW
The Most Happy Fella—MTI
My One and Only—TW
Nine—SF
The 1940's Radio Hour—SF
Of Thee I Sing—MTI
On a Clear Day You Can See Forever—TW
Once Upon a Mattress—RH
One Touch of Venus—RH
On the Town—TW
On the Twentieth Century—SF
On Your Toes—RH
Pacific Overtures—MTI
Paint Your Wagon—TW
Pal Joey—RH
Pippin—MTI

Porgy & Bess—TW
Promises, Promises—TW
Purlie—SF
The Robber Bridgroom—MTI
The Rothschilds—RH
The Secret Garden—SF
Seesaw—SF
Seven Brides for Seven Brothers—MTI
Shenandoah—SF
Silk Stockings—TW
Singin' in the Rain—MTI
Song of Norway—TW
Stop the World—I Want to Get Off—TW
Street Scene—RH
Sunday in the Park With George—MTI
Sweeney Todd—MTI
Sweet Charity—TW
Take Me Along—TW
Two Gentlemen of Verona—TW
The Unsinkable Molly Brown—MTI
The Wiz—SF
Wizard of Oz—TW
Wonderful Town—TW
Zorba—SF

SMALL MUSICALS

Baby—MTI
Dames at Sea—SF
The Fantasticks—MTI
I Do! I Do!—MTI
I'm Getting My Act Together and Taking It on the Road—SF
Little Shop of Horrors—SF
Nunsense—SF
Pump Boys and Dinettes—SF
Snoopy!!!—TW
You're a Good Man, Charlie Brown—TW

REVUES

Ain't Misbehavin'—MTI
A . . . My Name Is Alice—SF
Berlin to Broadway With Kurt Weill—MTI
Cole—SF
A Day in Hollywood/A Night in the Ukraine—SF
The Decline and Fall of the Entire World as Seen Through the Eyes of Cole Porter—RH
Duke Ellington's Sophisticated Ladies—RH

Eubie—MTI

Five Guys Named Moe—MTI

Forever Plaid—MTI

Jacques Brel Is Alive and Well and Living in Paris—
     MTI

Jerry's Girls—SF

The Mad Show—SF

Oh Coward!—MTI

Perfectly Frank—MTI

Red Hot & Cole—MTI

*Rodgers & Hammerstein's A Grand Night for
     Singing*—RH

Rodgers & Hart: A Celebration—RH

Side by Side by Sondheim—MTI

Some Enchanted Evening—RH

Sugar Babies—SF

Tintypes—MTI

Working—MTI

The World Goes 'Round—MTI

Ziegfeld, A Night at the Follies—MTI

OPERAS, COMIC OPERAS AND OPERETTAS

In addition to the above abbreviations, the following
are used in this list:

BH for Boosey & Hawkes, Inc.

GS for G. Schirmer, Inc.

Amahl and the Night Visitors—GS

The Barber of Seville—BH and GS

Billy Budd—BH

Candide—BH

Carmen—BH and GS

Cosi Fan Tutte—BH and GS

Der Rosenkavalier—BH

Die Fledermaus—BH and GS

Don Giovanni—BH and GS

Fidelio—BH and GS

Gianni Schicchi—GS

The Girl of the Golden West—GS

The Gondoliers—GS

Hänsel and Gretel—BH and GS

H.M.S. Pinafore—GS, RH and SF

Il Trovatore—BH and GS

Iolanthe—GS

La Bohème—GS

La Fille du Régiment—GS

La Traviata—BH and GS

Madama Butterfly—GS

The Magic Flute—BH and GS

The Marriage of Figaro—BH and GS

The Medium—GS

The Merry Widow—SF and TW

The Mikado—GS, RH and SF

Naughty Marietta—TW

New Moon—TW

Nixon in China—BH

No No Nanette—TW

Otello—GS

Pagliacci—BH and GS

Patience—GS

The Pirates of Penzance—GS, RH and SF

Red Mill—TW

Rigoletto—GS

Roberta—TW

Roméo et Juliette—GS

Rose-Marie—TW

The Saint of Bleecker Street—GS

Salome—BH and GS

Samson et Delilah—GS

Student Prince—TW

Sweethearts—TW

The Telephone—GS

Trouble in Tahiti—BH

The Turn of the Screw—BH

The Yeomen of the Guard—GS

Bibliography

MUSICAL THEATRE

Balk, H. Wesley. *The Complete Singer-Actor.* Minneapolis: University of Minnesota Press, 1977.

Berkson, Robert. *Musical Theater Choreography.* New York: Back Stage Books, 1990.

Bordman, Gerald. *American Musical Revue.* New York: Oxford University Press, 1985.

———*American Musical Theatre.* Expanded ed. New York: Oxford University Press, 1986.

———*American Operetta.* New York: Oxford University Press, 1981.

Bowers, Dwight Blocker. *American Musical Theater.* Washington, DC: Smithsonian Collection of Recordings, 1989. (With recordings.)

Citron, Stephen. *The Musical From the Inside Out.* Chicago: Ivan R. Dee, Inc., 1991.

Cohen, Selma Jeanne (ed.). *Dance as a Theatre Art.* New York: Dodd, Mead & Company, 1974.

Craig, David. *On Performing.* New York: McGraw-Hill Book Company, 1987.

———*On Singing Onstage.* New York: Schirmer Books, 1978.

Engel, Lehman. *American Musical Theatre.* Rev. ed. New York: The Macmillan Company, 1975.

———*Getting the Show On.* New York: Schirmer Books, 1983.

———*The Making of a Musical.* New York: Macmillan Publishing Co., Inc., 1977.

Filichia, Peter. *Let's Put On a Musical!* New York: Avon Books, 1993.

Frankel, Aaron. *Writing the Broadway Musical.* New York: Drama Book Specialists (Publishers), 1977.

Gishford, Anthony (ed.). *Grand Opera.* New York: The Viking Press, 1972.

Green, Stanley. *Encyclopedia of the Musical Theatre.* New York: Dodd, Mead & Co., Inc., 1976.

———*The World of Musical Comedy.* 4th ed. New York: Da Capo Press, Inc., 1984.

Hirsch, Foster. *Harold Prince and the American Musical Theatre.* Cambridge: Cambridge University Press, 1989.

Jacob, Ellen. *Dancing: A Guide for the Dancer You Can Be.* Reading, MA: Addison-Wesley Publishing Co., 1981.

Jefferson, Alan. *The Glory of Opera.* New York: Exeter Books, 1983.

Kislan, Richard. *Hoofing on Broadway.* New York: Prentice-Hall Press, 1987.

———*The Musical.* Englewood Cliffs, NJ: Prentice-Hall, Inc., 1980.

Kosarin, Oscar. *The Singing Actor.* Englewood Cliffs, NJ: Prentice-Hall, Inc., 1983.

Laufe, Abe. *Broadway's Greatest Musicals.* Rev. ed. New York: Funk & Wagnalls, Inc., 1973.

Lerner, Alan Jay. *The Musical Theatre.* New York: McGraw-Hill Book Company, 1986.

Lucha-Burns, Carol. *Musical Notes.* Westport, CT: Greenwood Press, 1986.

Mates, Julian. *America's Musical Stage.* Westport, CT: Greenwood Press, 1985.

Minton, Sandra. *Modern Dance: Body and Mind.* Englewood, CO: Morton Publishing Company, 1984.

Mordden Ethan. *Broadway Babies.* New York: Oxford University Press, 1983.

The New Kobbe's Compete Opera Book, ed. and rev. by the Earl of Harewood. New York: G.P. Putnam's Sons, 1976.

Novak, Elaine Adams. *Performing in Musicals.* New York: Schirmer Books, 1988.

Schmidt, Jan. *Basics of Singing.* New York: Schirmer Books, 1984.

The Simon and Schuster Book of the Opera. New York: Simon & Schuster, Inc., 1977.

Smith, Cecil, and Glenn Litton. *Musical Comedy in America.* Rev. ed. New York: Theatre Arts Books, 1981.

Stanislavski, Constantin, and Pavel Rumyantsev. *Stanislavski on Opera.* Tr. and ed. by Elizabeth Reynolds Hapgood. New York: Theatre Arts Books, 1975.

Zadan, Craig. *Sondheim & Co.* 2d ed. New York: Harper & Row, Publishers, 1989.

DIRECTING

Benedetti, Robert L. *The Director at Work.* Englewood Cliffs, NJ: Prentice-Hall, Inc., 1985.

Brook, Peter. *The Empty Space.* New York: Avon Books, 1968.

———*The Shifting Point.* New York: Harper & Row, Publishers, 1987.

Cohen, Robert, and John Harrop. *Creative Play Direction.* 2d ed. Englewood Cliffs, NJ: Prentice-Hall, Inc., 1984.

Dean, Alexander, and Lawrence Carra. *Fundamentals of Play Directing.* 4th ed. New York: Holt, Rinehart and Winston, 1980.

Jones, David Richard. *Great Directors at Work.* Berkeley: University of California Press, 1986.

Hodge, Francis. *Play Directing.* 3d ed. Englewood Cliffs, NJ: Prentice Hall, 1988.

Ilson, Carol. *Harold Prince: From Pajama Game to Phantom of the Opera.* Ann Arbor, MI: UMI Research Press, 1989.

Leiter, Samuel L. *The Great Stage Directors.* New York: Facts on File, Inc., 1994.

Morrow, Lee Alan, and Frank Pike. *Creating Theater.* New York: Vintage Books, 1986.

O'Neill, R.H., and N.M. Boretz. *The Director as Artist.* New York: Holt, Rinehart and Winston, 1987.

Rodgers, James W., and Wanda C. Rodgers. *Play Director's Survival Kit*. West Nyack, NY: The Center for Applied Research in Education, 1995.

PRODUCING

Engel, Lehman. *Planning and Producing the Musical Show*. Rev. ed. New York: Crown Publishers, Inc., 1966.

Farber, Donald C. *Producing Theatre*. Rev. ed. New York: Limelight Editions, 1981.

Langley, Stephen. *Producers on Producing*. New York: DBS Publications, Inc., 1976.

Laughlin, Haller, and Randy Wheeler. *Producing the Musical*. Westport, CT: Greenwood Press, 1984.

ACTING

Adler, Stella. *The Technique of Acting*. New York: Bantam Books, 1988.

Barton, Robert. *Acting: Onstage and Off*. 2d ed. New York: Harcourt Brace Jovanovich College Publishers, 1993.

Benedetti, Robert L. *The Actor at Work*. 5th ed. Englewood Cliffs, NJ: Prentice-Hall, Inc., 1990.

Cohen, Robert. *Acting Professionally*. 3d ed. Palo Alto, CA: Mayfield Publishing Co., 1981.

Crawford, Jerry L. *Acting in Person and in Style*. 4th ed. Dubuque, IA: Wm. C. Brown Publishing, 1991.

Gronbeck-Tedesco, John L. *Acting Through Exercises*. Mountain View, CA: Mayfield Publishing Company, 1992.

Hagen, Uta. *Respect for Acting*. New York: Macmillan Publishing Co., Inc., 1973.

Kahan, Stanley. *Introduction to Acting*. 3d ed. Newton, MA: Allyn and Bacon, Inc., 1991.

King, Nancy R. *A Movement Approach to Acting*. Englewood Cliffs, NJ: Prentice-Hall, Inc., 1981.

McGaw, Charles, and Larry D. Clark. *Acting Is Believing*. 5th ed. New York: Holt, Rinehart and Winston, 1987.

McTigue, Mary. *Acting Like a Pro*. Cincinnati: Betterway Books, 1992.

Miller, Allan. *A Passion for Acting*. New York: Back Stage Books, 1992.

Moore, Sonia. *The Stanislavski System*. 2d rev. ed. New York: Penguin Books, 1984.

Novak, Elaine Adams. *Styles of Acting*. Englewood Cliffs, NJ: Prentice-Hall Inc., 1985.

Richardson, Don. *Acting Without Agony*. Boston: Allyn and Bacon, Inc., 1988.

Stanislavski, Constantin: *An Actor Prepares*. Tr. by Elizabeth Reynolds Hapgood. New York: Theatre Arts Books, 1936.

———*Building a Character*. Tr. by Elizabeth Reynolds Hapgood. New York: Theatre Art Books, 1949.

———*Creating a Role*. Tr. by Elizabeth Reynolds Hapgood. New York: Theatre Arts Books, 1961.

Stanislavsky, Konstantin. *Stanislavsky on the Art of the Stage*. London: Faber and Faber, 1967.

Whelan, Jeremy. *Instant Acting*. Cincinnati: Betterway Books, 1994.

Yakim Moni, with Muriel Broadman. *Creating a Character*. New York: Back Stage Books, 1990.

AUDITIONING

Nielsen, Eric Brandt. *Dance Auditions*. Princeton, NJ: Princeton Book Company, 1984.

Oliver, Donald. *How to Audition for the Musical Theatre*. New York: Drama Book Publishers, 1985.

Silver, Fred. *Auditioning for the Musical Theatre*. New York: Newmarket Press, 1985.

VOICE AND DIALECTS

Anderson, Virgil A. *Training the Speaking Voice*. 3d ed. New York: Oxford University Press, 1977.

Blunt, Jerry. *Stage Dialects*. New York: Harper & Row, Publishers, Inc., 1967. (With tapes.)

———*More Stage Dialects*. New York: Harper & Row, Publishers, Inc., 1980. (With tapes.)

Hill, Harry, with Robert Barton. *A Voice for the Theatre*. New York: Holt, Rinehart and Winston, 1985.

Linklater, Kristin. *Freeing the Natural Voice*. New York: Drama Book, Specialists (Publishers), 1976.

Machlin, Evangeline: *Dialects for the Stage: A Manual and Two Cassette Tapes*. New York: Theatre Arts Books, 1975.

———*Speech for the Stage*. Rev. ed. New York: Theatre Arts Books, 1980.

Mayer, Lyle V. *Fundamentals of Voice & Diction*. 8th ed. Dubuque, IA: Wm. C. Brown Publishers, 1988.

Stern, David Alan. *Acting With an Accent*. Los Angeles: Dialect Accent Specialists, Inc., 1979. (With tapes.)

MANNERS AND CUSTOMS

Oxenford, Lyn. *Playing Period Plays*. London: J. Garnet Miller Ltd., 1958.

Russell, Douglas A. *Period Style for the Theatre*. Boston: Allyn and Bacon, Inc. 1980.

STAGE FIGHTING

Gordon, Gilbert. *Stage Fights*. New York: Theatre Arts Books, 1973.

Hobbs, William. *Stage Combat*. New York: St. Martin's Press, 1981.

Kezer, Claude D. *Principles of Stage Combat*. Schulenburg, TX: I.E. Clark, Inc., 1983.

Martinez, J.D. *Combat Mime*. Chicago: Nelson-Hall Publishers, 1982.

STAGE MAKEUP

Corson, Richard. *Stage Makeup*. 7th ed. Englewood Cliffs, NJ: Prentice-Hall, Inc., 1986.

Smith, C. Ray (ed.). *The Theatre Crafts Book of Makeup, Masks and Wigs*. Emmaus, PA: Rodale Press, 1974.

Swinfield, Rosemarie. *Stage Makeup Step-by-Step*. Cincinnati: Betterway Books, 1995.

TECHNICAL THEATRE

Arnold, Richard L. *Scene Technology*. Englewood Cliffs, NJ: Prentice-Hall, Inc., 1985.

Bellman, Willard F. *Scene Design, Stage Lighting, Sound, Costume & Makeup*. New York: Harper & Row, Publishers, 1983.

Collison, David. *Stage Sound*. 2d ed. New York: Drama Book Service,

1982.

Cunningham, Glen. *Stage Lighting Revealed*. Cincinnati: Betterway Books, 1993.

Gillette, A.S. and J. Michael. *Stage Scenery*. 3d ed. New York: Harper & Row, 1981.

Hawkins, Brenda. *Stage Costume*. Cincinnati: Betterway Books, 1996.

Ingham, Rosemary, and Liz Covey. *The Costumer's Handbook: How to Make All Kinds of Costumes*. Englewood Cliffs, NJ: Prentice-Hall, Inc., 1980.

Ionazzi, Daniel A. *Stagecraft Handbook*. Cincinnati: Betterway Books, 1996.

———*The Stage Management Handbook*. Cincinnati: Betterway Books, 1992.

Rose, Rich. *Drawing Scenery for Theater, Film and Television*. Cincinnati: Betterway Books, 1994.

Russell, Douglas A. *Stage Costume Design: Theory, Technique and Style*.

New York: Appelton-Century-Crofts, 1973.

Stern, Lawrence. *Stage Management*. 3d ed. Newton, MA: Allyn and Bacon, Inc., 1987.

Thomas, Terry. *Create Your Own Stage Sets*. Englewood Cliffs, NJ: Prentice-Hall, Inc., 1985.

Thurston, James. *The Theatre Props Handbook*. Cincinnati: Betterway Books, 1987.

Warfel, William B. *Handbook of Stage Lighting Graphics*. New York: Drama Book Specialists (Publishers), 1974.

———and Walter A. Klappert. *Color Science for Lighting the Stage*. New Haven: Yale University Press, 1981.

Welker, David. *Stagecraft*. Boston: Allyn and Bacon, Inc., 1978.

———*Theatrical Set Design*. Boston:

Allyn and Bacon, Inc., 1979.

MUSICAL ANTHOLOGIES

Gilbert, W.S. and Arthur Sullivan. *The Complete Plays of Gilbert and Sullivan*. New York: The Modern Library, 1936.

Richards, Stanley (ed.). *Great Musicals of the American Theatre*. Vol. 2. Radnor, PA: Chilton Books Company, 1976.

———*Great Rock Musicals*. New York: Stein and Day, Publishers, 1979.

———*Ten Great Musicals of the American Theatre*. Radnor, PA: Chilton Book Company, 1973.

Rodgers, Richard, and Oscar Hammerstein II. *Six Plays by Rodgers and Hammerstein*. New York: Random House, 1963.

Glossary of Theatrical Terms

Above. Upstage or away from the audience; to move above someone or a property is to move upstage of that person or prop.

Ad-lib. To improvise words and actions.

Apron (or forestage). Area between the proscenium arch and the front edge of the stage.

Architectural set. Permanent structure that can be altered to suggest different locations by adding scenic pieces, draperies and properties.

Arena stage. Playing area that is surrounded on all sides by spectators.

Aria. Operatic solo.

Aside. Short remark made by a character to the audience that other people onstage are not supposed to hear.

Back. To cross in back of a person or a property is to move on the upstage side of someone or something.

Backdrop (or drop). Large sheet of painted canvas or muslin that hangs at the back of a set.

Backstage. Areas behind the stage set, including the dressing rooms.

Balance. Aesthetically pleasing integration of performers, set, properties and lighting.

Ballad. Romantic, smooth-flowing song.

Bar. (1) In music, one bar is one measure. (2) (Often spelled *barre*) In dance, a handrail used by dancers in exercising.

Batten. Long pipe from which scenery, draperies or props may be suspended.

Below. Downstage or toward the audience; to move below someone or a property is to move downstage of that person or prop.

Belt. To sing in a forceful manner using the chest voice.

Bit part. Small role.

Blackout. Fast darkening of the stage.

Block. To plan the movements of performers.

Border. Drapery or short drop hanging across the stage above the acting area to mask the fly loft and overhead lights.

Box office. Place where tickets are sold for admission to performances.

Box set. Realistic representation of a room with three walls and often a ceiling.

Breakaway. Costume or prop that is specially constructed to come apart easily onstage and to be assembled quickly for the next performance.

Broadway. Street in New York City on which and near which major commercial theatres are located.

Build. To increase the loudness, rate and energy of a line, speech, scene or song in order to reach a climax.

Bump up. To bring stage lights up quickly.

Burn (or slow burn). Slow, comic realization that something bad has happened; the disgust and anger builds within the comedian until he or she explodes in rage.

Business. See **stage business**.

Call. (1) Announcement to performers or crews that they are needed for a rehearsal or performance. (2) Warning to performers to get ready for an entrance.

Callboard. Place backstage in a theatre where company rules, announcements, notes and messages are posted.

Cheat. To move slightly to improve the stage picture or to turn more toward the audience for better audibility.

Chorus. (1) Group of people who sing and/or dance. (2) (Also called the **refrain**) Main part of a song, often having thirty-two measures.

Climax. High point of an audience's involvement in a scene, act or play.

Closed turn. Turn made away from the audience so that the spectators see the back of the actor.

Combo. Small combination of instrumentalists who usually play piano, bass, percussion and, perhaps, another instrument or two.

Concept musical. Musical in which the emphasis is on expressing an idea with episodes serving to illustrate the concept.

Counter (or dress stage). Small movement made by an actor to better the stage picture after a cross by another performer.

Counterweight system. Device for lowering and raising scenery from and to the area above the stage by means of ropes, wires and pulleys.

Cover. (1) To stand in front of someone so that the audience cannot see that person. (2) To de-

ceive an audience by concealing an action, such as a stabbing.

Cross (sometimes abbreviated X). To move from one place to another on a stage.

Cross-fade. To take the lights down in one area of the stage while bringing them up in another area or to fade down one sound effect while fading in another.

Cue. Signal for performers and technicians to speak, enter, turn on lights, play a tape and so forth.

Curtain call. Bowing and receiving the audience's applause at the end of the show or, sometimes in opera, at the end of an act.

Curtain line. (1) Last line spoken by an actor before the curtain closes to end an act or scene. (2) Imaginary line formed where the act curtain touches the stage floor.

Cyclorama (abbreviation: cyc, pronounced "sike"). Curved curtain, drop, or wall that is often painted to look like the sky and is used at the rear and sides of the stage.

Deadpan. Impassive matter-of-fact manner with no facial expressions.

Denouement. Ending or resolution of the plot of a play.

Double. (1) To play more than one role in a production. (2) One who resembles a member of the

cast and takes his or her place in scenes needing special skills.

Double take. Delayed reaction to a line or situation after an initial failure to see anything unusual.

Dress rehearsal(s). Final rehearsal(s) in which performers wear costumes, makeup and hairstyles, the orchestra plays, and all technical elements are used to make the rehearsal(s) as close to a performance as possible.

Dress stage. See **counter**.

Drop. See **backdrop**.

Elevator stage. Stage in which sections of the floor may be raised or lowered to change scenery.

Ensemble. Group of singers, dancers, actors or musicians.

Entr'acte. (1) Orchestral opening to the second act of a musical. (2) A dance, musical number or interlude performed between the acts of a play.

Entrance. (1) Entering the stage. (2) Opening in the set that is used for entering.

Exit. (1) Leaving the stage. (2) Opening in the set that is used for leaving.

Exposition. Information given in a play by the writer to help the audience understand it.

Extra (or walk-on, supernumerary or super). Person who is onstage to provide atmosphere and background and who may speak only with a group.

Fade in (or up). To bring up the lights or sound gradually.

Fade out (or down). To darken the stage or to take sound out gradually.

Feed line. See **straight line**.

Flat. Wooden frame covered with canvas or muslin that is painted and used as part of a set.

Floor plan (or ground plan). Line drawing of a stage set as seen from above; it shows the placement on the stage floor of the scenic elements, such as walls, doors, windows, fireplaces, platforms, steps, furniture and other set props.

Fly loft (or flies). Space above the stage from which scenery and lights may hang.

Focal point. Place onstage of greatest interest to the audience at that moment.

Focus. (1) To look at someone or something. (2) To adjust the beam size of a spotlight.

Follow spotlight. Lighting instrument operated by an electrician to follow the movements of one or more performers.

Freeze. To stop all movement.

Front. (1) Front of the house includes the lobby, box office and auditorium. (2) To move in front

of a person or property is to walk on the downstage side.

Gelatin (or gel). Filter placed over stage lights to color the light.

Genre. Group or category of compositions that have common characteristics.

Give stage. To permit another actor to have the dominant position.

Greenroom. Traditional backstage waiting lounge and reception room for performers.

Ground plan. See **floor plan**.

Heads up! Warning to those onstage that something is falling or being lowered from the flies and that everyone should look up to determine if he or she is in danger of being hit.

Heavy. Role of a villain.

House. (1) Places where the audience is seated. (2) Audience.

Houselights. Lights that illuminate the auditorium of a theatre.

Inciting incident. Incident near the beginning of a play that gets the main action started.

Ingenue. Role of a young girl.

In one. In a wing and drop setting, it is the area that is downstage of the first set of wings.

Jackknife stage. Large wagon that, when facing the audience, is

permanently pivoted at one corner (usually a downstage corner in the right or left wing area) and is swung on and offstage in a motion resembling the opening and closing of a jackknife.

Juvenile. Role of a young man.

Kill. (1) To lose the effectiveness of a line, action or stage effect. (2) To eliminate something, such as a light.

Laugh line. See **punch line**.

Leg (or leg drop). Drapery hung at the side of a stage to mask the wings and vary the width of the acting area.

Libretto (Italian word meaning "little book"). Text of an opera or musical.

L-shaped stage. Rectangular playing area with audience sitting on two sides and scenic elements on other two sides.

Malapropism. Use of an incorrect word that sounds similar to the intended word.

Measure. Group of notes indicated on a musical staff between vertical bars.

Monologue. Long speech by one character.

Move in (or on or onstage). To move toward the center of the stage.

Move out (or off or offstage). To move away from the center of the stage.

Mug. To use excessive facial expressions.

Off-Broadway theatres. Small professional theatres in New York City.

Open turn. Turn made toward the audience so that the spectators see the front of the actor.

Open up. To turn toward the audience.

Operatic musical (or popular opera or theatre opera). Musical that has few or no spoken lines.

Orchestra. (1) Group of musicians who perform together. (2) Main floor of a theatre.

Orchestra pit. See **pit.**

Out front. Auditorium, lobby and other public areas.

Overplay. To exaggerate or use more force than is needed.

Overture. Orchestral beginning of a musical, opera or play.

Pas de deux. Dance for two people.

Phrase. (1) A group of words that contains a thought. (2) Small part, typically two to four measures, of a melody. (3) Small series of dance movements.

Pick up. To speed up or shorten the time between a cue and the next line.

Pit (or orchestra pit). Area where the orchestra usually plays that is located between the stage and the front row of seats.

Plane. Imaginary line that runs parallel to the front edge of the stage and is as wide as a standing actor.

Pointe (or point). Position in ballet in which dancers wearing toe-shoes dance on the tips of their toes.

Point up (or play up). To make a line or action more emphatic.

Practical. Any onstage prop, light or piece of scenery that can be used by performers and is not just decorative; for example, a table lamp that can be turned on or a window that can be opened.

Pratfall. Fall on the buttocks.

Projected scenery. Projection of film, slides or television pictures onto a surface to serve as part of the scenery.

Promptbook (or promptscript). Copy of the script in which all information, including the blocking, is recorded that is essential for the production of the show.

Prompter. Person who holds the promptbook offstage during rehearsals and performances and provides lines to forgetful performers.

Property (or prop). Article or object that is carried by performers (such as a cane sword or fan) or is used on the set (such as a piece of furniture, pillow, picture or drapery).

Proscenium. Permanent architectural arch that separates the stage from the audience.

Public domain. Older opera, play, musical, song, etc., that is no longer under copyright.

Punch line (or laugh line). Line that should get a laugh.

Recitative. Operatic dialogue that is sung in a style that suggests the inflections of speech.

Refrain (or chorus). Main part of a song, often having thirty-two measures.

Regisseur. European name for stage director.

Rendering. Perspective drawing of a stage set.

Reprise. Repetition of all or part of a song or dance.

Revolve. Circular platform that can be turned to change sets; it may be permanently built into the stage or mounted temporarily on the floor.

Revolving stage. Stage that has a revolve.

Ring down. Close the front curtain.

Ring up. Open the front curtain.

Road company. Travelling company of performers and

technicians who present a show in various theatres.

Rock musical. Musical that features rock music.

Running gag. Comic business that is repeated throughout the show.

Run-through. Rehearsal in which a scene, act or entire show is played without interruption.

Scrim. Curtain, drop or set made of net or gauze that is opaque when lighted from the front but becomes transparent when lighted from behind.

Script. Dialogue, lyrics and stage directions of a musical or play.

Share a scene. To have two or more performers equally dominant onstage.

Shtick (also spelled shtik or schtick). A repeated bit of comic business, routine or gimmick used by a star performer.

Sides. Half sheets of paper that have one character's speaking lines and lyrics with cues and stage directions.

Sight gag. Visual humor from a funny prop, costume, makeup, hairstyle or movement.

Sight lines. Imaginary lines from seats at the sides of the house and top of the balcony to the stage to determine what parts of the acting area will be visible to audience members sitting in those seats.

Simultaneous set. Setting that displays to the audience several different locales simultaneously.

Slapstick (from a device made of two slats that makes a loud noise when used by a performer to strike someone). Comedy that stresses horseplay and wild physical buffoonery.

Soliloquy. Revelation of thoughts and feelings by a character when alone onstage.

Space stage. Open stage that features lighting and, perhaps, projected scenery.

Special effect. Mechanical or electrical effect devised by designers, such as a sunrise, blood from a wound, fog or lightning.

Spectacle. Visual elements of a stage production (the scenery, properties, lighting, costumes, makeup, movements and dancing) and, by extension, those productions in which the visual elements are predominant.

Spike. To mark the stage floor with chalk or tape to indicate the position of furniture, properties or scenery so that they will be placed correctly during scene shifts.

S.R.O. Sign meaning "Standing Room Only" that is displayed at the box office when all seats have been sold for a performance.

Stage business. Not a major movement, but a smaller activity, such as smoking a cigarette, playing with eyeglasses, or sewing, that helps to establish characterization or mood.

Stage convention. Departure from reality that the audience will accept, such as a character in a musical suddenly breaking into song and being accompanied by an orchestra.

Stage picture. Arrangement on a stage of performers and the visual production elements (scenery, properties, lighting and costumes).

Standby. Performer who is prepared to substitute for a star in case of an emergency; unlike an understudy, the standby does not appear in the musical at other times.

Steal. (1) To steal a scene is to take attention away from the person who should receive it. (2) To move without attracting the audience's attention.

Straight line (or feed line). Line that sets up a punch line so it will get a laugh.

Straight man (or woman). One who delivers straight lines to a comic.

Strike. To remove a prop or light or to dismantle a set.

Style. Distinctive manner of expression in the writing, designing or performing; the characteristics of a show that make it different from others.

Subtext (literally, under the text). Underlying meaning of a scene.

Swing. Singer and/or dancer who is prepared to substitute for chorus members who are unable to perform.

Tag line. Final line of a scene, an act or a character's exit.

Take (or slow take). Slow, comic realization of what has been done or said.

Take stage. To assume the dominant position onstage.

Teaser. Curtain hung from a batten to adjust the height of the stage opening.

Technical rehearsal. Rehearsal for perfecting the technical elements of the show, such as the scene and property shifts, lighting, sound and special effects.

Tempo. Rate of speed used in performing a scene, song, dance or musical number.

Text. Words of the dialogue and lyrics.

Theme. Main underlying idea of a play or musical.

Thrust stage. Playing area with audience sitting on three sides

and a stagehouse or wall on the fourth side.

Timing. Selecting the right moment to say a line or do an action for maximum effectiveness.

Top. To speak with a louder tone, higher pitch, and more energy than the previous line.

Tormentors. Flats or drapes at the sides of the proscenium arch that may be used to alter the width of the stage opening.

Tracks. Slots in a stage floor created for guiding portable scenery, wagons and properties.

Trap. Opening in the stage floor through which performers, properties or scenery may enter or leave the stage.

Traveler. Horizontally drawn curtain.

Turn in. To turn away from the audience.

Turn out. To turn toward the audience.

Undercut. To speak with a softer tone and lower pitch than the previous line.

Underplay. To use a softer tone, less energy, and a more casual manner than previously.

Understudy. Performer in the show who studies another role and is prepared to substitute in case of emergency.

Unit set. Neutral type of stage

setting that can be altered by rearranging flats and adding scenic pieces and properties to suggest different locations.

Upstage. (1) On a proscenium stage, the areas farthest away from the audience. (2) To cross deliberately to a place upstage of another actor, thereby forcing the latter to turn to a three-quarter position to talk with the upstager.

Up-tempo song. Fast-moving song.

Verse. Lyrics and music leading to the chorus of a song.

Wagons (or rolling platforms). Platforms of different sizes on casters that can be rolled on and offstage with scenery and performers to change the sets.

Walk-on. See **extra**.

Wing-drop-border set. Setting that has wings at the sides of a proscenium stage, backdrops and borders hanging overhead.

Wings. (1) Offstage space at the sides of the stage. (2) Flats or drapes used at the sides of the stage to mask the offstage areas.

Work lights. Lights used for illuminating the stage when it is utilized for rehearsals and other nonperformance activities.

Index